THE RELIGION OF ISLÁM

THE
RELIGION OF ISLÁM

اَلْيَوْمَ اَكْمَلْتُ لَكُمْ دِيْنَكُمْ ـ وَرَضِيتُ لَكُمْ اَلْإِسْلَامَ دِيْنًا

(Súra v. 5.)

" This day have I perfected your religion for you; and it is My pleasure that Islám be your religion."

BY

F. A. KLEIN

LONDON
CURZON PRESS

First paperback edition 1985

Published by
Curzon Press Ltd · London and Dublin

ISBN 0 7007 0190 7

Printed and bound in Great Britain by
Biddles Ltd, Guildford and King's Lynn

CONTENTS.

CHAPTER. I.

THE SOURCES OR FOUNDATIONS OF ISLÁM.

CHAPTER II.

THE DOCTRINES OF ISLÁM.

CHAPTER III.

THE IMAMATE.

CHAPTER IV.

FIQH.

CONTENTS.

CHAPTER V.
THE SECTS OF ISLÁM.

The Religion of Islám.

CHAPTER 1.

THE SOURCES OR FOUNDATIONS OF ISLÁM.

Islám (اسلام),[1] the name applied by Muhammad himself to his religion means the religion of resignation, submission to the will, the service, the commands of God.

The sources[2] (أُصُول) from which the doctrines and precepts of Islám are derived, or the foundations (أَرْكَان) on which they rest, are the following four:

(1) the *Qur'án* (القرآن) (2), the *Sunna* (السُنَّة) (3), the *Ijmá'* (إجمَاع) (4), the *Qíás* (القِيَاس)

---

[1] سَلِم (IV) to resign, surrender, submit oneself. Inf: اسلَم = the act of resigning, submitting oneself.—The professor of Islám is a Muslim (مُسْلِم pl. مُسْلِمون). The true religion with God is Islám (Súra iii. 17). He who desires a religion other than Islám, it will not be accepted of him (Súra iii. 78, 79). In this sense Abraham and all the prophets down to Muhammad are considered to have been Muslims (Súra iii. 60).

There are three terms used by Muslim writers to designate religion, *viz.*, دين used to designate religion, as it stands in relation to God as دين الله ; مِلَّة as it stands in relation to the prophet or law-giver مَذْهَب as it stands in relation to the founders of مِلَّة الرسول , مِلَّة ابرهيم the religious systems of Islám, as مَذْهَب ابى حنيفة. (*See* Jowh. 12—14.)

[2] These four sources of Islám are called the four proofs (الأدلّة الاربعة) or the traditional proofs (الأدلّة النقليّة) *i.e.*, transmitted by tradition, in

The special branch[1] of theology, which treats of the interpretation of the principles of these four sources, and of all the questions (مسائل) connected with the same, is called علم الأصول, that is, فنّ اصول الدين and فنّ أصول الفقه ‏—‏ science of the principles of dogmatics, and science of the principles of fikh, which means practical theology, jurisprudence.

The Qur'án,[2] the first foundation of Islám, is the book which contains the revelations Muhammad professed to have received from time to time, chiefly through the mediation of the angel Gabriel, which he delivered as a divine message to those about him, and which is, therefore, called the Word of God (كلام الله).

___

distinction from the proofs of reason (الادلّة العقليّة) ; they are also called the proofs of (divine) Law (الادلّة الشّرعية). The first two sources, Qur'án and Tradition, are called the absolute, infallible proofs (الادلّة القطعيّة), because they contain the absolutely true and undoubted fundamental doctrines of Islám, while the other two are called the secondary (الادلّة الاجتهاديّة) i.e., obtained by exertion in searching and in reasoning by analogy. The former are called the Roots (أُصُول) ; the latter the Branches, (فُرُوع), on account of their being derived from the roots and dependent on them.

[1] A very useful commentary on this branch of Muslim theology is the book of the learned Banáni called حاشية العلّامة البناني على شرح الجلال المحلّى على جمع الجوامع للامام ابن السبكى

[2] The word Qur'án, from قرأ to read, means the 'reading', or rather that which is to be read, the 'lectionary.' It was used at first to designate a portion only of the Qur'án, a lesson to be read, but was subsequently, and is now, used to designate the whole collection of the revelations of Muhammad (Súra xcvi.)

There are various other terms by which this collection of revelations is designated, such as Furqán (الفُرقان) from فرق to separate, to distinguish,

The Qur'án, as we now have it, consists of one hundred and fourteen chapters of unequal length called Súras[1]

---

because it distinguishes between truth and error, or because it is divided into sections (Hebrew : Perek, Pirka = portion, section of Scripture); Al-Kitáb (الكتاب), the Book, the Biblia Sacra of Muslims; the Mushaf (المُصْحَف) the Volume, collection of sheets.

The learned Suyúti relates that when the Qur'án was collected into one book, Abú Bakr requested his companions to call it by an appropriate name. Some proposed to call it Sifr (سِفْر), others Mushaf, because the Abyssinians used to call their holy book by this name.

[1] سُورة (Heb. שׁוּרָה) means a row or series of stones in a building, steps, and also a line in books or letters, applied to the chapters of the Qur'án, each being, as it were, a distinct row or step in the building of the whole.

Another division of the Qur'án is that into thirty sections, called جُزْء pl. أَجْزَآء, made to enable Muslims to read the whole of the Qur'án during the thirty days of the fast of Ramadán. Each of these sections is subdivided into four parts called رُبْع pl. أَرْبَاع. There are various other divisions besides. The number of words in the Qur'án is said to be 77,934 or 77,437.

These Súras have each a special title, taken from a particular subject treated of in the same. Thus the second Súra is called the Súra of the Cow (سُورة البَقَرَة); the third, the Súra of the family of 'Imrán (سُورة آل عِمْران). This is no doubt in imitation of the custom of the Jews. Suyúti mentions various traditions in support of Muhammad's having himself called certain Súras or portions of the Qurán by the name which they now bear. The verses are called آيات, signs, miracles, as each verse is considered a divine miracle. Muhammad himself assured his adherents that it would be impossible for men and genii, if they exerted themselves to the utmost, to produce any thing like them (Súra xvii. 90). This inimitability of the Qur'án is called the اعجاز القرآن i.e., its rendering any one incapable of producing anything like one of its verses. The Qur'án itself is therefore considered a sufficient proof of its divine origin and a 'standing miracle' (آية بَاقِيَة). For a complete list of the titles of the Súras see Dictionary of Islám by Hughes, p. 490.

The last word of the verse is called Fásila (فاصلة pl. فَوَاصِل), or separating word (فاصلة الآى). Suyúti says : " God has given to His Book.

(سُورَة pl. سُوَر). These are divided into verses (آيَة pl. آيَات). Each of the Súras has a special title. Muhammad and the Muslim doctors after him assert that everything contained in the Qur'án rests on direct

the whole of it, as well as its parts, different names from what the Arabs used to give to their books, for He called His Book as a whole قرآن, while the Arabs called their books Diwan (ديوان, collection of poems); the larger portions which they called Qasida, (قصيدة), He called Súra, and the smaller portions which they call Bait (بيت pl. أبيات) he called Áyat, (آية); the Fásila (فاصلة) of the Qur'án corresponds to the Qáfia (قافية), or rhyme of their poems."

The style in which the Qur'án is written is a kind of rhyming prose (سجع) *i.e.*, language having a final rhyme (فاصلة), without being measured, a style much in use in the time of Muhammad, and liked by the Arabs, and in which their soothsayers and poets (كاهن pl. كُهَّان - شاعر pl. شُعَرَآء) used to speak. Some Muslim doctors, however, strongly object to the style of the Qur'án being called سجع, or rhyming speech, as they consider it improper to ascribe to God artificial language.

The Qur'án is considered to be, not only the source of the knowledge of true religion, but of all knowledge and science in general. It is looked up to as the standard of the Arabic language, grammar, style, logic and is said to contain the elements of innumerable other sciences. As to its excellency Muhammad says : "He who reads a letter or syllable of the Qur'án receives for it the recompense of a good action, and this action is worth ten other good actions."—"The Qur'án contains a thousand times and twenty thousand letters; he who reads it with the desire of receiving a reward from God, and with patience, will receive (in Paradise) a ' Houri' as wife." For further details *see* Itqán II, 88 ff. ; Ghazáli Ihyá I, 168; Nöldeke : Dictionary of Islám ; Muir, the Qur'án.

Each of the Súras, except the ninth, begins with the basmala (بَسْمَلَة) or the words : " In the name of God, the Merciful, the Compassionate." There are twenty-nine Súras which have one or more letters of the alphabet prefixed to them. They are considered to have some mysterious mean-ing, which however only God and his Prophet know. Thus Súras 2, 3, 29, 30, 31, 32 begin with ١ ل م ; Súra 13 with ١ ل م ر ; Súras 10, 11, 12, 14, 15 with ١ ل ر ; Súra 19 with كهيعص. For a curious explanation of this last set of letters, *see* Sell's Essays on Islám, p. 225. For a com-plete list and suppositions as to the meaning of the letters generally *see*

revelation from God, (وَحْي), communicated to His Prophet in a miraculous manner, chiefly by the mediation of the 'Holy Ghost' (الرُّوح القُدُس), also called 'the faithful spirit' (الرُّوح الأمِين) by which is, however, meant, according to Muslim authorities, the Angel Gabriel. Súras (ii. 91, xvi. 104, xxvi. 193).

The chief modes of this divine inspiration (مَرَاتِب الوَحْي) were, according to Suyúti (Itqán i. 55), the following :

(1) By the mediation of an angel[1] coming to the Prophet, with a peculiar sound like the tinkling of bells (مِثْل صَلْصَلَة الجَرَس).

Itqán II, 10-14. Sale, p. 42-43. Dictionary of Islám, 517, 518. Nöldeke, 215. Faith of Islám, p. 64.

[1] The Angel Gabriel, on account of his being considered the chief mediator of inspiration, is called 'the Angel of Inspiration' مَلَك الوَحى.

Other learned doctors, like Kastalláni, the author of the famous biography of Muhammad :—the كتاب المواهب اللدنيّة—enumerate the following modes, such as :

Dream, vision (الرُّؤياء الصادقة حُلَم), inspiration of Gabriel into the heart of the Prophet without his seeing him (يلقيه الملك فى قلبه من غير ان يراه), and the appearance of Gabriel to the Prophet in human shape. He is said to have appeared to him several times in the shape of a certain Duhayyá (كان يتمثّل له الملك رجلاً. فقد كان ياتيه فى صورة دَحْيَّا). Inspiration is said to be accompanied by tinkling of bells or by the Prophet's seeing Gabriel in his true shape (with six hundred wings) ; or the Prophet's receiving revelations in heaven (ما واحاه الله اليه و هو فوق السموات); or God's speaking to the Prophet directly (كلام الله منه اليه بلا واسطه), as He did to Moses, or God's speaking with the Prophet face to face, without a separating curtain (تكليم الله له كفاحًا بغير حجاب). (Mawáhib i. 271—278).

Besides the above enumerated modes of inspiration, Suyúti says that "possibly the Angel received the revelation from God in a supernatural

(2) By instillation (نَفَثَ) into the heart of the Prophet,
whispering, suggestion. (يَنْفُثُ فِي رُوعِهِ الكَلَام)

(3) By the mediation of an angel in human shape.
(يأتِي فِي صُورَةِ الرَّجُلِ)

(4) By the appearance of an angel to the Prophet
while asleep. (يأتِي المَلَكُ فِي النوم) [1]

(5) By direct communication from God to the Prophet
in his waking or sleeping state. (ان يُكَلِّمَهُ اللهُ)

As regards the beginning of the revelations, 'Áyesha,
one of Muhammad's wives, says : "The first revelations
which the Prophet received were in true dreams, and he
never dreamt, but it came like the dawn of day. After this,
the Prophet became fond of retirement, and used to seclude
himself in a cave in Mount Hirá and worship there day
and night—till one day the Angel came to him and said :

---

manner, or learned it from the Preserved Tablet (اللَّوح المحفوظ) on
which it was written, and that he came down and transmitted it to the
Prophet." Some are of opinion that Gabriel transmitted to Muhammad
both the meanings and the words of the Qur'án in Arabic ; others, however,
are of opinion that only the meanings were communicated to him, and
that he expressed them in Arabic. Others mention a variety of other
modes of inspiration, as many as forty-six different kinds.

[1] Muhammad at first had some doubt as to whether the angel that
appeared to him was a good angel or the devil, as he had also feared his
being possessed by an evil spirit (مجنون). It is curious to observe how
Khadíja, his wife, undertook to decide the question as to the character
of the angel and to prove the genuineness of the inspiration. Ibn Hishám,
in his biography of the Prophet (i. 154), relates that when the angel once
appeared to Muhammad, she caused him (Muhammad) to sit on her left
thigh, then on her right thigh, then on her lap ; when Muhammad
assured her that the angel had not retired but remained in his place, she
took off her veil, (another version says ' caused Muhammad to slip into her
chemise') and asked Muhammad whether he still saw the angel ; on his
declaring that the angel had disappeared, Khadíja said : "Be of good
cheer, my cousin, by God it is an angel and not a devil."

'Read,' but the Prophet said : ' I am not a reader.' Then said Muhammad : "he took hold of me and squeezed me as much as I could bear, and he then let me go and again said : ' Read,' and I said : ' I am not a reader.' Then he took hold of me a second time and squeezed me as much as I could bear and then let me go and said : 'Read,' and I said : ' I am not a reader.' Then he took hold of me a third time and squeezed me as much as I could bear, and said :

'Read! in the name of thy Lord who created ;
Created man from a clot of blood.
Read! for thy Lord is the most beneficent,
He hath taught the use of the pen ;
He hath taught man that which he knoweth not.'
(Súra xcvi. 1-5)

Then the Prophet repeated the words himself, and with his heart trembling returned (*i.e.*, from Hirá to Mecca) to Khadíja and said : ' Wrap me up ! wrap me up !' and they wrapped him up in a garment till his fear was dispelled, and he told Khadíja what had occurred, and he said : ' Verily I was afraid I should have died.'"[1] Then Khadíja said : ' No, it will not be so. I swear by God, He will never make thee ashamed. For verily thou art kind to relatives, thou bearest the afflictions of the people, thou art hospitable and assisteth thy fellow-men.' After this Khadíja took the Prophet to Waraqa (ﻭﺭﻗﺔ) bin Naufal, her cousin, and said to him : ' O my cousin, hear what thy brother's son says.' Then Waraqa said to the Prophet : 'O son of my brother! what doest thou see ;'

---

[1] A tradition mentions that Muhammad said : "They wrapped me up and poured cold water over me.—Bukhári mentions that Waraqa bin Naufal, the cousin of Khadíja, had embraced Christianity in the days of ignorance," *i.e.*, before Islám, and that he used to copy from the Hebrew book (Thorah) and from the New Testament (ﺍﻹﻧﺠﻴﻞ), Bukhári i, 2.

then the Prophet told Waraqa what he had seen, and Waraqa said : ' This is the Námús (ناموس) which God sent to Moses.' "[1]

'Áyesha also says : " Verily I saw him (Muhammad perspire when the revelation came down to him, he became melancholy and turned pale in the face " and also : " When the revelation came down to him, he used to cover his head and his face, his teeth became cold and the perspiration ran down on his skin in drops like pearls." Another Tradition says that " froth appeared before his mouth and he roared like a young camel." (Bukhári i. 2. Mishkát).

After this first appearance of the Angel, tradition says that the revelations stopped for sometime (six months, two or three years, according to different authorities), which made Muhammad so sad that he determined to commit suicide by throwing himself from the top of ¯a hill; ¯but when he went up in order to carry out his intention, Gabriel is said to have appeared to him and to have said to him : " O Muhammad, verily thou art the Prophet of God in truth." At these words he was comforted and at ease. The Imám Ahmad says : " God appointed the Angel Isráfíl to be the Prophet's companion for three years, during which interval he instructed him ; but no Qurán was sent down to him through his instrumentality ; then God sent Gabriel to be with him, and through the instrumentality of this Angel the Qur'án was sent down to him for the space of twenty years.[2]

---

[1] For the Arabic text see Bukhári ii. 2-3. Námús evidently means the νόμος, or the Law, Mawáhíb i. 254-259.

[2] Some portions are said to have been communicated to Muhammad directly from the " Treasury of Mercy below the throne of God," (من كنز الرحمة من تحت عرش اللّه) which is considered a privilege granted to no other prophet but Muhammad.

The Qur'án is said to have been extant in the highest heaven from eternity,[1] written on the Preserved Table (اللوح المحفوظ) near the throne of God, and from thence to have been sent down to the lowest heaven, in the month of Ramadán, in the night of Al Qadr (ليلة القدر, night of the decree) and stored up there in the Temple of Majesty (بيت العزة), from whence it was revealed to Muhammad in smaller or larger portions in the course of twenty to twenty-five years. (Jowh, 89. Itqán i. 47-49).

Muhammad never undertook the task of collecting and systematically arranging his revelations in one book, and the Qur'án, as we now have it, did not, therefore, exist in his life-time. The several portions had been written down from his lips,[1] from time to time, by an amanuensis, or some friend or follower present, on any material that happened to be at hand such as palm-leaves, bones, stones, leather, etc. For the space of about a year also after Muhammad's death no need was felt for collecting and arranging these portions, as they were preserved in the retentive memories of the many 'Readers' of the Qur'án. When however various readings crept into the holy text, and numbers of the readers who had learned the Qur'án from the Prophet's lips had fallen in the many battles

---

[1] The Qur'án is now held by all orthodox Muslims to be eternal and uncreated (قديم - غير مخلوق) when the essential word of God is meant; but when the written and pronounced Qur'án is meant, it is not eternal but created.

مذهب اهل السنة ان القرآن بمعنى الكلام النفسى ليس بمخلوق - و امّا
القران بمعنى اللفظ الذى نقرؤه فهو مخلوق (Jowh 68. 88)

Ghazáli says on the subject : "The Qur'án is read and pronounced with the tongue, written in books, and kept in memory and yet is eternal, subsisting in God's essence' (i.e., the meanings of the Qur'án are in God,) co-essential and co-eternal with him, but the written book containing them is recent and created."

that were fought in those times, it was felt by many that,
if the various portions of the Holy Book were not collected
and arranged, and the various readings sifted and the true
text fixed and written down, much of the text might be
lost, and the greatest confusion of various readings be the
result of such neglect. 'Umar bin al Khaṭṭáb was the
first to give expression to the want thus felt. He advised
Abú Bakr, who was the Khalif at the time, to order the
Qur'án to be collected into one book. Abú Bakr hesitated
at first, but at last he consented and ordered Zaíd bin
Thábit (زيد بن ثابت) to undertake the task. The various
portions of the Qur'án were collected from the materials
on which they had been written, and from the memories[1]
of men and written down by Zaid on ' sheets ' (صحف) and

---

[1] Among those to whom Muhammad had occasionally dictated his
revelations were 'Ali and 'Uthmán. Among the amanuenses who were
formally engaged for such work we see Zaid bin Thábit, who is also said to
have learned Hebrew for the purpose of conducting the Prophet's corre-
spondence with the Jews. As many as twenty-four persons are mentioned
as having occasionally acted as scribes. At Mecca, when Muhammad had
no regular scribe, he had the assistance of Khadija, Waraqa, 'Ali and Abú
Bakr, who all could read and write. At Muhammad's death the materials
on which portions of the Qur'án had been written down were found
heaped up in the room of Hafasa, one of his wives.

Even during Muhammad's lifetime various readings had crept into
the text of the Qur'án which gave occasion to him to declare ' that the
Qur'án had been revealed in seven versions ' (أنزل على سبعة احرف).
Bukhári iii. 188, Itqán i. 56—59.

Abú Bakr, at first, hesitated to give the order for collecting and editing the
Qur'án, as he said that he had received no authority or command on the
subject from the Prophet. Zaid, an intelligent young man, who had been
accustomed to write down the revelations, being aware of the difficulties
and the importance of the task at first refused to undertake it; but, on
being urged again and again, consented and collected whatever he could
from the scattered portions of the Qur'án, written on palm-leaves, bones
etc., and from the memories of men. One portion he found with a single
man only. (For further details see : Itkán i. 71-74; Bukhári iii. 186—
188 ; Muir's Life of Muhammad, 551 ff. Dictionary of Islám, 486—489).

delivered to Abú Bakr who preserved them during his lifetime.

The Shí'ah sects pretend that 'Ali collected the Qur'án into a volume during Muhammad's lifetime and at his command. (*See* Nöldeke, 191, Sprenger III. p. xliv.)

On what principles Zaid performed his task of collecting and editing the Qur'án, and what was the exact character of this first edition, it is difficult to ascertain, as no copies of the same have been preserved. What we can collect on the subject from various records still extant is:

(1) That the collector and editor, Zaid, one of Muhammad's scribes was, on the whole, a man well-qualified for such kind of work; that he was a young man "intelligent, honest and unbiassed" and, therefore, not suspected of having any inclination to tamper with the text of the Qur'án.

(2) That he had been instructed not to receive anything as belonging to the Qur'án unless two witnesses at least testified to this being the case.

(3) That in putting together the portions of the Qur'án, he in general followed the original from which he copied, but occasionally added verses to a longer Chapter, or portion, without regard to sense and connection.

(4) That he does not seem to have arranged the Qur'án into Súras, but to have only collected the materials he found in parts or portions (صُحُف sheets, leaves, bundles). This is confirmed by a tradition which says : ' he collected it, not arranged into Súras, after immense trouble.'

. (جمعه غير مرتّب السور بعد تعب شديد)

(5) That his edition, though complete on the whole, did not contain every verse which had been 'revealed.' Some parts may have been suppressed by Muhammad, others forgotten.

(6) That it is not likely that either Zaid or 'Umar intentionally altered any part of the text, or made additions or omissions.

(7) That Zaid's edition does not, however, seem to have been generally received as the authoritative text and standard edition, for a number of the Qur'án readers continued to read certain verses in a different way, in which they pretended to have heard them from the Prophet, without regard to the text fixed by Abú Bakr. Still, there is no doubt that this first compilation was of very great importance, as it formed a generally reliable basis for a later revised edition.

(Itqán i. 71-74; Muir's Life of Muhammad, pp. 555-577 ; Nöldeke, 189-204 ; Dictionary of Islám, 486-487. Sell's Essays on Islám, pp. 218-241, in which the Arabic text of the lost Súra, the Súratu'n Núrain, is given).

Notwithstanding this attempt of Abú Bakr to fix an authoritative text of the Qur'án, which would be generally received, and to do away with all "readings" differing from it, the differences in reading the Qur'án not only continued, but increased and spread in the various countries subjected to the Muslim rule to such a degree that the greatest confusion ensued, and angry strife and controversy was the result thereof.[1]

---

[1] 'Uthmán also had recourse to Zaid b Thábit with whom he associated a syndicate of three members of the Quraish. He sent to Hafasa requesting her to send those portions which she had, (الصحف) saying : " I shall have a number of copies taken of them and then return them." 'Uthmán then ordered Zaid and 'Abdu'lláh bin Jubair and Said ibn-ul-Aás, 'Abdu'r Rahmán al Hárith to take copies of them. (Itqán i, 74-76). To these he said : " When you and Zaid differ in anything concerning the language of the Qur'án, then write it in the language (dialect) of the Quraish, for it was revealed in their language." They did as 'Uthmán had commanded them, and the old original was returned to Hafasa. Transcripts of the new recension were then forwarded to the chief cities in the empire and the previously existing copies were all, by the Khalif's command, committed to the flames. Bukhári says that the copy of Abú Bakr's recension, committed to the keeping of Hafasa, was soon after destroyed by Marwán, governor of Madina, lest it should make people to doubt. Copies of this new edition were sent to Kúfa, Basra, Yaman, Bahrain and Damascus ; one copy remained at Madína. The secopies seem, however, to have been soon lost, and no trace of them is to be found now.

This edition of 'Uthmán has been handed down to us. Notwithstanding the care which had been taken to produce an absolutely correct edition, it seems that it did not prove to be quite free from mistakes, (orthographical, grammatical, idiomatic), for 'Uthmán, on examining the copies written at his command, said : " I perceive mistakes in them but the Arabs will correct them." (اری حنّا و ستقیمة العرب).

A comparison of a number of copies of the Qur'án will show that it is, as little as any ancient book, free from various readings ; (- روایات - روایة - قراءة - قرآت) They do not, however, amount to any important alteration of the sense of the text, and are, chiefly, the result of the ignorance or negligence of the transcribers, or their desire to correct what they considered not quite clear or correct.

In consequence of the alarming spread of the differences in reading the Qur'án and the great confusion caused by the same, the Khalif 'Uthmán was persuaded to have a new recension of the Qur'án made, which was to be accepted as the authorized and standard text of the Holy Book, and which was to do away with all readings differing from the same.[1]

The chief Qur'án-readers (حُفَّاظَ قُرَّاء) who were recommended by Muhammad himself, as regards their correct and extensive knowledge of the Qur'án, and of whom he said : " Learn the Qur'án from them " (خُذُوا القُرآن عن اربعة) are the following four :—[2]

1. 'Abdu'llah bin Mas'úd (عبد الله بن مسعود)

2. Sálim bin Ma'qal (سالم بن معقل)

3. Ma'áz bin Jabal (معاذ بن جبل)

4. Ubai ibn Ka'b. (أبي ابن كعب)

Addani in his book المُقْنِع فى رسم المصحف treats at large on this subject. (Itqán i. 12-7 ff.) Nöldeke in his Geschichtes dés Qur'áns gives a full list of the varianta extracted from that work, see pp. 237-266.

[1] At last Hudaifa bin al Yaman (حَذِيفَة) who had warred both in Armenia and Azerbijan, and had observed the difference between the readings of the Syrians and the men of Irak, alarmed at the number and extent of the variations, warned the Khalif 'Uthmán to interpose, " before they should differ (regarding their Scriptures) as did the Jews and the Christians."

[2] The first two were of the Refugees (مهاجرين) and the other two of the Ansár (انصار, Helpers, Madína men). Sálim, died at the battle of Yamama, and Ma'áz during the Khalifate of 'Umar, Ubai and 'Abdu'lláh bin Mas'úd during the Khalifate of 'Uthmán. Zaid outlived them all, and became the chief authority on the Qur'án. Suyúti says: " those of the Companions (اصحاب) of the Prophet who who were celebrated for their knowledge of the Qur'án are seven : 'Uthmán, 'Ali, Ubai, Zaid, Ibn Ma'súd, Abú Dardai, Abú Músa-ul-Ash'ari. From them the knowledge of the Qur'án was transmitted to a number of the 'Followers (التابعين) For details see Itqán i. 88 sqq.

Among the Qur'án readers in the various dominions of Islám the following seven are considered as of higher authority than all others, and their readings are considered the standard readings. They are called the seven Imáms (الأئمة السبعة) Itqán i, 92) *Náfi'* (نافع) *Abú 'Amar* (ابو عمر) *Ibn 'Ámír* (ابن عاصر) *'Ásim* (عاصم) *Hamza* (حمزة) *Al Kisá'i* (الكسائي). To these some add three more, so that we often read of the ten Imáms. The generally recognized ones however are the above mentioned seven.

For further details on this subject *see* Itkan 88-104. Nöldeke, p. 234-299. Sell's Faith of Islám, pp. 332-358.

The varianta are divided into several classes, according to the authority on which they rest, and the value they consequently possess. They are called :

(1) قراءة when resting on the authority of one of the seven Imáms.

(2) رواية when transmitted by some one on the authority of one of these Imáms.

(3) طريق when mentioned by some learned doctor of later authority.

(4) وجه when the reader is at liberty to choose between the various readings. (Itqán i, 93-97).

The Súras of the Qur'án are neither arranged chronologically nor according to matter; but chiefly as to length or shortness. The long Súras were placed first and the short ones last. Within the Súras, some portions have been arranged in chronological order, others on the ground of similarity of matter; but in a variety of instances passages are joined together without any regard to either chronology or similarity of subject. Thus we find verses revealed at Mecca in the midst of Madína Súras, and passages revealed at Madína mixed up in the earlier Mecca

Súras, and occasionally most heterogeneous materials put together without any regard to logical connexion at all.

It is, however, of great importance, for the sake of the exegesis of the Qur'án, to ascertain, as far as this is possible, the chronological order in which the Súras, or various parts of the Súras, have been revealed.[1]

In general the Súras may be divided into :

(1) *Mecca Súras* (سُور مَكِّيَّة) *i.e.*, Súras revealed at Mecca, or more correctly the Súras revealed before Muhammad's flight to Madína.

(2) *Madina Súras* (سُور مَدَنِيَّة) *i.e.*, Súras revealed at Madína, or more correctly all Súras revealed after the flight to Madína, whether revealed in that city itself, or in some other place.

Commentators have laid down certain rules by which they say that the Meccan Súras can be distinguished from the Madína Súras such as

(1) What begins by " O ye believers" (يا ايها الذين آمنوا) belongs to the later Madína Súras.

---

[1] For classification of the Súras according to Arabic authorities *see* Itqán i. 10-12.

Though it is not possible to fix with absolute certainty the time at which each portion of the Qur'án has been revealed, still we have material which will help us in ascertaining, for the greater part of the same, the period and the occasion at which they were ' revealed'.

Many works have been written on the subject by learned doctors of Islám. Abú-l-Kásim Neisaburi says : " One of the most noble branches of the sciences of the Qur'án is the knowledge of the manner, the occasion and the place of the revelation of the Qur'án and the chronological order in which the Súras have been revealed at Mecca, and what at Madína, and what at other places. He who does not know these things is not allowed to speak on the Book of God." (Itqán i. 10.)

(2)   What begins with : " O ye sons of Adam," or " O ye people " (آدم يا بني ‬ـ‬ يا ايها الناس) belongs to the Mecca Súras.

(3)   Passages in which the " by-gone generations " (الامم والقرون) are referred to are of Meccan origin.

(4)   Passages which contain laws and ordinances' (سنن و فرائض) belong to the later Madína Súras. According to Ibn 'Abbás, there are twenty-seven Madína Súras ; the remainder are Meccan.

European Scholars, such as Weil, Nöldeke, Muir, Rod-well, Palmer adopt different classifications, which vary in several points from that of the Muslim doctors.

Sir W. Muir gives the following approximative chrono-logical order of the Súras :

First Period.   Eighteen Súras : 103, 100, 99, 91, 106, 1, 101, 95, 102, 104, 82, 92, 105, 89, 90, 93, 94, 108.   These are all short rhapsodies.   They may have been composed before Muhammad had conceived the idea of a Divine Mission.

Second Period.   The opening of Muhammad's minis-try, Súras 96, 113, 74, 111.

Third Period.   From the commencement of Muham-mad's public ministry to the Abyssinian emigration, Súras, 87, 97, 88, 80, 81, 84, 86, 110, 85, 83, 78, 77, 76, 75, 70, 109, 107, 55, 56.   These are chiefly composed of descriptions of the Resurrection, Paradise and Hell, with references to the growing opposition of the Quraish.

Fourth Period.   From the 6th to the 10th year of Muhammad's ministry, Súras, 67, 53, 32, 39, 73, 79, 54, 34, 31, 69, 68, 41, 71, 52, 50, 45, 44, 37, 30, 26, 15, 51. With this period begin narratives from Jewish Scriptures and rabbinical and Arab legends.   The temporary compro-mise with idolatry is connected with Súra 53.

Fifth Period. From the 10th year of Muhammad's
ministry to the flight to Medina, Súras 46, 72, 35, 36, 19,
18, 27, 42, 40, 38, 25, 20, 43, 12, 11, 10, 14, 6, 64, 28, 23,
22, 21, 17, 16, 13, 29, 7, 113, 114. The Súras of this
period contain some narratives from the Gospel.

Sixth Period. Súras 98, 2, 3, 8, 47, 62, 5, 59, 4, 58,
65, 63, 24, 33, 57, 61, 48, 60, 66, 49, 9.[1]

In Rodwell's Qur'án translated from the Arabic, the
Súras are arranged in chronological order. Professor
Palmer in his translation of the Qur'án into English gives
an abstract of the contents of each Súra of the Qur'án,
which may also be found in the Dictionary of Islám,
p. 492-515.

There are in the Qur'án passages suggested by men.
Suyúti mentions that in several cases the 'Truth' was also
revealed through the instrumentality of other persons
than the Prophet.[2]

---

[1] For more details see Muir, The Qur'án, 43-47. Nöldeke 45-174.
Sell's Historical Development of the Qur'án, S. P. C. K.

[2] Thus he mentions that Ibn Merdawiyya said : " 'Umar used to have
an opinion on a certain subject and lo ! a Qur'án revelation came down in
accordance with the same." Bukhári also reports on this subject :
" 'Umar used to say : 'I and my Lord (God) agreed in three things."
I said ' O Apostle of God, that we might adopt the Makám of Abraham,
the Ka'ba, as a place of worship '—and a revelation came down to that
effect : ' Take ye the Makám (sanctuary) of Abraham for a place of worship.'
(Súra ii. 119) ; then I said : 'O Apostle of God,' I see the pious and the
wicked enter thy house and look at thy wives ; it would therefore be better
if thou didst command them to put up a curtain, and lo ! —the verse of
the curtain (الحجاب آية) was revealed : ' When ye ask them (the
Prophet's wives) for an article, ask them from behind a curtain ' (Súra
xxxiii. 53) ; then when I saw the wives of the Apostle of God collect
around him in a state of jealousy I said : ' Perhaps God will make him
divorce you and give him better wives than you are ' and lo ! —a revelation came down in these terms ' (Súra lxvi. 5). 'Umar further says :
" When the verse ' Truly we have created man of a choice sort of earth '
(Súra xxiii. 12) was revealed, I exclaimed : ' Blessed be God the most
excellent of creators ! ' and this (exclamation) was literally received into

Though the Qur'án is, on the whole, a complete collection of the revelations of Muhammad, still some smaller portions seem to have been omitted when it was collected into a volume, so that it cannot be considered as absolutely complete.[1]

---

the Qur'án." Al Bará also says: " When the verse 'Those of the believers who remain at home and those who fight in the way of God are not alike ' (Súra iv. 97) was revealed, the Prophet said : ' Call Zaid and let him bring the tablet and the inkstand,' then he said to him : ' write, Those of the believers who remain at home and those who fight in the way of God are not alike.' Hereupon Amrú bin Umm Maktúm, a blind man who stood behind him exclaimed : ' What dost thou command me O- Apostle of God, for I am a blind man.' In consequence of this, the verse was changed to ' Those of the believers who remain at home, except those who have a defect, ∴. (Súra iv. 97.) See Baidáwi's Commentary on the verse.

Several other instance of this kind are mentioned by Suyúti, showing that Muhammad had no objection to embody in the Qur'án opinions and expressions from other people, when he considered them suitable and expressive. It seems difficult to reconcile this with the orthodox doctrine that every single word of the Qur'án was from eternity written on the Preserved Table and communicated to Muhammad by direct divine revelation (Itqán i. 43 et seqq.)

1 Suyúti (Itqán ii, 30-32) mentions that 'Umar is reported to have said : " some of you say ' I possess the whole Qur'án,' but how can he know what is the whole Qur'án since a great portion of the same has disappeared. Let him rather say: ' I possess of it what is still extant;' also of 'Áyesha that she said : 'the Súra of the Confederates (xxxiii) consisted at the time of the Prophet of two hundred verses; when 'Uthmán wrote the Mushaf, he was only able to collect of it what it now contains ' (i.e. 73 verses); also that ' Ubai bin K'ab said to Zarr bin Jeish : How many verses dost thou count the Súra of the Confederates? He replied seventy-two or seventy-nine." ' Ubai said : ' It used to be as long as the Súra of the cow (286 verses), and we used to read in it the ' verses of the stoning ' of the adulterer (آيَةُ الرَّجْمِ). Zarr said : ' what is the verse of the stoning,' to which 'Ubai replied : ' If the old man and the old woman commit adultery, stone them.' "

'Umar himself was so convinced that this verse was part of the Qur'án that he said : " If I were not afraid that people would say 'Umar has added something to the Book of God, I should write it down in the Qur'án."

There are in the Qur'án a number of passages which contradict each other (ناقص). In order to remove from the Holy Book the reproach of contradiction and inconsistency, Muhammad himself set up the theory of abrogation (نَسخ). In Súra ii. 100, God is made to say : " Whatever verse we abrogate (ما نَنسَخ), or cause thee to forget, we will bring a better one than it, or one like it." This theory was subsequently worked out more systematically by Muslim theologians.[1]

Another passage which 'Áyesha affirms they used to read as part of the Qur'án, and which is no more to be found in the same, is a verse commanding mothers to suck their children for the space of ten months (Itqán ii. 26). One very remarkable instance of the suppression of a verse, which Muhammad used to read for sometime as part of the Qur'án, is that of the verse : " Those idols (of the Meccan idolaters) are the noble beings, and verily their intercession may be looked for." (تلك الغرانيق العُلَى و ان شفاعتهم لَتُرتَجَى) Later on Muhammad declared it not to have been a divine revelation but a satanic suggestion. (Mawáhib i. 336. Muir's Life of Muhammad, pp. 86-91. Nöldeke, p. 80). Suyúti mentions various other verses which formed originally part of the Qur'án, but which are no more extant in the same. The learned doctors of Islám explain such omissions by saying that God has taken away (رفع) the passages alluded to, causing them to be either quite forgotten or at all events not to be written down in the Book.

[1] 'Abú-l-Kásim Hibatu'lláh bin Salama, the author of the book كتاب الناسخ والمنسوخ, divides the abrogated passages (ناسخ abrogating; منسوخ abrogated) into three classes :

(1) Passages the sense of which is abrogated, but the words remain— ما نُسِخ حُكمُهُ دون تلاوته, e.g., the Jerusalem Qibla, abrogated by the Ka'ba Qibla.

(2) Passages the words of which have been abrogated, but the sense remains ما نُسِخ تلاوتهُ دون حُكمه e.g., the command of stoning adulterers, the words of which are no more extant in the Qur'án, but the command still remains obligatory.

(3) Passages abrogated both as to the sense and the words— ما نسخ تلاوتهُ و حكمهُ معاً e.g., the verse commanding the mothers to suck

An important subject in connexion with the exegesis of
the Qur'án is the knowledge of what are called the
obscure or, ambiguous and the clear verses of the Qur'án
(المتشابه والمحكم).   In Súra iii. 5 it is said : " He it is
who has revealed to thee the Book of which there are
some verses that are clear (perspicuous) these are the
mother (basis) of the Book—and others are ambiguous
(figurative) ;—as for those in whose heart is perversity,
they follow what is ambiguous and do crave for sedition,
craving for their own interpretation of it, but none know
the interpretation of it but God.   But those who are well

---

their children for the space of ten months. (For more details *see*
Itqán ii. 24-32).

As regards abrogating and abrogated passages, great differences of
opinion exist between the many authors who have made this doctrine
the special subject of their studies, some holding that only a passage
of the Qur'án is able to abrogate another passage of the Qur'án, others
maintaining that the Sunna also, *i.e.*, saying of Muhammad, being also
'of God' is able to abrogate even a passage of the Qur'án.

Only such passages, however, as contain a command (أَمَر) or prohibition
(نَهَى) can be abrogated.   Historical portions, reports (خَبَر) promises (وَعَد)
threatening (وعيد) can never be abrogated. (Itqán ii. 25, a list of the
abrogating and the abrogated passages, according to the Itqán, is to be
found in Dictionary of Islám p. 520.   Faith of Islám, pp. 74-77).

It is, therefore, a mistake when some Christian controversialists state
that the Muslims hold that the Old Testament (توراة) has been abrogated
by the New Testament (انجيل) and that both have been abrogated by the
Qur'án.

They hold no such opinion as, according to the abovementioned rule,
only such passages of the Old and New Testaments (divinely inspired
books) as contain a command or a prohibition could be abrogated, and all
other portions, history, promises, threats can never be abrogated in the
technical sense of the word abrogation.

There are a number of passages in the Qur'án which the learned say are
only 'apparently' contradictory ; but which can by proper interpretation
be brought into harmony.   If this should, however, be impossible, one of
the contradictory passages must be declared abrogating " as it is impossible
to admit that the Qur'án contradicts itself." (Itqán ii. 32-37).

grounded in knowledge say : ' We believe in it ; it is all from our Lord ; but none will remember but those who possess minds.' "[1]

Though Muhammad pretended that every word of the Qur'án was the result of divine inspiration,[2] it must become evident that by far the greater portion of it consists of materials collected from Jews, Christians, Sabeans, Magi and pagan Arabs.

---

[1] There are various opinions with regards to these two kinds of verses, but the more generally adopted one is that the clear, perspicuous (مُحْكَم) ones are those clearly understood without any allegorical interpretation, and the ambiguous, figurative ones, those which God has reserved to His own knowledge, such as the verses which refer to the Last Day, the appearing of Antichrist, the letters at the beginning of the Súras, also such expressions as face, hand, right hand, when applied to God. " These verses are to be believed, but not to be explained." (For more details *see* Itqán ii. 2-15, and, alao Ibn Khaldún ; also Faith of Islám pp. 169-70 for a different reading in Súra iii. 5 and the important result which followed from it.)

[2] The Muslim divines declare that Muhammad being the ' illiterate Prophet ' (النبى الامى) unable to read and to write, he could not have obtained the contents of the Qur'án, except through divine revelation, and that the Qur'án, under these circumstances, must be considered one of the greatest proofs of Muhammad's prophetic character.

Whether Muhammad knew how to read and to write is a controverted question. Most Muslims deny it ; some however affirm it. As a number of people at Mecca were conversant with the art of reading and writing, and Muhammad was a most intelligent man and had acted for a long time as mercantile agent for Khadíjá it is not unnatural to suppose that he too was able to read and to write. That he did not, however, possess any part of the Old or New Testament from which he might have derived much of his information, is pretty certain. Still, it is a fact that he had many opportunities at Mecca, on his journeys to Syria, and during his stay at Madína of obtaining religious information from Kos, bishop of Negran, Waraqa, Salmán the Persian and the Jews at Madína. (*See* Ibn Hishám i. 144. Sprenger i. 60 and 102-137. Rodwell Qur'án, Introduction p. xviii., Geiger's Was hat Muhammadans dem Judenthum aufgenommen in English Translation (S. P. C. K., Madras). Gerock Christologie des Qur'án, Nöldeke 1—15, Tisdall's Sources of Islám).

It has been said with much truth " that Islám owes more to Judaism than it does to either Christianity or Sabaism and that it is simple

Commentaries on the Qur'án are numerous. Very soon after Muhammad's death, some of his companions and chief followers began to comment on certain passages of the Qur'án. Among the first who did so are mentioned the four first Khalífs, 'Ali, Mas'úd, Ibn 'Abbás, Zaid ibn Thábit, Abú Musa bin Ash'ari.[1]

The commentaries chiefly consulted at present are :

Al Jalálain - الكتاب الجلالين في تفسير القرآن العظيم
It is the joint work of Jalálu's Suyúti and Zatalu'l Mahalli. (864 A.H.) It is printed at Boulak.

Al Baidáwi (685 A.H.) كتاب انوار التنزيل واسرار التاويل
للبيضاوي Ed. Fleischer, Leizig 2 vol.

Al-Baghawi (515 A. H.) تفسير البغوي

Az-Zamakhshari (604 A.H.) الكشاف عن حقائق التنزيل
للزمخشري I. II. Calcutta.

Muhammad Rázi Fakharu'd Din (606 A.H.) مفاتيح الغيب
للامام محمد فخر الدين الرازي Boulak.

Talmudic Judaism adapted to Arabic, *plus* the apostleship of Jesus and Muhammad, and that where Muhammad, departs from the monotheistic principles, as in the idolatrous practice of the pilgrimage to the Ka'ba, it is evident that it is done as a necessary concession to the national feelings and sympathies of the people of Arabia." (Deutsch.)

[1] Among these, the chief man is no doubt Ibn 'Abbás (68 A.H.) a cousin of Muhammad, for their fathers were brothers. He lived at Madína and is said to have been only thirteen years of age at the time of the Prophet's death. He fought in North Africa and was appointed by 'Ali, the Governor of Basra. After the death of 'Ali, he retired from public service and devoted himself entirely to the study of the Qur'án. He was the great authority on the Qur'án and was therefore called ' the Interpreter of the Qur'án ' (ترجمان القرآن), and ' the Ocean ' (البحر), and may be considered the Father of the exegesis of the Qur'án. (Itqán ii. 221. Sprenger iii. cvi). For a list of the chief of the earlier commentators (2nd and 3rd century A. H.) *See* Itqán ii. 222-226—Sprenger iii. 104-120. Of these, however, we only know the names; their commentaries are lost.

The best European edition of the Arabic Qur'án is the *Corani Textus Arabicus.* ed. Gustav Flügel Lipsiæ 4to. A book which will be found most useful in the study of the Qur'án is a concordance on the same, Concorantiæ Corani Arabicæ Ed. Fluegel Lypsiæ. Of English translations, with introductory remarks and more or less copious explanatory notes on the text, these may be mentioned :— The Qur'án by George Sale. The Qur'án by J. M. Rodwell. The Qur'án by E. H. Palmer. Some useful books are :—The Qur'án, its Composition and Teaching by Sir W. Muir, London, published by the Religious Tract Society : also Sell's Historical Development of the Qur'án, (S. P. C. K.). Tisdall's Sources of the Qur'án (S. P. C. K.).

Before concluding this chapter it may be interesting to hear what As-Suyúti, in his famous Introduction to the Qur'án (Itqán) says on the variety of subjects the student of the Qur'án must make himself acquainted with, before he is able thoroughly to understand the meanings of the Holy Book. Among these he mentions the following, which form so many chapters of his work :

The Mecca and the Madína Súras, Súras revealed at home, on a journey, in the day time, at night, in summer, in winter, in bed, in a dream, on earth, in heaven ; first revealed, last revealed ; the occasion of the various revelations ; what was revealed by the mouth of some person other than Muhammad ; what was twice revealed, what became law before it was revealed in the Qur'án, and what became law after it had been revealed in the Qur'án ; portions revealed ' en bloc' and portions revealed separately ; what had been revealed to other prophets also and what was revealed to Muhammad only ; the manner in which the Qur'án was revealed ; the names of the Qur'án and the titles of the Súras ; the collecting and arranging of the Qur'án ; the Qur'án readers ; the authorities for the various readings, the varianta, the science of reading the Qur'án ; what is written in a language not Arabic ; what is clear and what is ambiguous ; passages abrogating and passages abrogated ; passages apparently contradictory ; what is meant in a literal and what in a tropical sense ; the similes and parables used in the Qur'án ; the beauties and excellencies of the Qur'án, the rhymes ; the sciences derived from the Qur'án, &c. (Compare also the article الكتاب in Bannáni i, 117-127 and the chapter آداب تلاوة القرآن in Ghazáli's Ihyá i, 168-182).

The Sunna, (سُنَّة), the second foundation of Islám, is
next in importance to the Qur'án.[1] The term signifies the
custom, habit, usage of the Prophet. It designates his
behaviour, mode of action, his sayings and declarations
under a variety of circumstances in life, which are
considered to be so many rules to be observed, and examples to be imitated by all pious Muslims. It is also called
Hadíth (حديث), piece of information, account, narra-
tive, story and record of the actions, doings and sayings
of the Prophet, as recorded and handed down by tradition
and which have become the rule of faith and practice
of Muslims.

The science of Tradition (علم الحديث) is considered the
noblest and most excellent after that of the Qur'án, and
its study the next in importance to that of the Holy
Book. Muhammad himself is said to have encouraged
his followers to keep and transmit his sayings.[2]

----

1 سُنَّة (pl. سُنَن) from v. سَنَّ to institute, establish a custom, a
practice, a usage to be followed; way course, rule, mode of acting or
conduct, statute, ordinance (Ban. ii. 64. السُنَّة اصطلاحاً تطلق على المجموع)
من اقواله صلعم و افعاله و تقريراته) Both terms سنة and حديث are often
used promiscuously, as if they were synonymous, which strictly speaking
they are not, for sunna properly designates the mode of action,
practice and the sayings and declarations (اقوال - تقريرات) of the Prophet,
while, Hadíth designates the narration, account and record of such
actions, practices or sayings.

An account, record of such an act or saying, is called a Hadíth or a
Tradition (حديث pl. احاديث). The term حديث is also used to designate
a whole collection of Traditions, such as the Collection of Traditions
of Bukhári, Muslim, &c.

2 He is reported to have said : " May God bless him who hears my
words and keeps them, and understands them, and transmits them,"
and also : " Transmit from me if it be but one verse." (بلغوا عنى ولو اية)
When once asked who would be his successors, he replied : " Those who

Very soon after the death of Muhammad, the want of possessing more detailed and reliable information on the exact meaning of certain passages of the Qur'án and certain doctrines and practices of Islám made itself felt and gradually stimulated the desire to have the Traditions (احاديث), which had hitherto not been generally accessible and had only been transmitted by word of mouth, collected, sifted and written down, so as to preserve them from corruption and loss and to have them fixed as a code of law. About one hundred years after

report my sayings (احادیثی) and instruct men in the same." Sufiánu'th, Thúri (سفيان الثورى) says: "I do not know a more excellent science than the science of Tradition (علم الحديث), for people are in need of it even with regard to their food and drink; it is more excellent than prayer and fasting." Hákim says: "If it were not for the great companies of Traditionists (مُحَدِّث pl. مُحَدِّثُون), the light of Islám would have been extinguished." Muhammad used to say: "science (religious science of Islám) consists of three things: well ordered verse, well observed sunna and just law." (العلم ثلاثة آية مُحكَّمة اوسنَّة قائمة اوفريضة عادلة)

Under the term Sunna are comprised:

(1) all utterances, sayings, declarations, oral laws emanating from the Prophet. These are called سنَّةُ القول, Sunna of saying.

(2) His acts, customs, practice سنَّةُ الفعل, Sunna of action.

(3) His silent approbation and sanction of certain acts of others سنة التقرير, Sunna of approbation, confirmation (Ban. ii. 65.)

These traditions are, on account of their importance, also called وَحى غير مَتَلو (unread revelation) *i.e.*, uninspired record of inspired sayings of the Prophet.

To obey the Sunna is a duty laid upon every pious Muslim, in imitation of the Prophet. It is not, however, a duty of the same obligation as the commands of the Qur'án, which are فرض *i.e.*, duty of absolute obligation. The duty of observing the Sunna and conforming to its rules is of various degrees of importance: such as the سنّة الهدى or Sunna of guidance; سنة موكّدة the Sure Sunna, or those duties which cannot be neglected without committing a fault (Faith of Islám, pp. 17-21); the سنة زائدة or additional Sunna which may or may not be observed.

Muhammad, the Khalíf ' Umar II. (99—101 A.H.)[1] gave orders to have them collected and committed to writing.

1. This Khalíf requested Abú Bakr ibn Muhammad (120 A. H.) to write down what he could find of the ' Sunna or Hadith.' The task thus begun, continued to be vigorously prosecuted, and Traditions were collected from all parts of the Muslim Empire, but we possess no authentic remains of any compilation of an earlier date than the middle of the second century. Then indeed ample materials had been amassed, and they have been handed down to us both in the shape of Biographies (سيرة pl. سِيَر) and of general collections of traditions, which bear upon every imaginable point of Muhammad's life and habits, and give details of the minutest incidents of that life, as well as of the doctrines and practices of the religion of Islám. (For details *see* Muir's Life of Muhammad, p. 566 *et seqq.* Dictionary of Islám, 643. Sprenger III. lxxvii. Bukhári's Traditions with the Commentary of Castellani, i. 6. Ban. ii. 64. Ibn Khaldún i. 368).

The text of a Tradition is called مَتْن ; the authority, the guarantee on which a Tradition rests is the support, or اسْناد (pl. أَسَانِيد) ; the chain of reporters who vouch for the correctness of the Tradition is the سِلْسِلة الاسانيد ; the relator of a Tradition is the رَاوٍ (pl. رُوَاة) and his version the رِوَاية (pl. رِوَايات).

Traditions are divided into various classes[1] (مراتب), according to the degree of authority they possess, the persons from whom they are derived, the manner in which they have been transmitted, and other characteristics. (*see* Bukhári's Commentary i. 7 Ibn Khaldún I, 368 *et seqq*).

---

[1] Traditions may be : Genuine, sound (صحيح) ; handed down by pious men, distinguished for their integrity (عدول ضابطين) ; good, mediocre (حَسَن) not coming up to the authority of the first degree ; weak (ضعيف) or inferior as to their trustworthiness (قصر عن درجة الحسن). They may also be traced up (مرفوع) to Muhammad himself ; or restricted (موقوف) ; or intersected (مقطوع). They may also be connected (متّصل) or interrupted (منقطع). They may be generally accepted (متواتر); or well-known (مشهور); or strange (غريب); or invented, false (موضوع). For the

The collections of Traditions, now considered as of the greatest authority, in fact the standard canonical collections and called the six books:—

(الصِّحاح السِّتَّة - الكُتب السِّتَّة - الكُتب المُعتَبَرَة)

are those of :—

1. *Bukhári* (محمد بن اسمعیل البُخاري) who was born A.H. 194.

His plan was only to collect genuine Traditions and his book is, therefore, called صحیح البُخاري or the sound traditions of Bukhári. He is said to have chosen out of 600,000 traditions only 7,275 which he considered genuine. As these are repeated under various heads, they can be reduced to about 4,000. A learned doctor of Islám says : " The collection of Buhkári is the most excellent book of

exact meaning of these terms and others used in this science which it would lead us too far to explain here in detail, see Bukhári's Commentary i. 7-16. Dictionary of Islám, 640. Faith of Islám, pp. 86-7. Among the earliest collectors of traditions may be mentioned Málik bin Anas (مالك بن أنس) in Mádína, Abdu'l Malik bin Jaríh (عبدالملك بن جریح) 150 A.H.) in Mecca, 'Abdu'-r-rahmánu'l Wazá'í (عبدالله الرحمن الوزاعی) at Damascus ; Sufián ath Thúri (سُفیان الثوری) at Kúfa ; Haminád bin Salama bin Dínár (سَلَمَة بن دینار) at Basra. Some of them mentioned the Traditions together with the chain of witnesses, others, like Al Baghawi, (البغوی) give the text only.

(For a list of learned doctors who have written special works on the Science of Tradition see Bukhári's Commentary i. 7.)

At the end of the 3rd century A.H. there existed already a large number of systematically arranged collections of Traditions. Among these may be mentioned the Muwattá (كتاب المُوطّا) of the Imám Málik (179 A.H.) The Imáms Idrís ash Sháfi'í, Ahmad bin Hanbal and others had made such collections, each in support of his special system of Theology and Jurisprudence ; this kind of collection of Traditions is called a Musnad (مُسنَد), as its object is to furnish the ' supports ', ' dicta probantia' of the theological system of the respective authors. (See Faith of Islám, pp. 26-30. Osborn's Islám under the Khalifs of Baghdad, Chapter I.)

Islám after the Book of God." (Bukhári's Commentary, i. 19. Sprenger iii, cii. Ibn Khaldún i, 369).

2. *Muslim* (مسلم بن الحجاج القشيري) who died in 261 A.H.

The Imám Muslim, a disciple of Bukhári, followed the plan of his master in writing his Masnad, receiving in his collection, the صحيح مسلم, only what he considered genuine traditions, of which he collected 4,000. The collection of Bukhári was in high repute and preferred to all others in Asia and Egypt; that of Muslim chiefly in Spain and North Africa.

3. *Abu Dáud* (ابو داود السجستاني) He died in 275 A.H. His collection is called the Sunana Abi Dáud سنن ابي داود and contains 4,000 traditions.

4. *Tirmidhi* (ابو عيسى القرمذي), who died in 279 A.H., was a disciple of Ahmad ibn Hanbal. His work is called جامع القرمذي.

5. *An Nisá'i* (ابو عبدالرحمن النسائي) who died in 303 A.H. He was the author of the سنن النسائي

6. *Ibn Májá* (ابن ماجاة القزويني) died 273 A.H. His collection, the كتاب السنن, is also highly esteemed.[1]

---

[1] The much esteemed collection by Ibn Málik, the Muwatta, الموطّا, is a so-called مسند *i.e.*, a collection made in support of a certain theological system, arranged under special chapters of the Fiqh, and thus more a *corpus juris* than a *corpus traditionum*. A later, but also very much esteemed collection of traditions, is the Mishkátu-'l-Masábíh (مشكاة المصابيح) the niche of lights, written by the Shaikh Wáli'u'd-din, 737 A.H. There is an English translation of this work, translated by Captain A. N. Mathews, printed at Calcutta, 1809.

The third foundation of Islám is the Ijmá' اِجْماعٌ[1]
or the unanimous agreement of the Muslim nation,

A very handy collection of traditions (text only) is the كَشف الغُمّة
الامّة جميع عن by the Shaikh 'Abdu-l-Wahháb ash Sha'ráni (عبدالوهّاب
الشعرانى) printed at Cairo, 1281 A.H.
The Shi'ah sects, though they do not accept the traditions of the
Sunnis, do not reject Tradition. They have their own collections which,
however, cannot be considered as of much value, for the study of this
branch of theology is of recent date with them. They consider their
Imáms (successors of 'Ali) as infallible and their sayings, consequently, as
of the same authority as the Qur'án. They have not at times, scrupled
to invent lies in support of their systems (Sprenger iii. ciii).
Their standard collections of traditions are :
Al Ka'fí by Abu Ja'far Muhammad ibn Ya'qúb (329 A.H.), Man la
Jastahziruho-l-Faqíh by Shaikh ' Ali (381), the Tahzib of Abu Ja'far-ibn
Husain (466), the Istibsár by the same, the Nahju-l-Balágha by Syedu'r-
Rázi (406).
In the sixth century we hear of the ten canonical collections
(المصنّفات العشرة), which were adopted in the west; but were not con-
sidered as of the same authority with the six in the East. The following
ones were added to the six (الرجال الستة) the Muwatta, the Sunan of
Bazzár (440), the Musnad of Abú Shíba (264), the Sunan of Darakotni
(385), the Sunan of Baihaki (458). The collection of Ibn Májá was then
not included in the list of the ten standard works.
A most able treatise on the subject of Tradition is found in Ignaz
Goldziher's Muhammedanische Studian, Halle, 1890; II. Theil p. 1-203.
On the value of Tradition see Muir's Life of Mahomet, Vol. I. Bánnáni
treats of the various questions connected with the Sunna in his famous
work, the Commentary on جمع الحوامع vol. II. p. 164-190.

[1] جمع to agree, to be of one mind ; اِجْماع n. a., agreement, being of one
opinion. Ijmá' designates the unanimous agreement of the Muslim
nation, الأمّة, or rather of the representatives of the same, the learned
doctors of Islám, called the Mujtahidín (المجتهدين), on certain legal or
theological questions, and corresponds with the Christian term 'the
unanimous consent of the apostolic Fáthers'—

(الاجماع هو اتفاق المجتهدين فى عَمر على حكم شرعى)

The importance and value of such a collective opinion of the Muslim
nation or congregation or its representatives, the chief doctors of Islám,

or rather the Mujtabídín or the great doctors of the nation.

rest on the saying of Muhammad: "My people will never agree on falsehood." (امتى لا تجتمع على ضلالة لا تجمع امتى على خطا) This agreement is to be arrived at by اجتهاد or exertion, or conscientious examination and meditation on the subject under consideration.

The chief men among the company of the Mujtahidín are the Companions of the Prophet, (اصحاب pl. صحابى) and the first four Khalifs. Such agreement is said to be three fold :

(a) Agreement of word (الاجماع القولى , اتفاق القول) or declaration of opinion in words.

(b) Agreement of action, practice (اتفاق الفعل) or expressed in unanimity of action, practice.

(c) Agreement of silence (اجماع سكوتى اتفاق السكوت) or tacit assent by silence or non-interference. There is also the so-called ' composed agreement.' (اجماع مركَّب) or unanimous agreement as to the matter, but difference as to the cause (علّة) ; and simple agreement (اجماع غير مركَّب) which denotes absolute agreement in everything.

It has been very properly remarked that the setting up of this agreement of the learned doctors of Islám as a foundation of the Faith and practice must be a source of religious dissension and sectarian strife. Though it is now accepted by the orthodox Muslims, there have not been wanting learned doctors who have altogether rejected it, as they said it was a matter of impossibility to collect the opinions of all the persons, even in the same generation (فى عصرٍ), who would have the right to vote on the subject.

Great diversity of opinion exists about the persons who may be considered as Mujtahids, with regard, to the time (عصر) in which they are to be found. Some are of opinion that only the Companions of the Prophet can be considered as men of such high authority, others add to these the Ansár (أنصار) that is, the men of Madína who assisted the Prophet ; others again include the Refugees (المهاجرين) the people of Mecca who fled with the Prophet to Madína. Some consider the authority of the people of Madína to be the higher, as they had had the best opportunities of hearing the sayings and observing the practices of the Prophet. The majority of Muslim theologians, however, are of opinion that there may be true Mujtahidín in any age and in any place, and that their unanimous agreement is to be accepted

Three classes of Mujtahíds are mentioned by writers on this subject :

1. The absolute Mujtahíd—

,المجتهد في الشرع ـ المجتهد المطلق

the Mujtahíd of general and absolute authority, whose sphere of exertion embraces the whole Law.

2. The Mujtahíd of a special school of theology المجتهد في المذهب, who is an authority within the sphere of one of the special theological systems, مذهب (pl. مذاهب), as, for example, of the system of Abú Hanifa, of Sháfi'í and of others.

3. The Mujtahíd of special questions, and cases, المجتهد في المسائل, which have not been decided by the founders of the four great orthodox schools. (*See* Ban. ii. 120-134. Dictionary of Islám, pp. 198 and 418).

The fourth source, or foundation of Islám, is the Qíás[1] (measuring), by which is meant the reasoning by analogy of the learned doctors of Islám, the Mujtahidín, with regard to certain difficult and doubtful questions of doctrine and practice, by comparing them with similar cases already settled by the authority of the Qur'án, Sunna or Ijmá' and thus arriving at the solution of undecided questions.

---

as conclusive in any legal or theological question. (*See* the view of Mírzá Kázim Beg, in Faith of Islám, pp. 41-46). مجتهد from اجتهد, to exert oneself, to take pains, is a conventional term for a learned Muslim, who exerts the faculties of his mind to the utmost, for the purpose of forming an opinion in questions of law respecting a doubtful and difficult case. اجتهاد is the exertion of the Mujtahid in solving such a question by means of reasoning and comparison.

[1] قياس n. a.-Measuring, measure, reasoning by analogy from قاس to measure, compare, conclude. This method of solving difficult and undecided questions is considered to be in harmony with the Qur'án which

Muhammad himself is reported to have sanctioned and encouraged the reasoning and the exerting of the faculties of one's mind (اجتهاد), in order to find the proper solution of difficult and doubtful cases of Law. A Tradition states that the Prophet wished to send a man named Mu'áz to Al Yaman to receive some money collected for alms which he was then to distribute to the poor. On appointing him he said: "O Mu'áz, by what rule wilt thou act"? He replied : "By the law of the Qur'án." "But if thou findest no direction therein?" "Then I will act according to the Sunna of the Prophet." "But what if that fails?" "Then I will make an 'Ijtihad' (exertion) and act on that." The Prophet raised his hands and said: "Praise be to God who guides the messenger of His Prophet in what He pleases!"

enjoins: "Take examples, ye who are men of insight." (Súra lix.) (اعتبروا يا اولى الابصار), which is said by commentators to mean "Compare one thing with another."

In the Qíás four points are to be considered—(اركان القياس اربعة)

(a) the thing compared with, المقيس عليه

(b) the thing compared, المقيس

(c) the point of similarity between the two, the thing common to both, المعنى المشترك بينهما

(d) the decision resulting from the comparison of both.

حكم يتعدى بواسطة المشترك الى المقيس (Ban. ii. 139 ff. and 215.)

The Qíás is either (a) Jali (جَلِى) that is, evident, clear, apparent, e.g., wine (خمر) is forbidden (حرام) in the Qur'án. Now خمر means anything intoxicating; it is clear, therefore, that opium and any intoxicating drug is also forbidden.

(b) Khafi (خَفِى) or hidden, concealed, e.g., by Tradition it is established that one goat in forty must be given to God as alms, poor rate (زكاة), so it may be concluded that the value of the goat may be given instead of the goat (Ban. ii. 217).

There are four conditions of the Qíás :—

(a) That the precept or practice upon which it is founded must be of general (عام) and not of special application.

(b) The cause (عِلّة) of the injunction must be known and understood.

(c) The decision (حكم) must be based upon either the Qur'án, the Hadíth or the Ijmá'.

(d) The decision arrived at must not be contrary to anything declared elsewhere, in the Qur'án or the Hadíth.

The learned doctors of Islám were, as regards the legality of deciding religious questions by Qíás, divided into two camps :

(1) the people of Qíás (اهل القياس), also called the people of private opinion (اهل الراي) and (2) the people of the Tradition (اهل الحديث).[1]

There are four theological Schools or Rites (مَذهب pl. مذاهب), to one of which every Muslim must belong. The founders of these four orthodox schools or rites are the so-called four great Imáms (امام pl. أَئِمّة). They are :

(1) The Imám Abú Hanífa (الامام الاعظم ابو حنيفة النعمان)

---

[1] Reasoning by analogy is also called اعتبار الامثال, or the comparing similars with similars. Among the great Imáms who allowed reasoning by analogy (الراى) was Abú Hanífa, Málik ibn Anas and the Imám ash Sháfi'í, who was, however, less liberal on this point than Abú Hanífa, as he only allowed it in cases of very great necessity. He, therefore, obtained the title of 'Protector of Tradition' (ناصر الحديث). To the people of the tradition, who held that the Qur'án and the Sunna were the only rules of faith and practice, belonged chiefly the men of the Záhiriyya School (مذهب الظاهرية), the heads of which were Dáúd bin 'Ali al Záhiri (270) and his son, Ibn Hazm (حَزم). Their opinions were violently opposed and entirely disappeared after a time. (See Ibn Khaldún i. 372. Banán. ii. 134-215. Goldziher: Die Záheriten).

A very useful book on the four foundations of Islám, in fact an introduction to the Science of Fiqh, is the "Annotations of al Bannáni on the Commentary of Zalálu'l Muhalli on the work of the Imám ibnu's Sabki called : جمع الجوامع (Cairo. 1308 H.)

حاشية العلّامة البنالى على شرح الجلال المحلّى على جمع الجوامع للامام ابن السبكى

(2) The Imám Muhammad bin Idris ash Sháfi'í

(الامام محمد بن ادريس الشافعي)[1]

1 The subject of the works of these four great Imáms is not so much what is to be believed (the Creed) but what is to be practised. They do not treat of the articles of faith, but of the duties of the Muslim: prayer, fasting, alms-giving and the laws by which all their concerns, civil, and social are to be regulated. They are the great jurisconsults of Islám, and their sphere is jurisprudence (فقه) and practical theology, on which they give the minutest details.

The Imám Abú Hanífa was born at Kufa (80 A.H.=700 A.D.) under the Khalifate of 'Abdu'-l-Málik and died at Bagdad (150 A.H.) poisoned by order of 'Abdu'lláh II.

He is the founder of the Hanafi School (المذهب الحَنَفى), which was adopted by the 'Abbáside Khalifs and other Muslim sovereigns of the East, and to which the rulers of the Ottoman Empire adhere to this day, and which, therefore, enjoys the highest authority in Turkey. His great work is entitled, الفقه الاكبر, "the great work on jurisprudence."

The most celebrated of his disciples, who are also considered great oracles of orthodox jurisprudence, are: the Imám Abú Yúsuf (ابو يوسف), the author of the آداب القاضى (the duties of the judge) and the Imám Muhammad, the author of several important works, the chief of which are الجامع الكبير and the الجامع الصغير. The Hanafites (الحَنَفِيّة) are called by Sharastáni "the men of speculation, of reasoning" (اصحاب الراى), as they allowed themselves to be guided by their own judgment, in distinction from the other schools, which rejected the use of private judgment and adhered more tenaciously to the dictates of Tradition. The latter, therefore, were called the أهل الحديث, "men of Tradition" (Shahrastáni i. 160, 161, Ghazáli i, 18. Ibn 'Ábidu'ddín i, 37, 49.)

The Imám ash Sháfi'í was born at Askalon in Palestine (150 A. H.), studied at Gaza, then went to Mecca, Baghdad, Egypt and died at Cairo (204 A.H.) where his tomb is still to be seen. He was a great enemy of scholastic divines, and one of the great supporters of Tradition (ناصرالحديث). The adherents of the Sháfi'í rite are chiefly to be found in Arabia and Persia. His first work was the أُصُول 'Fundamentals,' containing the principles of the Muslim civil and canon law. His next literary productions were السُنَن and مُسنَد, both works on traditional law. His principal disciples were the Imám Ahmad and az Zuhairi.

The Imám Málik Ibn Anas was born at Madína (90 or 94 A.D.=716 A.D.) and died there (175) under the Khalifate of Harúnu'r-Rashid. He is the

(3) The Imám Málik ibn Anas (الامام مالك ابن أنَس)

author of the collection of Traditions called المُوَطّا. His adherents (المالكـيّة) are chiefly to be found in Barbary and the other Northern States of Africa. (Ghazáli i, 18. Dictionary of Islám 312).

The Imám Hanbal was born at (Baghdad 164 A.H. = 780 A.D.) and flourished during the Khalífate of 'Abdu'lláh iii, al Mamúm and Muhammad al Mu'tasim. During the reign of the above Khalifs, the disputes concerning the Qur'án's being eternal or created ran very high, and Hanbal was severely persecuted, imprisoned and scourged for refusing to adopt the Khalif's opinion on the creation of the Qur'án. The Khalíf Mutawakkil, being more tolerant, set the persecuted doctor at liberty and even received him at his court. He had several eminent pupils, particularly Ismail al Bukhári and Muslim ibn Dáúd. (Ibn Khaldún i, 372. Ghazáli i, 19. Dictionary of Islám 188).

To these great Imáms, some add Sufián ath Thúri (سُفيان الثوري), as of equal rank, but he had only few adherents and, therefore, did not become the founder of an additional school of theology or rite, and the four mentioned above maintain their rank as the four Imáms (الائمّة الاربعة). They belong to the class of مجتهد فى الشرع, or مجتهد مطلق. They are agreed on all fundamental doctrines of Islám, and only differ on secondary questions, religious rites, of ceremonies and laws of jurisprudence. There is between them about the same difference as between the Lutheran, Calvinistic and Zwinglian schools in the Protestant Church. Such differences are not, however, considered as defects to be regretted or injurious to the system; but, on the contrary, as advantages and mercies, as they leave more liberty to people to follow their personal opinions and inclinations in matters of duty and discipline. Muhammad himself is reported to have said: 'The differences of my people are a mercy.' (اختلاف أمتى رحمة)

The abovementioned four great Imáms belong to the first class of learned divines (طبقَة الفقهاء الاولى) or Jurisprudents; they have laid down the Foundations of the religious systems (قواعد الاصول) and belong to the class of مجتهد مطلق, whose authority extends over the whole law. Besides these, six other classes are mentioned. To the second (فقهاء الطبقة الثانيه) who are مجتهد فى المذهب, authorities within the boundaries of the system, rite, they have adopted. To this class belong the Imáms Abú Yúsuf and Muhammad and others. They adhere to the fundamental rules laid down by their respective Imáms, though they may differ from him in secondary questions.

(4) The Imám Ahmad ibn Hanbal (الامام احمد ابن حَنبَل).

To the third class (فقهاء الطبقة الثالثة) who are مجتهد فى المسائل, or investigators of special questions and cases, belong men like Khassáf, Taháwi, Sarchási. To the fourth class, called اصحاب التخريج, that is, those who give explanations of the various meanings (وجه), belong men like Rázi. The men of the fifth class are called اصحاب الترجيح, men of comparison, who weigh things against each other. To this class belong men like Abú'l-Hasanu'l-Kudúri, the author of the Hidáya. To the sixth class belong men like the author of the Kanz (صاحب الكَنز) and the author of the Mukhtár (صاحب المختار). To the seventh class belong learned Shaikhs (شيوخ - فقهاء - علماء), chiefly the authors of lengthy Commentaries (مطولات) on the works of their predecessors, like مجمع البَحرين. The last two classes of men belong to what are called مُقَلِّدون or imitators.

The كتاب تنوير الابصار, composed by the Shaikh Shamsu'd-din Muhammad bin Abdu'lláh al Gházzi (995 A.H.), is one of the most celebrated and useful books, according to the Hanífi system. This work has many commentaries; of which one of great celebrity is the دُرّ المختار, written by Muhammad bin Aláu'd-dín Shaikh 'Ali al Haskafi (الحسكفي). A highly esteemed and much used commentary on this commentary is "the Raddu'l Muktár 'ala'd-Durri'l-Mukhtár رتّ المُختار على الدرّ المختار written by the Shaikh Muhammad Amín. (Ibn 'Abidín (ابن عابدين) i. 57. Dictionary of Islám, 199 and 286-292).

CHAPTER II.

THE DOCTRINES OF ISLÁM.

The two general divisions under which Muslim doctors treat of the various subjects connected with the doctrines and practices of Islám are [1]: the theoretical or dogmatical part, and the practical part. The former deals with the creed, articles of faith, called the roots, foundations of religion (أُصُول الدِّين), or Tauhíd the Science of, the Unity of the Godhead (عِلم التَّوحِيد), or science of the articles of belief, of dogmas. (عِلم العَقَائِد).[1] It is also called the science of the word (عِلم الكَلام). This term is chiefly used to designate scholastic theology. This part treats of all the articles of faith (عِلم العَقائد ـ عَقائد الايمان ـ شُروط الايمان), which every true Muslim must believe. They are said to be

---

1 عَقِيدَة pl. عقائد article of faith. تَوحِيد from وحّد = to declare to be one, n. a., the action of declaring God to be one. The term is applied to dogmatics in general, because the article of the Unity of God is the chief article treated therein. The term for scholastic theology is علم الكلام, either because the subject of كلام is much treated of in this part, or because, as others say, the old dogmatists used to head their disquisitions on the various dogmatical subjects with the title: "the investigation on the discourse (word) on such and such a subject."

(مِن مباحثة الكلام فى كذا و كذا).

The dogmatical part is considered the 'roots' (أصول), out of which the second part (the practical) grows, which are, therefore, called ' branches ' (فروع).

These articles of faith every Muslim must know "in a general way" (اجمالِيًّا), but it is not required of all that they should be acquainted with the details (تفصيليًّا), or proofs of the same.

all comprised in the formula of the creed - (الشهادتان),

كَلِمَةُ الشهادة) "There is no God but God, and Muham-

mad is the apostle of God." (لا الَه الّا اللّه و محمّد رسول اللّه)

and are the following :—(1) Belief in God, (2) in His
Angels, (3) in His Scriptures, (4) in His Apostles, (5) in the
Resurrection and the Day of Judgment, (6) in God's
absolute decree and predestination both of good and evil.

(آمنت باللّه و ملائكته و كُتُبه ورُسُله واليوم الآخِر والقَدَر

خيرِه و شرّه من اللّه تعالي والبعث بعد الموت)

The second or practical part consists of precepts and
commandments to be obeyed, rules and customs to be
observed, duties to be fulfilled.[1] It is generally called
'Fiqh' نقه ـ (علم الفقه) Science, Knowledge, Jurisprudence,
and treats of the following subjects : Prayer, Alms-
giving, Fasting, and the Pilgrimage to Mecca. Some
add to these, Jihád, or Holy War. The articles of faith
to be believed and the duties to be practised are included in the formula : "Islám is built up on five foundations : the confession that there is no God but God
and that Muhammad is His Apostle, the performing of
Prayer, the giving of Alms, the keeping of the Fast of
Ramadán and the performance of the Pilgrimage where
there is a possibility of doing so."[1]

(بُنِيَ الاسلام على خمس ـ الشهادة ان لا اله الّا اللّه وان محمّداً رسول اللّه ـ

واقامُ الصلاة وايتاءُ الزكاة وصومُ رمضان وحجُّ البيت من استطاع اليه سبيلاً.)

---

[1] Sharastáni says : Religion (دين) may be divided into (1) Knowledge
(معرفة) and (2) Obedience (طاعة). Knowledge is the root (اصل) and obedience, practice is the branch. He who treats of knowledge and Unity
is a dogmatist (اصولى) and he who treats of obedience and the Law—
(الطاعة والشريعة) is a Jurist (فروعى). The object of the roots is the

Before we proceed to treat of the several articles of
faith, which have to be considered in this chapter, it is of
importance to know what is the exact meaning of Faith[1]
(ايمان), and its relation to Islám, and also who is a true
Muslim and who is a true Believer (مؤمن), and whether
the two terms Faith and Islám, Muslim and Believer are
synonymous, or whether there is a difference between
them.

---

science of the dogmas and the object of the branches is ' Fiqh.' (Sharastáni, i. 58.) Besides these two great divisions, there are others, under
which the various subjects connected with theoretical and practical
religion may also be considered :

(1) اعتقادات, Belief, embracing the six articles of faith.

(2) آداب, Morals, embracing the consideration of all the virtues and
moral excellencies enjoined in the Qur'án and Tradition.

(3) عبادات, including acts all of devotion to God.

(4) مُعَاملات, including such duties as are required in dealings between
man and man.

(5) عُقوبات, denoting the punishments instituted in the Qur'án and
Traditions for various crimes and transgressions.

(For details see Ibn 'Ábid i. 38. Dictionary of Islám, 285).

[1] There are various opinions concerning the exact meaning of Faith.
Some held it to be simply belief of the heart, mind (التصديق القلبى)
i.e., intellectual conviction and assent of the truth of every thing Muhammad taught concerning religion—

(1) Others say that it implies belief of the heart (mind) combined with
confession of the tongue (التصديق بالقلب والشهادة باللسان), without any
regard to outward works. This is the opinion of Abú Hanífa and a
number of his disciples.

(2) Others again are of opinion that faith implies belief of the heart,
combined with confession of the tongue and good works,

تصديق بالجنان و اقرار باللسان و عمل بالاركان - اعتقاد و نطق و عمل

and that no one deserves to be called a Believer unless he possess these
qualifications. This is the opinion of most men of the earlier days of
Islám, the Traditionists and the Mu'tazila. The author of the شرح المواقف
gives as many as eight different opinions on the meaning of faith with
the dicta probantia from the Qur'án for each of these different opinions.
(Mawak, 593. Jowhara 42-44. Ghazáli i. 76, et seqq.)

The orthodox doctrine on Faith, now generally accepted, is that it is the belief of the heart or mind, (العقد بالقلب
التصديق بالقلب) of the articles of the creed; the intellectual conviction of the truth, quite irrespective of the
confession of the tongue, or the performance of good
works.[1] المراد بالايمان مُطلق التصديق A man, therefore, may
be a believer, though he neither confesses his faith nor

---

[1] The author of the Jowhara says: "Faith is the belief of everything the Prophet taught 'as belonging necessarily to religion,'
(تصديق النبى صلعم فى كل ماجاء به و علّم من الدين بالضرورة) This belief
implies not only intellectual conviction, but belief combined with reception and approbation" قبول و اذعان, (Jowh. 40. Mawak. 596), or else
many of the infidels who knew the truth of Muhammad's being a Prophet
would also be believers.

Ghazáli in his discussion of the subject of Faith enumerates the following classes of believers :—

(1) He who combines inner belief with outward confession and good
works, (Ghazáli i. 76 et seqq. عقد و شهادة و عمل), is a true believer and
enters Paradise.

(2) He who combines inner belief with outward confession and some
good works عقد و شهادة و بعض الاعمال; but commits one or more great
sins, كبيرة او كبائر, does not thereby cease to be a believer, though his
faith is not of the higest degree (كمال). The Mu'tazíla deny that such
a one can be considered a believer, but that nevertheless by committing
deadly sins he does not become an unbeliever (كافر) but is in an intermediate state between a believer and an infidel هو على منزلة بين المنزلتين.
An infidel is an impious person (فاسق) and goes into everlasting hell-
fire (هو مُخلّد فى النار).

(3) The opinions with regard to the person who combines inner belief
with outward confession, but has no good works are divided. Abú Tálibu'l
Makki says : "Good works are part of the faith, and faith cannot exist
without them." The Sunni doctors of Islám, however, reject this opinion
as absolutely false, for they say that it is a truth, accepted by general
agreement, that a man, who believes and confesses and dies before he has
done any good work, is a true believer and enters Paradise; that good
works cannot consequently be considered as a necessary part of faith,
and that faith can exist without them.

performs any good works; but, on the contrary, be an
evil-doer, so that consequently faith and wicked works
may be combined الإيمان والمعاصي يجتمعان, (Jowh. 43).
This is the faith of the lowest degree, but still it is true
faith, and he who possesses it is a real believer. He,
however, who combines belief with confession and good
works, has reached perfection (الكمال) in faith. Muhammad said: "Faith is that thou believest in God,
and His angels, and His Scriptures, and His Apostles, and
the last Day, and the Resurrection after death, and the
account and the Predestination of good and evil."

(4) He who believes in his heart, but. dies before he has either con-
fessed or performed good works, is nevertheless a true believer and enters
into Paradise. Those who consider confession a necessary part of faith
naturally consider that such a one has died without faith, an opinion
absolutely contrary to the Sunni dogma.

(5) He who believes in his heart, and has time and opportunity of
confessing, and knows that it is the duty of the Muslim to do so, and does
not confess his faith is nevertheless a believer in the sight of God, and
will not be cast into everlasting hell-fire, for faith is the mere belief,
intellectual conviction and assent, and this belief does not cease to exist
through the want of outward confession. Such a man is a believer in the
sight of God, but an unbeliever in this world before the court of justice
and with regard to the rights of Muslims. In case of an impediment of
the tongue, a sign with the hand is as good as confession with the tongue
(Jowh. 42-43. Ibn Khaldún i. 384). The sect of the Murji'a (طائفة المرجئة)
go too far by saying that a believer, even if he act wickedly, will never
enter hell-fire. The orthodox doctrine on this subject is that everyone,
even the most perfect believer, will enter hell-fire, for no one is free from
committing some sins, for which he must enter fire; only infidels,
however, will remain in it for ever.

(6) He who confesses with the tongue saying: " There is no God but God,
and Muhammad is His apostle," but does not believe it in his heart is an
infidel in the sight of God and will be cast into eternal hell-fire. In this
world, however, he is to be considered and treated as a believer and a Muslim, for man cannot penetrate into the secrets of the heart, and the confession of the mouth must be taken to be the interpreter of the thoughts of
the heart. In order, however, to make a man a Muslim in this world,
before the Law, in the sight of the Qádi, confession is necessary.

One of the questions which have been much discussed in connection with the subject of Faith is whether Faith and Islám are synonymous terms, and whether every believer is consequently a Muslim.[1]

The author of the Jowhara mentions five degrees of faith :

(1) Traditional faith ايمان عن تقليد which is accepted on the authority of a teacher, or Shaikh, without investigation and knowledge of the evidences. It is the faith of the unlearned people التقليد للعوام.

(2) Faith resting on knowledge, ايمان عن علم. This is the faith of the learned class اصحاب الادلة.

(3) Faith resting on inner vision ايمان عن عيان, that is, the seeing God with the heart, the constant communion with God مراقبة القلب لله.

(4) Faith resting on Truth ايمان عن حق, or seeing God with the heart مشاهدة الله بالقلب

(5) Faith resting on reality ايمان عن حقيقة, which is attained when the heart sees nothing but God. This state of being absolutely devoted to God is called the annihilation, or the being absorbed in God مقام الفَنَاء, or the state of vanishing.

[1] The controversy on the subject embraces the following two questions : (Ghazáli i. 75.)

(1) Is Islám the same thing as Imán or not? (هل الاسلام هو الايمان او غيرة).

(2) If Islám and Imán are not the same thing, can they exist separately, or must they necessarily be combined?

(هل يوجد الاسلام منفصل عن الايمان - يوجد دونه او مرتبط به يلازمه). Some say that Islám and Imán are synonymous (الايمان والاسلام شئ واحد), and that consequently every believer is a Muslim, and every Muslim a believer (لا يوجد مؤمن ليس بمسلم ولا مسلم ليس بمومن). This is the opinion held by the orthodox School. Others say that they are different, and may exist separately انهما شيئان لا يتوصلان, others again say that they are distinct things but joined together.

Ghazáli solves the difficulties connected with this subject in the following manner :

From the linguistic point of view Imán means belief (تصديق), intellectual conviction and assent. (الايمان عبارة عن التصديق); Islám means submission, subjection, obedience, as the following quotation shows :—

الاسلام عبارة عن التسليم والاستلام والاذعان والانقياد. The seat of Imán is the heart, mind and the tongue is its interpreter. Islám comprises belief

Faith is also capable of increasing and decreasing—
(الايمان يزيد و ينقص), for the inner conviction concerning
the truths of Islám is sometimes strong and sometimes
weak. It also increases by man's obedience[1] to the will
of God and decreases by his disobedience to the same.
(الايمان يزيد بطاعة الانسان و ينقص الايمان بنقص الطاعة)

Infidelity (كفر) is the contrary of faith and consists
in disbelieving anything the Prophet has taught as necessarily to be believed.

(.Mawak. 597 عدم تصديق الرسول في بعض ما علم مجّئه ضرورةً)

---

with the heart, and confession with the tongue, and good works by the
members of the body, and is consequently a more comprehensive term
than Imán. Imán is one of the component parts of Islám and Islám,
therefore, includes it; but Imán being a more restricted term does not
include Islám. From a linguistic point of view the two terms are therefore not synonymous. (كل تصديق تسليم و ليس كل تسليم تصديقاً) From
the point of view of the Law and religion (شرع), and in a theological
sense the two terms are sometimes used as being synonymous
(على سبيل الترادف والتوارد), and sometimes as having different meanings
(على سبيل الاختلاف), and sometimes as being intermingled, comprised in
each other (على سبيل التداخل). (For proofs from the Qur'án and
Tradition in support of each of these definitions see Ghazáli i. 75).

Imán and Islám are found united in the individual, who believes in his
heart and outwardly observes the precepts of Islám; Imán exists separately in the individual, who only believes in his heart; but neither
confesses, nor does good works, and Islám exists separately in him
who outwardly observes the precepts of Islám, without inner belief.
الايمان والاسلام يجتمعان فى من صدّق بقلبه و انقاد بظاهره - و ينفرد الايمان فى
(.Jowh. 44) - من صدّق بقلبه والاسلام فى من انقاد بظاهره فقط

[1] Obedience to the will of God consists in doing what God commands, and abstaining from what He prohibits—الطاعد فعل المامور به
و اجتناب المنهى عنه (Ghazáli i. 78. Jowh. 47). With regard to the possibility of faith increasing and decreasing three classes may be distinguished:

(1) Men and Jinns, whose faith is capable of increasing and decreasing.
(2) Angels whose faith can neither increase nor decrease.
(3) Prophets, whose faith is capable of increasing, but not of decreasing.

No Muslim can be called an Unbeliever or Infidel, even if he opposes the truth.[1]

The learned author of the Sharhu'-l-Mawákif says on this subject: "Mankind may be divided into two classes, namely, those who believe in the prophetic mission of Muhammad, and those who do not believe in it. Those who do not believe in it are, either such as admit the divine mission (نبوّة) of other prophets, that is, Jews and Christians; or such as do not believe in any divine mission or revelation, such as the Buddhists (البراهمة) and the Atheists (الدهريّة). Those who reject the prophetic mission of Muhammad are of two kinds: (1) such as reject it from mere hostility and obstinacy (عن عناد), and (2) such as do so from sincere conviction, after due investigation and consideration. The portion of the former will be eternal punishment, that of the latter will not be eternal punishment.

[1] Among true Muslims there are such as err in fundamental doctrines; they are Heretics (اهل بدعة) innovators, but not infidels. As every sect of Islám agrees that infidelity means the contrary of faith, there are various opinions as to the exact meaning of infidelity. Those who consider faith as consisting in the knowledge of God, naturally say that infidelity consists in ignorance concerning God (الجهل بالله). Those who describe faith as obedience, say that infidelity consists in disobedience to the will of God. So the Khawárij and some of the Mu'tazila sect who say that every sin is infidelity (كل معصية كفر) which however is false.

The Mu'tazila hold that there are three kinds of sins (معصية pl. معاصي):

(1) Sins which are the result of ignorance concerning God and His Unity and the divine mission of His Apostle. These they consider amount to infidelity.

(2) Sins consisting in committing, besides good works, some deadly sins such as murder, adultery, etc. This class of sinners, they say, are not exactly infidels, but belong to an intermediate class between believer and infidels (منزلة بين المنزلتين) and are called impious (فاسق).

(3) Sins consisting in smaller transgressions, venial sins (معيرة pl. صغائر), which do not deprive a Muslim of his character of a believer and do not cause him to become an infidel.

The believer (اهل الصلاة - اهل القبلة), who commits a deadly sin, is therefore:

(1) According to the orthodox doctrine still a believer, but impious.

(2) According to the Khawárij an infidel.

(3) According to Hasanu'l Baria, a hypocrite (منافق).

In the lifetime of Muhammad and the Companions,[1] and their early followers, in the first century of the Hijra, the religion of Islám was very simple, and all the religious knowledge the believers possessed consisted of the Qur'án, of which some learned by heart a few verses,

---

(4) According to the Mu'tazila he is a man in an intermediate state. (*See* Mawákif. 597-600.)

[1] Abú'l-Hasan says: "After the death of Muhammad, the Muslim nation became divided into many sects, each one considering the others heretics, and separating itself from them; but Islám was common to them and united them" (جمهور المتكلمين و الفقها مجمعون على انّهُ)

لا يكفّر احدٌ من اهل القبلة فان الشيخ ابو الحسن قال اختلفوا المسلمون بعد نبيهم عليه السلام فى اشـياء مثل بعضهم بعضاً وتبرّأ بعضهم عن بعض فصاروا فرقاً متباينين الا ان الاسلام يجمعهم و يعمّهم. (Mawákif 600).

According to Súra v. 76, 77: "They indeed are infidels who say that God is the Messiah, the Son of Mary. . . . . . Whosoever shall join other Gods with God, God shall forbid him Paradise, and his abode shall be the fire." The Christians must be considered infidels, though in many passages they are described as 'the people of the Book' (اهل الكتاب) as those who possess an inspired book (الانجيل) and thereby belong to a class standing high above idolaters and infidels.

The learned author of the Sharhu'l-Mawákif sums up his discussions on Faith and Infidelity and the many heresies of Islám, by stating it as the orthodox doctrine on the subject that a Muslim, though he may lead a wicked and ungodly life, and entertain many opinions opposed to the commonly received doctrines of Islám, may never thereby become an infidel, deserving eternal fire. He only becomes an infidel (1) by denying the existence of the Almighty God, (2) by associating other gods with the One only true God, (3) by denying the divine mission of the Prophet, (4) by denying what has been received by general agreement, *i.e.*, by declaring lawful what has been by common consent declared prohibited. However he may differ in other points, he can never be considered an infidel but only a heretic, innovator. لا نكفّر احداً من اهل القبلة الّا بما فيه نفى

للصانع القادر العليم او شرك او انكار للنبوة او ما علم مجئةُ عليه السلام بهِ ضرورةً او المجَتَمع عليه كاستحلال المَحرّمات ۔ و امّا ما عداةً فالقائل بهِ مبتدع غير كافر. (Mawákif 634).

others larger portions, and the necessary explanations
which were given by Muhammad. Neither the Qur'án
nor the sayings of Muhammad were then written down
in books, but were chiefly learnt by heart and communicated to others by word of mouth. Later on the Qur'án
and the Traditions were collected and written down in
books, and, towards the end of the first century, people in
some quarters had begun to speculate on the truths which
had at first been simply received and believed without
investigation, and at the beginning of the second century
a kind of theological school had already formed itself.
Hasanu'l-Basri (حَسَنُ الْبَصْرِي 110 A.H.) may be considered
the founder of the same.[1]

The leaven of speculation and independent thought,
and the application of simple philosophical principles
to the primitive dogmas of Islám had by this time already worked in various directions. Dissatisfaction had
been shown with the old doctrines, and the introduction of new and vivifying elements into the same were
required. Wásil ibn 'Atá (واصل ابن عطا 80 A.H.), a disciple
of Hasanu'l-Basri, publicly gave expression to these feelings of dissatisfaction with the old teaching, and long-
ing for the introduction of new elements, and separating
himself from his master, became the founder of a new
school, the free-thinkers of Islám, called the Mu'tazila

---

[1] Hasanu'l-Basri lived and taught at Basra. He was the son of a freed
slave of Zaid ibn-Thábit, the editor of the Qur'án. His mother had been
the slave of one of the wives of the Prophet. He possessed all the
learning of his time and may, in a certain sense, be considered the
founder of Scholastic theology, which was more fully worked out at a
later period. There were at the time at Baghdad one hundred and twenty
learned doctors, who lectured on dogmatical and legal subjects, while
there were only a few who made inward piety and spiritual religion the
subject of their lectures (علم اليقين و احوال القلوب و صفات الباطن
Ghazáli i. 31).

(المُعْتَزِلَة) or Separatists[1] from (اعتزل) to secede, to separate oneself.

The Mu'tazila, after having had a time of success and power, were finally expelled from Baghdad, but continued to flourish in Basra, when a blow was dealt to them there by Abú'l Hasanu'l-Ash'ari (ابو الحسن الأشعري), one of their own body, from which they have never recovered. With Abú'l Hasanu'l-Ash'ari, who adopted the scholastic

---

[1] The story of Wásil's separating himself from his Master and becoming the founder of the Mu'tazila is thus told: "al Hasan was one day seated in the Mosque at Basra when a discussion arose on the question as to whether a believer who committed a mortal sin thereby became an infidel or not." When the question was proposed to al Hasan for decision, he kept silence for a moment to consider it; but before he had had time to give an answer Wásil ibn 'Atá rose up and said: 'I am of opinion that a Muslim who has committed a mortal sin should be regarded neither as a believer nor as an infidel, but as occupying a middle station between the two.' (مَنْزِلَة بين المَنْزِلَتَيْن) He then retired to another part of the mosque and was joined by a number of his friends to whom he explained his opinion on the subject. Katáda, entering the Mosque, went up to them, but, on becoming acquainted with the state of things he said: 'These are Seceders.'

The system of the Mu'tazila very soon spread in all directions, and gained numerous disciples and was by degrees more fully worked out, especially when later on the works of the Greek philosophers, chiefly of Aristotle, were translated and thus became accessible to the doctors of Islám. The system was then so construed as to be in harmony with the demands of sound reason and the principles of philosophy.

This theological school of the Muslim rationalists and free-thinkers found no favour in the eyes of the Ummayad Khalifs, who persistently discouraged and, when possible, persecuted its adherents. Under the reign of later Khalifs (198-132 A.H.) they were in high favour at court, but were finally discouraged, persecuted and suppressed. Their final blow however came not from a Khalif, but by one of their own disciples, al Ash'ari, who seceded from them and became the bitter opponent of their system and a defender of the old system. (For the doctrines of Ash'ari see Faith of Islám, pp. 181-2. For failure of the Mu'tazila and their revival in India also see Faith of Islám, pp. 191-9).

methods, began a new period in the Muslim science of theology. It was the beginning of a new and vigorous start and of the triumph of orthodoxy, and of the decline and fall of the more liberal and rational School of the Mu'tazila. The teaching of al Ash'ari (مذهب الاشاعرة), spread very widely and rapidly and soon gained many disciples.[1]

---

[1] The story of Abú'l Hasan's leaving the camp of the Mu'tazila and becoming the defender of the old school of orthodoxy is thus related: 'Abú 'Aliu'z-Zubbai was lecturing one day to his students when Abú'l-Hasanu'l Ash'ari, one of his disciples, propounded the following case to his master: "There were three brothers, one of whom was a true believer, virtuous and pious; the second an infidel, a debauchee and a reprobate, and the third an infant; they all died. What became of them?." Al Jubbai answered: "the virtuous brother holds a high station in Paradise, the infidel is in the depths of hell, and the child is among those who have obtained salvation." "Suppose now," said al Ash'ari, "that the child should wish to ascend to the place occupied by the virtuous brother, would he be allowed to do so?" 'No,' replied al Jubbai, "it would be said to him." 'Thy brother arrived at this place through his numerous works of obedience to God, and thou hast no such works to forward.' "Suppose then," said al Ash'ari, that the child should say: 'This is not my fault; you did not let me live long enough, neither did you give me the means of proving my obedience." "In that case," said al Jubbai, "the Almighty would say: 'I knew that if I allowed thee to live, thou wouldst have been disobedient and have incurred the punishment of hell; I acted therefore for thy advantage." "Well" said al Ash'ari, and suppose the infidel brother were to say: 'O God of the universe! since Thou knewest what awaited him, Thou must have known what awaited me; why then didst Thou act for his advantage and not for mine? Al Jubbai was silent, though very angry with his pupil, who was now convinced that the Mu'tazila dogma of man's free will was false, and that God elects some for mercy and some for punishment, without any motive whatever. Disagreeing with his teacher on this point, he began to find other points of difference, and soon announced his belief that the Qur'án was not created, as the Mu'tazila pretend. This occurred on a Friday on the great Mosque at Basra. Seated on a chair he cried out in a loud voice, 'They who know me know who I am; as for those who do not know me, I shall tell them: I am 'Ali Ibn Ismá'ilu'l Ash'ari and I used to hold that the Qur'án was created, that the eyes shall not see God

Seventy-three sects are said to have sprung up in Islám at different times,[1] and on various subjects, most of which have since disappeared. The adherents of these sects, though considered as heretics, or innovators, are nevertheless acknowledged to be Muslims, and not infidels. The system of theology now acknowledged to be orthodox is that of the Ash'ariyya (الاشـاعرة الشـعرية)

Dogmatics (توحيد) may be divided into three parts:

(1) الهيّات, Theology treating of doctrines connected with the Godhead (في المسائل المتعلقة بالالاه).

(2) النبوات, Doctrines connected with the prophetical office. (البحـث في المسائل المتعلقة بالانبياء)

---

and that we ourselves are the authors of our evil deeds. Now I have returned to the truth, I renounce these opinions, and take the engagement to refute the Mu'tazila and expose their infamy and turpitude. He enlisted on the side of orthodox Islám all the dialectical skill of the Mu'tazila and gave to the side of the orthodox the weapons of the sceptic. He then adopted the scholastic methods, and started a school of thought of his own, which was in the main a return to orthodoxy. He thus overthrew the liberal school, and his principles and methods have ruled the greater part of the Muslim world ever since." (Faith of Islám, pp. 179, 180).

[1] Muhammad predicted that his followers would be divided into numerous religious sects. According to a tradition recorded by 'Abdu'lláh ibn 'Umar he said: " Verily it will happen to my people even as it did to the children of Israel. The children of Israel were divided into seventy-two sects, and my people will be divided into seventy-three. Every one of these sects will go to Hell except one sect." The Companions said: "O Prophet, which is that?" He replied: "The Religion which is professed by me and my Companions."

(ستفرق امتى على ثلث و سبعين فرقة الناجية منها واحدة و الباقون هلكى و قيل ومَن الناجيةُ قال اهل السنة والجماعة.)

The chief subjects on which these sects differed from the orthodox dogmas were (1) The attributes of God and His Unity (الصفات والتوحيد فيها), (2) Predestination and God's justice (القدر والعدل), (3) God's promises and threats (الوعد و الوعيد), (4) Revelation, reason and (5) The Imamate (السمع والعقل والرسالة والامامة).

(3) السمعيّات, Other dogmatical subjects.

(المسائل التي لا تتلقّي احكامها الّا من السمع)

The name by which God, the one and only true God, is
called in the Qur'án, is Alláh (الله), originally اله with the
article اَل prefixed to it.[1]

The doctrine concerning God, His unity, His essence,
His attributes, and His works forms a very important
part of the Qur'án, which speaks in many of its passages
of His absolute Sovereignty and Majesty. He is the
Creator and Preserver of every thing that exists, the
Almighty, All-wise, and Omniscient.[2]

---

[1] As many as thirty opinions have been started respecting the derivation and meaning of الله, most of them agreeing that it is not a derived
but a proper name (إِلَٰهِيم - إِلَٰوهٌ). Another word frequently used in
the Qur'án for God is Lord (الربّ).

The title Alláh is called the essential name of the essence (اسم الذات),
all other titles being considered names designating attributes of God
(اسماءالصفات). They are called the excellent names (الاسماء الحسني) Súra
vii. 179). Abú Huraira reports that Muhammad said: "Verily there are
ninety-nine names of God, and whosoever recites them shall enter
Paradise."

According to tradition, God has among the many names by which He
is known, one called the Exalted Name (الاسم الاعظم), which is generally
considered to be unknown to any but the Prophet and possibly some of
the distinguished saints. Some however say that it is Alláh.

It is a generally received opinion that it is not allowed to call God by
any other name besides those mentioned in the Qur'án. These are called
fixed, settled names (اسماء توقيفيّة). The Mu'tazila and others hold that
there is no objection to one's applying expressive names to God besides
those mentioned in the Qur'án. (See Mawáqíf. 540-545 where a list is also
given of the ninety-nine names of God.)

[2] It would lead us too far to quote all the verses of the Qur'án referring
to this subject. It may suffice to quote a few verses, and the curious will
find a fairly complete list of those passages in the Dictionary of Islám,
p. 142 et seqq.

The doctrine concerning God, as it has been developed
on the foundation of the Qur'án and Tradition, by the
learned doctors of the Ash'ariyya School, among whom
may be mentioned as chief representatives Ibn Mujáhid,
the Qádi Abú Bakr al-Báqiláni Abú'l-Ma'áli, known
as the Imámu'l-Haramain. Ghazáli says: that the two

"Verily your Lord is God, who created the heavens and the earth in
six days. . . . He created the sun and the moon and the stars, subjected to
laws by His commands. Is not all creation and its empire His?" Súra
vii. 52, "Omniscient, Judge of all, Author, Preserver of all things."
Súra vi. 59-64. The Mighty, the Wise, the Subtile. Súra vi. 95-103:
"God everlasting, self-subsisting, all by his sovereign will; His throne
embraces heaven and earth." Súra ii. 256. "God brings forth the living
from the dead—and the dead from the living." Súra iii. 25.

The most important doctrine laid down by Muhammad in the Qur'án,
to which he refers again and again, on which he insists as the great truth
to be believed, and which he endeavours to prove and illustrate in a variety
of ways, is the doctrine of the unity of God (وحدانيّة اللّه). 'There is no

God but God' (لا الـٰه الّا اللّه) is a formula said to contain the negation

of false gods (نفى), and the affirmation (إثبات) of the one true God.

Súra ii. 158 "Your God is one God; there is no God but He, the Merciful,
the Compassionate." Súra cxii., called the (سورة الاخلاص) the chapter
of clearing oneself, i.e., of belief in any but the one true God, states the
dogma thus :—

> "Say : ' He is God alone
> God the eternal !
> He begetteth not and He is not begotten !
> And there is none like unto Him."

Everything opposed to the oneness of God is strongly denounced in the
Qur'án, so the statues and idols (انصاب), which the pagan Arabs set up
for worship, are called an "abomination of Satan" رجس من عمل الشيطان
Súra v. 92. Idols (اصنام), and their worship are spoken of with contempt and reprobation (Súras vi. 74; xiv. 38). Three hundred and sixty
such idols are said to have been erected in and around the Ka'bah on the
day when Muhammad conquered Mecca.

Some of these pagan Arab idols are called by name in the Qur'án, such
as Lat, ' Uzza, Manat (مناة, العزّى, اللّات Súra liii. 20) ; Wadd, Suwá,
Yaghúth, Ya'úq, Nasr (نَسر , يعوق , يغوث , سُوَاع , وَدّ. Súrá lxxi. 23-4) ;

sentences of the Confession (الشهادة كلمتَنِ) (1) there is
no God but God, (2) Muhammad is the apostle of God,
notwithstanding their shortness, comprise the doctrines
of :

(1)   The Essence of God   (ذات الله)

(2)   The Attributes of God   (صفات الله)

As'áf and Fá'ila (فائلة، اساف) were two idols erected on the hills Safá
and Marwa (صفا و مَروة), round which the pagan Arabs used to go in procession and which hills Muhammad retained as holy places to be visited
during the pilgrimage to Mecca.

Another false opinion Muhammad denounced as opposed to the Unity
of God is that entertained, apparently by the pagan Arabs, that God had
taken angels as his wives or had begotten daughters. "What! has your
Lord chosen to give you sons, and shall he take for himself daughters
from among the angels." Súra xvii. 42: "He begetteth not and He is
not begotten." Súra cxii. 3:

Another false system Muhammad denounced as irreconcilable with the
Unity of the Godhead is that of ascribing to Him associates, partners,
companions in His dominion (شُركَاء) : "Yet they made the Jinn partners with God . . . . and in their ignorance they have falsely ascribed
to Him sons and daughters." Súra vi. 100. Polytheists are therefore called
Mushrikín مُشركين, or those who ascribe partners, associates to God.

Not only the idolatrous Arabs and pagans in general, but the Jews also
as well as the Christians are considered as holding opinions which
militate against the Unity of God. So the Jews are accused, falsely so, of
believing that Ezra (عُزير) is the son of God. "The Jews say Ezra is a
son of God and the Christians say " The Messiah is a son of God. . . . .
God do battle with them! How they are misguided !" Súra ix. 30-31:
(On this verse see "Sell's Historical Development of the Qur'án, S. P. C. K.
p. 193.)

In many passages of the Qur'án Muhammad accuses the Christians
also of being Polytheists, on account of their holding the doctrines of
the Trinity (التثليث ـ الثالوث) and the divine sonship of the Lord
Jesus. It is evident that Muhammad was mistaken in his opinion of the
doctrine of the Trinity held by Christians, which he represents as God,
Jesus and the Virgin Mary and confounded it with Tritheism (See
Súras v. 77 ; xix. 36, 91, 94 ; vi. 101 ; lxxii. 3 ; v. 116 ; iv. 169 ; xxxix. 5.)

(3) The Works of God (افعال الله)

(4) The Truthfulness of the Apostles (صدق الرسل)

In giving a somewhat condensed exposition of these doctrines, we make use of the following Arabic books: Ghazáli's إحياء علوم الدين Sunúsi's أمّ البراهين and Shaíkh Ibrahim al Lakáni's جوهرة التوحيد

The doctrine of the Unity (وحدانيّة ـ وَحْدَة) of the God-head is a most important dogma. God is one in his essence (nature ذات), that is, not composed of parts; one in his attributes (صفات), that is, not having two powers, two knowledges, and so on. He is one in his works (افعال), no other being besides God having any influence on God (ذاتُه تعالي مخالفة لسائر الذوات). For proofs of the Unity of God from the Qur'án *see* Súras ii. 110, 111, 158-160 ; iii. 1, 4, 16 ; iv. 51, 52, 116. Ghazáli says that the doctrine of the Essence of God comprises the following points : existence of God, His existence from eternity and for ever, His being neither substance nor body nor accident, His not being tied to space, nor resting in a place, His being seen at the last day.

الركن الأوّل في معرفة ذات الله تعالي و مدارهُ علي عشرة اصولٍ و هي العلم بوجوده الله و قدمه و بقائه و انه ليس بجوهر ولا جسم ولا عرض و انه سبحانه ليس مختصًا بجهة ولا مستغرًا علي مكان و انه واحد .

These various subjects are dealt with under ten different heads : [1]

---

[1] (1) The Self-existence of God. (قيامُه بنفسه ـ وجودُ الله تعالى), must be admitted as a matter of necessity (الله واجب الوجود), for we can-

not admit that there was a time when God did not exist, nor that a
time will come when He will not exist. (Jowh. 49 الله تعالى واجب الوجود
لا يجوز عليه العدم فلا يقبل العدم لا ازلاً ولا ابداً) For proofs from the
Qur'án and reason (see Ghazáli, i. 68. Súras xiii. 2-4; xxii. 18; lxvii.
19, 30; vi. 72-78). This attribute (mode of being of God) is called an
essential attribute (صفة نفسية), as it refers to the essence of God. It is
also one of the positive attributes (صفة ثبوتية) He is self-existing :—
(ان وجوده لذاته لا لعلة) not by reason of some cause that called him into
existence (ان الغير ليس مؤثراً فى وجوده). (Ghazáli i. 68. Jowh. 49-59.
Mawáqif 478-479).

(2) His 'Eternity (ان الله قديم أزلى - قدم الله) of old, without beginning (اول كل شئ عدم افتتاح الوجود - عدم أزليّه للوجود). If he were not
the first He would require a creator, and this creator another creator.
This is one of the negative attributes (صفة سلبية) as it negates in God
an attribute, which it would not be becoming to ascribe to him
(الله صانعُ العالم و مبدئهُ و بارئه و مُحدثهُ و ميدعهُ) (Ghazáli, i. 68. Jowh. 51-52.
Maw. 474.)

(3) His Eternity (بقاءُ الله) in the sense of his having no end.
(باقٍ انه تعالى مع كونه ازليًا ابديًا ليس لوجوده آخر واحد لله عدم الأخروية
و عدم اختتام الوجود) For proofs see Jowh. 52-54. 59 Mawáqif 474.

(4) God is not a substance, an element (ان الله ليس بجوهر يتحيّز). He is
not contained in space (حيّز). Every substance comprehended in a space,
either rests or moves, and is, consequently, subject to changes and accidents
(ساكن او متحرك فى حيزة). This cannot be admitted of God. " He who
calls God a substance, an element (جوهر), without meaning His being
contained in space, may not be mistaken in what he means thereby, but
he makes a mistake in employing these terms." (Ghazáli i. 69. Maw. 474.)

(5) God is not a body (جسم) composed of elements or parts.
(انه ليس بجسم مؤلّف من جواهر) (Ghazáli i. 69. Maw. 473.)

(6) God is not an accident (عَرَض), inherent in a body, or dwelling in
a place (انه تعالى ليس بعرضٍ قائم بجسم او حال). (For further explanations
see Ghazáli i. 69. Maw. 474).

The attributes of God are known as the Sifátu'lláh (صفات الله تعالي) and concerning them there are ten points:[1] (هذا الزكن مدارة علي عشرة اصول).

(7) God is not restricted to certain regions. (انه تعالى منزه الذات عن الاختصاص بالجهات). He cannot be said to be on high or below, on the right or left, etc., (Ghazáli i. 69) For a full discussion of the negative qualities of God (صفات سلبيّة or صفات تنزيهية) see Mawáqif 471.

(8) God is sitting on His Throne (عرش) in the sense in which He means His sitting on the Throne (انه مستو على العرش بالمعنى الذى اراده الله بالاستواء) Súras xx. 4; 11-27. (For explanation see Ghazáli i. 69-70. Dictionary of Islám, 145.)

(9) God will be truly seen in the next world with the eyes and sight. Though God has no shape, and cannot be (انه تعالى مرئى بالا عين والابصار فى دار الآخرة دار القرار) seen in this world, yet in the world to come the blessed will truly see him with their own eyes as it is stated in the Qur'án: "The faces then resplendent will regard their Lord " (Súra lxxv. 22-23). The author of Jowhara (p. 107-112) says: " It is possible to see God in this world as well as in the next. In this world it has been granted to Muhammad only. In the future world however all believers will see him; some say with the eyes only (حدق), others with the whole face (وجه), others with every part of their whole body " (بكل جزو من اجزاه البدن).

(10) God is one, having no partner (شريك); one, single (فرد), having no equal. (انه تعالى واحد لا شريك له فرد لا ند له) In proof of this doctrine the verse of the Qur'án (Súra xxi. 22) may suffice: " Had there been in heaven or in earth gods besides God, both surely had gone to ruin, for one would have opposed the other." Jowh. 55. Mawáqif 475. Ghazáli i. 70).

[1] (1) God is omnipotent, Almighty, powerful (ضابط الكل - قدير - قادر). Súras ii. 19; lxxv. 40; iii. 159. The proof of this is the wonderful mechanism of the world. This attribute implies God's power to create and annihilate whatever is possible (Jowh. 60-62. Dictionary of Islám, 145).

(2) God is omniscient (عليم - عالم) He knows all things in the present, the past and the future, in general as well as in detail (اجمالا و تفصيلا).

This knowledge is not acquired (مكتسب) like that of man. His know-ledge comprises all things necessary, possible and impossible. (العلم صفة

ازليّة متعلقه بجميع الواجبات والجائزات والمستحيلات على وجهالاحاطة)
(Súras vi. 59; lviii. 8).

(3) God is living (حى). Súras ii. 256; xxv. 60, روح حياة الله لذاته ليست

(Jowh. 66-67. Ghazáli i. 70). (وحياتنا ليست لذاتنا بل بسبب الروح)

(4) God is endued with a will (الله تعالى مُريد لافعاله - مُريد) : will is

(مشيعة - ارادة. This will subsists in His essence from eternity.

(ارادة الله تعالى صفة قديمة زائدة على الذات قائمة به) Súras lxxxv. 16; vi. 35;
xiv. 4. His will is not synonymous with His omniscience, or His com-mand or His pleasure (رضى) as the Mu'tazila of Baghdad pretend, for God's knowledge extends to everything whether necessary, possible or impossible (واجب - جائز - مستحيل); while His will comprehends only what is possible. As to His will being synonymous with His pleasure, this is refuted by the Sunni doctrine that God wills certain things, though he has no pleasure in them (الارادة قد تتعلق بما لا يرضى به تعالى). His

will comprises everything possible, good or evil (شمل الممكن الخير والشر).
The Sunni dogma that His Will is eternal refutes the opinion of the Karramiyya sect, that His will had a beginning (ارادته حادثة); just as the orthodox teaching, that the Will of God is an attribute added to his essence (زائدة على الذات) refutes the doctrine of some Mu'tazila, who say that His will is His very essence (ان الارادة نفس الذات). The Mu'tazila also hold, contrary to the orthodox dogma, that the will of God does not comprise what is evil or shameful but only what is good. (ان ارادة الله

لا تتعلق بالشرور والقبائح)

(5) God sees and hears everything (بانه تعالى سميع بصير) ; even the most secret thoughts of the heart. Each of these attributes is eternal, inherent in His essence, extending to every existing thing.

(تتعلق بالموجودات الذوات و غيرها)

(6) God speaks by speech (انه تعالى متكلم بكلام) but His speaking is not like that of man composed of sounds and words. (كلامه تعالى صفة

ازلية قائمة بذاته ليست بحرف ولا صوت) The speech is in reality the inner speech of the soul (كلام النفس); the outward speech is only the inter-preter of the inner one. The Mu'tazila, on the contrary, hold that the speech of God is composed of sounds and words, and is not eternal but recent (حادث). The speech, word of God is one (لا‌تعدّد فيها), but it has, according to the circumstances of the case, various modes, as command, prohibition, information, promises, and threats (امر - نهى - خبر - وعد - وعيد). God's word (كلامة) has two meanings, *i.e.*, the eternal word inherent in God's essence (الكلام النفسى القديم القائم بذاته) and the spoken word, (الكلام اللفظى), created by God. In this sense is to be understood the saying of 'Áyesha مابين دفتّى المصحف كلام الله "what is comprised between the two covers of the Qur'án is the word of God," combining both the above mentioned meanings, by participation (بالاشتراك), or truly (حقيقى) of the eternal word (الكلام النفسى); figuratively (مجازى) of the spoken (or written) word. Anyhow, he who denies that "what is contained between the two covers of the Qur'án," (written or printed) is an infidel. Though the words of the Qur'án which are read are recent, it is not permitted to say that the Qur'án is recent (حادث), except for the sake of instruction, such as a professor gives to his students (Jowh 67-68).

(7) The speech (word) of God is eternal (ان الكلم القائم بنفسه قديم) like all His other attributes. What is recent are the sounds and words which express it. The words of God, to Moses: "Take off thy shoes from thy feet" existed from eternity in the essence of God, though they were addressed to Moses in his days in words and sounds (Ghazáli i. 70-72).

(8) God's omniscience (knowledge) is eternal (علمهُ تعالى قديم). He knew everything before it came into existence.

(9) God's will is eternal (ان ارادة اللّه قديمة). From eternity God willed the events that were to take place, in due course, according to his omniscience.

(10) God knows by knowledge, lives by life, is omnipotent by reason of His omnipotence, wills by will, speaks by speech, hears by hearing, sees by sight, (Ghazáli i. 71) ان اللّه تعالى عالم بعلم حىّ بحياة قادر بقدرة مريد بارادة متكلّم بكلام سميع بسمع بصير ببصر. God's knowing cannot be separated from his knowledge. The Mu'tazila, in opposition to this orthodox dogma, hold that God knows, lives, is omnipotent, wills, speaks, hears, sees, by reason of His essence ان اللّه عالم بذاته حىّ بذاته (Jowh. 72-73). The glorious names of God are, like His attributes eternal that is, not the articulation of these names, but the meanings; and men are, therefore, not permitted to designate God by any other names than those mentioned in the Qur'án. The Mu'tázila, on the contrary, hold that the names of God are recent, applied to God by men, and that there is no objection to apply to God any appropriate name even if not mentioned in the Qur'án or Traditions. Expressions in the Qur'án or Traditions which seem to ascribe to God a body, are to be

The works of God are called the Afa'álu'lláh انعال الله
and concerning them there are ten points :—[1]

(الركن الثالث و مداره علي عشرة اصول)

---

understood in a figurative sense, (تاويل) ; and to be explained in accordance
with the other expressions, such as 'Thy Lord comes, descends (جاء ينزل)
to the lowest heaven' 'God has created Adam in his image' (على صورته)
'the face of God remains' (و يبقى وجه ربّك) 'the hand of God is above
their hands' (يد الله فوق ايديهم), 'all hearts of mankind are between
two fingers of the fingers of the Merciful' (بين اصبعين من اصابع الله).

[1] (1) Everything that exists and takes place in the world is God's
doing and creation; He has created man and his actions.

ان كل حادث فى العالم هو فعله تعالى و خلقه و اختراعه لا خالق له سواه ولا
محدث الّا ايّاه - خلق الخَلق و مُنَعهم و اوجد قدرتهم و حركتَهم)

All acts of man are created by God as the Qur'án says : " God has created
you and what you do." (Ghazáli i. 71-74).

(2) Though God has created the movements, acts of man, still he has
done so in a manner that they are, at the same time, the acquisition of man.

(ان انفراد سبحانه باختراع حركات العباد لا يخرجها عن كونها مقدورة للعباد
على سبيل الاكتساب)

God has created the power which man possesses to act, and has created
the act itself (خلق القدرة والمقدور جميعاً) ; He has created the choice and
the thing chosen. خلق الاختيار والمختار جميعاً (For details see Ghazáli
i. 72).

(3) Though the acts of man are his own doings, acquired by him, and
the result of his own choice (كَسْبًا للعبد), still they are nevertheless
willed by God (ان فعل العبد و ان كان كسبًا فلا يخرج عن كونه مُراد الله).
Not the least thing happens in the world except by the decree and will
and power of God. (بقضاء الله وقدرته و ارادته و مشيئته) He decrees the
good and the evil, what is profitable and injurious, faith and infidelity
and idolatry, obedience and disobedience, salvation and perdition. He
does what He wills, and no one can alter what He has decreed, or change
what He has predetermined. He guides aright whom He wills, and He
causes to err whom He wills. No one has a right to question His doings,
but man will be questioned as to his doings, he will have to render an
account and is responsible for his acts. (منه تعالى الشرّ والخير والنفع والضرّ

والاسلام والكفر والعرفان والنكر ـ والطاعة والعصيان والشرك والايمان والفوز
والخسران ـ لاراد لقضائه ولا معقب لحكمه ـ يُضِلّ من يشاء ويهدى من
يشاء ـ لا يُسْأَل عمّا يفعل وهم يُسْأَلُون).

The Qur'án says: "If God had willed He would have guided all men.'
Ghazáli says that reason also proves that God must be the author of good
and evil, else Satan who wills evil would be mightier than God, which
cannot be admitted. To the objection "How can God forbid what He wills
and command what He wills not," the answer is that there is a difference
between God's command and his will (الأَمرُ غير الارادة) Ghazáli i. 72).

(4) God's creating man and imposing on him the duties of religion is
an act of His free will and grace, nothing made it incumbent on Him.

(ان الله تعالى متفضّل بالخلق والاختراع و متطوّل بتكليف العباد ولم يكن
الخلق والتكليف واجبًا عليه) The Mu'tazila, on the contrary, pretend
that this was incumbent on God, as the highest interests of man require
it. (انه وجب عليه ذلك لمّا فيه مصلحة العباد)

(5) God has the right to require of His creatures more than they are
able to perform. This the Mu'tazila deny, (انه يجوز على الله سبحانه و تعالى
ان يكلّف الخلق مالا يطيقون) saying that God, in accordance with His
justice, cannot require of man anything exceeding his ability. (Ghazáli
i. 72).

(6) God has the right to inflict pain and punishment on His creatures
without any guilt on their part, and without bestowing on them any
reward afterward. (ان لله ايلام الخلق و تعذيبهم من غير جُرم سابق ومن
غير ثواب لاحق). God is the absolute Sovereign over all His creatures, and
cannot, therefore, be accused of acting unjustly towards them, howsoever
He may deal with them, 'as every possessor of an object is forced to do
with his own property as he likes.' The Mu'tazila reject this doctrine, as
contrary to God's justice. To this Ghazáli replies that injustice is a
man's dealing so with the property of another person, but as long as he
deals so with his own property, no one can accuse him of dealing with it
cruelly or unjustly.' (Ghazáli i. 72-73).

(7) God has the right to deal with his creatures as He wills,
and is not bound to take into consideration what is best for them,
انه تعالى يفعل بعباده ما يشاء فلا يجب عليه رعاية الا صلح لعباده. Nothing can
be said to be incumbent on God. His will is the sole rule for His dealings, He is not responsible to any one for what He does. The Mu'tazila, on
the contrary, hold that God according to His justice is bound to have
regard to what is best for the welfare of His creatures (الا صلح واجب عليه)

The learned Shaikh Sunúsi [1] gives a somewhat different classification of the attributes of God.

---

and to punish and reward them, not according to His sovereign will, but according to their deserts. (For details *see* Ghazáli i. 73).

(8) To know and obey God, is the duty of man, not in accordance with the dictates of reason, but in consequence of God's command and law. (ان معرفة الله سحانه واجبة بايجاب الله تعالى و شرعه لا بالعقل) Ghazáli says in explanation of this statement that reason is not sufficient to guide man to the acquisition of the knowledge of God and the true way of obeying and pleasing him, it is only the positive law of God which can do this. 'Obedience and disobedience are the same to Him.' (الكفر والايمان الطاعة و المعصية فى حقه يتساويان اذ ليس له الى احد هما ميل ولا به لاحد هما اختصاص).

The Mu'tazila, on the contrary, ascribe a great influence to reason in guiding a man to the obedience of God.

(9) There is no absurdity (impossibility) in God's sending the prophets (انه لا يستحيل بعثة الانبياء عليهم السلام). Reason alone is insufficient to guide man to salvation, prophets are, therefore, required to instruct them. The proof of the prophet's divine character is his ability to perform miracles (يعرف صدق النبى بالمعجزة) Ghazáli i. 74.

(10) God has sent Muhammad as the last of the prophets and thereby abolished the former laws (dispensations) of the Jews, Christians and Sabeans, and has confirmed him as to his prophetical mission by evident signs and miracles. ان الله تعالى ارسل محمداً صلعم خاتماً للنبيين و ناسخاً لما قبله من شرائع اليهود والنصارى والصابئين و ايّده بالمعجزات الظاهرة و الايات الباهرة In explanation of this Ghazáli says: "God has established Muhammad's prophetic character by miracles, such as the splitting of the moon, and the praising of the stones, the gushing out of water from between his fingers. One of the greatest miracles, proving his divine mission, is the Qur'án, for none of the Arabs were able to produce anything like it. Another sign of his prophetic character is his being able to foretell things which are to come to pass, such as his victorious entry into Mecca, the defeat of the Greeks and their subsequent victories. (Súra xxx. 1-2. Ghazáli i. 74).

[1] Sunúsi says: The judgment of reason comprises three classes of things, *viz.*, those that are (1) Necessary (الوجوب - واجب), (2) Impossible (الاستحالة - مستحيل), (3) Possible (الجَوَاز - جائز). Every responsible

Abú 'Abdu'llah Muhammad Yúsuf al Sunúsi (about 895 A.H. 1489-90 A.D.) wrote a short treatise entitled الرسالة في معاني كلمتَي الشهادة. Another treatise on the subject is called: كتاب أمّ البراهين with the commentary of the Shaikh Muhammad al Dasúki.

Muslim (كل مُكَلَّف) is bound to know what it is necessary, possible and impossible to ascribe to God and to His Prophet.

Attributes which must necessarily be ascribed to God are—Existence (وجود), Eternity (القدم), Eternity (البقاء), being distinct from created things (مخالفتة تعالى للحوادث), Self-existence (قيامة تعالى بنفسه), Unity (وحدانية), in His essence, attributes and works. Of these attributes the first essence is called an essential attribute, an attribute of essence (صفة نفسية); as it refers to His essence it is also called affirmative, positive (صفة ثبوتية); the other five are called privative, negative attributes صفة سلبية. There are seven attributes which must be ascribed to God, called ideal attributes (صفات معنوية), which are intimately connected with the attributes just mentioned, viz., God's being omnipotent (قادر), willing (مُريد), omniscient (عليم), living (حيّ), hearing (سميع), seeing (بصير), speaking (متكلّم). These are attributes which must necessarily (واجب) be ascribed to God.

Attributes which it is impossible to ascribe to God (مستحيل) are those which are the contrary of those just enumerated, viz., non-existence (العدم), coming into existence (الحدوث), vanishing in time (الفناء - طرو والعدم), similarity to created things (المماثلة للحوادث), not being self-existent, (يستحيل عليه تعالى ان لا يكون واحداً بان not being One عدم القيام بذاته) يكون مركّبا في ذاته او يكون له مماثل في ذاته او صفاته ; want of power (عدم القدرة - عجز), want of will (عدم الارادة), ignorance (جهل), death (موت), deafness (صَمَم), blindness (عَمَى), dumbness (بَكَم). It is also impossible to ascribe to God the contrary of the ideal attributes.

Attributes it is possible to ascribe to God are called الجائز في حقة تعالى.

It is allowed to ascribe to God the doing or not doing of anything possible الجائز في حقّه تعالى فعل كل شيءٍ و تركهُ Jowh. 89-92. Sunúsi 4-5.)

Many learned doctors have deviated from the orthodox doctrine on these subjects in a variety of ways. They are the founders of separate schools and sects (فِرْقَة pl. فِرَق) and their peculiar opinions are considered by the Sunni theologians as heresies (بِدْعَة pl. بِدَع innovations, inventions). The chief among these are those mentioned below.[1]

The learned author of the commentary of the Jowhára sums up the above statements thus:

فاعلم ان الاستغناء يستلزم وجوب وجوده و قدمه و بقائه و مخالفته للحوادث و قيامه بنفسه و تنزيهه عن النقائص و يدخل فى ذلك السمع والبصر والكلام و لوازمها وهى كونه سميعاً و بصيراً و متكلماً . فهى احدى عشرة عقيدة من الواجبات - فاذا وجبت هذه الصفات استحالت اضدادها . فهذه احدى عشرة عقيدة من المستحيلات . ويلزم ايضاً نفى وجوب فعل شىء من الممكنات او تركه . فهذه عقيدة الجائز . فجملة ما استلزمه الاستغناء ثلاث وعشرون عقيدة - و اما الافتقار يستلزم الحياة والقدرة والارادة والعلم و لوازمها وهى كونه حياً و قادراً و مريداً و عالماً . ويستلزم ايضاً الوحدانية . فهذه تسعة من عقائد الواجبات . ومتى وجبت هذه الصفات استحالت اضدادها . فهذه تسعة من العقائد المستحيلات . فجملة ما استلزمه الافتقار ثمانى عشرة عقيدة . فاذا ضمت للثلاثة والعشرين السابقة كان المجموع واحداً و اربعين الواجب له تعالى منها عشرون . والمستحيل عليه عشرون والجائز عليه واحد .

(Jowh. 119 et seqq). For a somewhat condensed statement on these subjects see Ghazáli's al Maksudu'l-Asna, translated into English in Dictionary of Islám, pp. 144-147. See also Palgrave's observations on the Muslim doctrine of the Unity and absolute Sovereignty of God, and the influence of this doctrine on the character of Muslims. Faith of Islám, p. 161.)

[1] The Mu'tazila (المُعْتَزِلَة) who, as a body, entirely reject the eternal attributes of God, in order, as they say, to avoid the distinction of persons made by the Christians, and they hold that eternity is the proper attribute of God's essence (القِدَم اخصّ وصف ذاته), that God is omniscient, not by reason of His knowledge, is omnipotent, not by reason of His omnipotence, as the Sunnis say, but by reason of His essence, because of these attributes shared in His eternity, they would also share in His divinity and there would be a plurality of gods. On account of this opinion, the orthodox school call the Mu'tazila, the 'Mu'attila' (المُعَطِّلَة)

=divestors). They also hold that all those verses of the Qur'án which contain a comparison of God to creatures (تشبيه) must be explained allegorically (تاويل الايات). These are the opinions of the Mu'tazila, as a body. There are, however, a number of groups, which though Mu'tazila, have peculiar opinions. In addition to these, some declared God's omniscience and omnipotence to be declarative of His eternal essence, (اعتبر ان للذات القديمة) or states (حالتان); others reduced the two into one, *viz.*, omniscience (عالمية) This, says Sharastáni ii. 32, is the very opinion of the philosophers. Another branch of the Mu'tazila: the Hodhailiyya (الهذيلية) say that God is omniscient by His omniscience, and His omniscience is His essence and so with His omnipotence (قادر بقدرة و قدرته ذاته ۔ الله عالم بعلم وعلمه ذاته) which opinion, Sharastáni says he took from the philosophers, who affirm the essence of God to be simple, and that His attributes are not accessory to His essence, subsisting therein, but are His essence itself.

ii. 34). الصفات ليست وراء الذات معانٍ قائمة بذاته بل هى ذاته)

The Há'itíyya (الحائطية) and the Hadathiyya (الحدثية) ascribed a divine character to Christ, in conformity with opinions of the Christians " who believe that he will come to judge all creatures at the last day." Ahmed bin Haid believed that Christ was the eternal word incarnate, and that he had assumed a true and real body. They asserted the existence of two gods ; the one eternal, the most High God, and the other not eternal, that is Christ. (اثبتوا حكماً من الاحكام الالهية فى المسيح عليه السلام موافقة للنصارى على اعتقادهم ان المسيح عليه السلام هوالذى يحاسب الخلق فى الآخرة ۔ وزعم احمد بن حائط ان المسيح تدرّع بالجسد الجسمانى و هوالكلمة القديمة المتجسّدة كما قالت النصارى)

He believed that this was the meaning of Súra lxxxix. 23 " thy Lord, cometh with angels rank on rank," (*See* Sharastáni ii. 42. Sale, 114).

The Bishriyya (البشرية) hold that the Will of God was one of His works, (ارادة الله تعالى فعل من افعاله) that since God is omniscient and knows what is profitable for man, it is impossible to suppose that He does not will it (Sharastáni ii. 45. Mawáhib 622. Sale, 115).

The Mushshabbiha (المشبهة) are called Assimilators. As regards the verses of the Qur'án containing a comparison of God to creatures, the early Muslims had said : " we believe what the Qur'án and the Sunna contain, and do not take our refuge in allegorical interpretation; everything comes from God our Lord, we believe in the evident sense thereof,

Angels (مَلَك pl. ملائكه) are beings endued with subtle bodies created of light,[1] (اجسام لطيفة نورانية) who neither eat nor drink, in whom there is no distinction of sexes and who, therefore, do not propagate their species (لا يوصفون بذكورة ولا بابوتة). Their chief characteristic is complete obedience to the will of God; their dwelling place, as a rule, is heaven; their chief work consists in praising God day and night and in executing His orders.

---

and also in the hidden meaning; we leave to God the knowledge of the true sense, and we are not obliged to know it, as it is not a condition of faith or an article of the Creed." Some of the Mu'tazila followed the early Muslims in this way. Others, however, allowed a resemblance (تشبيه) between God and his creatures, supposing Him to be a figure composed of members or parts, either spiritual or corporeal, (اعضاء و ابعاض امّا روحانية و امّا جسمانية) and capable of motion. Some of this sect inclined also to the opinion that the divine nature might be united with the human in the same person (Shahrastáni ii. 76-77. Mawáqif, 633. Sale, 120).

The Karrámiyya (الكرّامية), followers of Muhammad ibn Karrám, called the Mujassima (المجسمة corporealists) not only admitted a resemblance between God and created beings but declared God to be corporeal (التشبيه - التجسيم). They are subdivided into as many as twelve different sects, each holding somewhat modified ideas about the corporeality of God. (For details see Sharastáni ii. 79. Mawáhib 633. Sale's Introduction.)

[1] The Qur'án (Súra ii. 28-31) says that when God determined to create man he said to the angels: "Verily I am about to place one in my stead on earth" to which they demurred. He then made them ashamed by asking Adam to name all things, which they had not been able to do. He then asked the angels to bow down and worship Adam, which they did, except Iblis, who was, therefore, expelled from Paradise and cursed (Súras xv. 34-35, xvii. 63-67). Satan tempts Adam to sin and causes him to be expelled from Paradise (Súra xx. 115-122).

He who asserts the existence of male angels is impious; he who asserts the existence of female angels is an infidel 'because he contradicts the Qur'án.' (Súras xliii. 18 ; xxi. 26 ; xxxvii. 150-159 ; liii. 28 ; xvii 42.) 'Hath

They are able to adopt a variety of beautiful forms; some live on earth. The Mu'tazila and others, consider them superior in rank to the prophets because they are free from evil propensities. The Ash'ariyya school consider them inferior to the prophets, in accordance with the saying of the Prophet : "The works God loves most are those performed under the greatest difficulties." The prophets have the evil propensities in their hearts, but they fight and conquer them, and are therefore superior to the angels, who have no evil propensities to resist.

There are four Archangels (رُؤَسَاءُ الملائكة) :

Jibríl (جبريل), God's messenger, said to be meant by الروح القدس mentioned in the Qur'án; called also the Angel of Revelation (ملك الوَحْي) Súra ii. 91, 92.

Miká'íl (ميكائيل) and ميكال (ميكال), said to have been the friend and protector of the Jews.

Asráfíl (أسرافيل) who will sound the trumpet at the day of resurrection.

'Azrá'íl (عزرائيل), the angel of death (ملك الموت).[1]

---

then your Lord preferred you for sons, and taken for himself daughters from among the angels? Indeed, you assuredly say a dreadful saying." (Súra xlii. 3.)

[1] 'Azrá'íl is said to separate men's souls from their bodies; and also those of the angels and all other creatures (Súra vi. 93). He is said to be terrible in appearance; so large that his head is high in heaven opposite the Preserved Tablet, and his feet in the deepest regions under the earth; to a believer however he appears in a pleasing shape. The learned Sunúsi and other learned Shaikhs say that the best remedy, enabling one to meet death and its anxieties and terrors which come after it, without fear, is to perform a prayer of two rak'as after sunset on the night of Friday, and after it to read the Fátiha and the Súratu'z Zalzál (κcix) fifteen times. This Súra is said to be worth half the Qur'án (Jowh. 153). Of neither of the three latter Archangels is the name mentioned in the Qur'án.

Besides the Archangels there are Guardian Angels (حفظة Súras vi. 61 ; lxxxvi. 4) who continually attend man, and of whom each man has, some say, two others four, to guard him from dangers and such calamities, as are not decreed by God, i.e., such things as are ' suspended ' (معلق), for from what is absolutely decreed by God no one can save him. The Jinn also are said to have such guardian angels to protect them. As these Angels are said to succeed each other in their watch they are called the Mu'aqqibát (معقبات), Muhammad is reported to have said that every man has ten angels (according to some traditions twenty or as many as four hundred), who have charge over him by day and by night, from the first beginning of his life to the moment of his death. Angels intercede for man, but their intercession is of no avail unless God is pleased to accept their intercession ; they also assist believers against infidels (Súras xxxiii. 42 ; xlii. 3 ; liii. 26 ; viii. 9-12, 52 ; iii. 119-120).

Besides these there are also Recording Angels (الكاتبون Súra xliii. 80), who constantly observe and write down men's actions. Of such angels every man is said to have two, one standing on the right to write down his good actions (ملك الحسنات), the other on his left to write down his bad actions (ملك السّأَت) ; they are constantly watching (رقيب) and always present (عتيد) except on certain occasions. These angels never change, but remain with man till his death and then stand at his grave, praising and writing down his reward, if he was a believer ; cursing him to the day of the resurrection if he was an infidel. Some say that every man has four such angels who relieve each other in the morning and the evening. The good acts are said to be noted down at once, but when a bad act is committed, the angel of the bad actions asks the angel of good actions whether he is to write it down, whereupon this one orders him to wait for the space of six hours, in the hope that the sinner may repent and ask for pardon. If within this time he does not repent, his bad action is irrevocably written down. The recording of good and evil is to be understood literally, i.e., that it is done on paper with pen and ink (الكتب حقيقيّ بآلة و قرطاس و مداد). Some, however, understand it figuratively. As to the place where these angels abide, opinions differ. Some say that they stand on the last molar teeth (ضرس pl. ضراس) right and left, others on the shoulders. They are called in the Qur'án كرام كاتبين (Súra lxxxii. 11-12), exalted writers.

Another class of angels are the Throne Bearers (حملة العرش) who are said to be at present four, but will on the day of resurrection be strengthened by an additional four who will then bear the Throne of God above them. 'Above them on that day shall eight bear the Throne of the Lord.' (Súras lxix. 77 ; xl. 7.)

Besides angels and devils a distinct order of creatures is said to exist, whose nature places them between man and angels. They are called Jinn[1] (جِنّ Genii). They

---

Another kind of Angels are the Cherubim (الكروبيين) who surround the throne.

Ridwán (رضوان) is the Angel in charge of heaven; the treasurer, keeper or guardian of Paradise (خازن الجنة).

Málik (مالك) is said to preside over Hell and superintend the torments of the damned (خازن النار Súra xliii. 77). And the inhabitants of hell shall say, ' O Málik, would that thy Lord would make an end of us.' (Súra lxxiv. 30, 31).

Munkar and Nakír (مُنكَر نكير) are two fierce looking angels, who visit every man in his grave, and who, immediately after the return of the funeral party from the burial, are said to examine the dead person as to his or her belief in God and Muhammad and to torment him, if his answer is not satisfactory.

As to the sinlessness of angels (عِصْمَة, immunity, exemption from sin) the orthodox doctrine is that angels are free from sin (معصوم). Some, however, reject this idea, on account of their having remonstrated with God on His creating Adam, which is a sin. To this objection the Sunnis reply that the angels did not withstand God, but only wished for an explanation.

As to the superiority or inferiority of angels to the prophets, the prevalent opinion is that prophets stand higher in rank than angels. On both these subjects the author of the Mawáqif says that every one is at liberty to hold whatever opinion commends itself to his own mind.

The Devil is called Iblís (ابليس) and also Shaitán (الشيطان), and is said to have been created of fire. His name was originally 'Azázíl (عزازيل) and he belonged to a class of angels and, according to the Qur'án, was expelled from Paradise and stoned (رجيم).

[1] جِنّ (from جَنّ to conceal, to hide) are so called because they are hidden from men. "We created man of dried clay, and the Jinn had been before created of subtle fire " (Súra xv. 26, 27). They eat, drink and propagate their species and are subject to death. They are considered to be, like men, capable of future salvation and damnation, wherefore Muhammad pretended to have been sent for the conversion of the Jinn as well as of men (Súras lxxii. 1-17; xv, 27). The Jinn are said to listen to what is going on behind the curtain in heaven, which

were created of fire some thousand years before Adam
came into existence. There are good ones and evil ones,
believers and infidels among them.

Every Muslim is bound to believe in the divinely
inspired[1] Books which God has sent down from time to

---

hides the presence of the most High, in order to steal God's secrets, and
so the good angels are said to throw stones at them (*i.e.*, stars), wherefore
they are also called the stoned ones.' (رجيم) from رجم, to throw stones
at. رجم shooting stars. Súras lv. 14; li. 56; xi. 120; xlvi. 28-29; lv.
33-41; xv. 16-17-18 xxxviii. 78 lxvii. 5). *See* Baidáwi's Commentary on
these passages. The Jinn are said to be divided into five distinct orders:
(1) Jánn (جان) Súra xv. 27. (2) Jinn (جن). (3) Shaitán (شيطان). (4).
'Ifrít (عفريت) pl. عفاريت. (5) Márid (مارد). The terms Jinn and Jánn
are often used to designate the whole species, good and bad. The weakest
among them are the Jánn, the strongest the Márid. Their chief abode is
said to be the mountains of Qáf, which are supposed to encircle the world.
See Bukhári's Commentary, v. 291. Sprenger ii. 238. Dictionary of
Islám, pp. 133-138. Faith of Islám, 199-206.

Muhammad and his followers have evidently borrowed from the Jews
the whole doctrine concerning angels, devils and Jinn. The Jews in their
turn learned the greater part from the Persians. Thus the Talmud
teaches that angels were created of fire and that they have various offices,
that they attend on man .... that the Jinn are an intermediate order
between angels and men .... that they know what is to happen in the
future, because they listen to what is going on behind the curtain to steal
God's secrets. (*See* Geiger's Judaism and Islám, 62-64, Simpkim Marshall
London; Tisdall's Sources of the Qur'án, 84).

[1] Inspiration is called Wahi (وحى). The number of such inspired books
(كتب صحف) is said to have been one hundred and four. Of these ten
are believed to have been given to Adam, fifty to Seth, thirty to Idris
(Enoch), ten to Abraham. The other four: the Pentateuch, the Psalms,
the Gospel and the Qur'án were revealed successively to Moses, David,
Jesus and Muhammad who, is now the last, the seal of the prophets.
(خاتم الانبياء) These revelations are now closed, and no more are to be
expected. All these divine books, except the four last, are believed to be
now entirely lost, and their contents unknown. As regards the Pentateuch, the Psalms and the Gospel, the learned doctors of Islám pretend
that they have undergone so many alterations and corruptions that no
credit is to be given to the present copies in the hands of the Jews and
Christians.

time to men, through his apostles : " We believe in God
and what has been revealed to Abraham and Ishmael and
Isaac and Jacob and the tribes, and what was brought

The Suhuf (مُحُف pl. of صحيفة), small books, sheets, pamphlets given
to the ancient prophets, are often mentioned in the Qur'án (Súras lxxxvii,
18, 19; liii. 36-40 ; xxxii. 23-25 ; xlv. 15, 16). (For a list of the passages of
the Qur'án referring to these books, and especially to the Old and New
Testaments, *see* Sir William Muir's " The Coran and the testimony it bears
to the Holy Scriptures," and also Dictionary of Islám, pp. 440-448).

The Pentateuch (التورة) is thus referred to :—" And verily we gave
Moses the Book : wherefore be not in doubt as to the reception thereof
and we made it a direction to the Israelites " (Súras xxxii. 23 ; xli. 45 ;
xlv. 15). In Súra xxxvii. 117, the Thorah is called الكتاب المستبين,
the perspicuous book. (Súra vi. 91, 155). " Then we gave Moses the book,
complete as to whatever is excellent and an explanation of every matter
and a direction and a mercy." (Súras xl. 56 ; xxv. 37). The following Old
Testament characters are mentioned by name in the Qur'án, Adam, Abel,
Cain, Abraham, Aaron, Therah, Korah, David, Goliath, Enoch, Elias,
Elijah, Ezra, Gog, Magog, Isaac, Ishmael, Jacob, Joseph, Job, Jonah,
Joshua, Lot, Moses, Noah, Pharaoh, Solomon, Saul. The following
incidents of the Old Testament are some of those related in the Qur'án
with more or less correctness.

Creation of the world (Súras xvi. 3 ; xii. 3 ; xxxv. 1-12) Adam, his fall
(Súras vii. 18 ; ii. 34) Cain and Abel (Súra v. 30), Deluge (Súras liv. 9 ;
lxix. 11 ; xi. 42). Noah's Ark (Súra xi. 40). Abraham visited by Angels
(Súras xi. 72 ; xv. 51). Abraham ready to sacrifice his son (Súra xxxvii.
101). Jacob goes to Egypt (Súra xii. 100). Joseph's history (Súras vi.
84 ; xii. 1 ; xl. 36). Moses strikes the rock (Súra vii. 160). Pharaoh
(Súras ii. 46; x. 76 ; xliii. 45 ; xl. 38). Manna and quails (Súras vii. 160 ;
xx. 82). Aaron makes a calf (Súras xx. 90). Korah (Súras xxviii. 76 ;
xliii. 45; xl. 38). David's praise of God (Súra xxxiv. 10). Solomon's
Judgment (Súra xxi. 78). Queen of Sheba (Súra xxvii. 22). Jonah and
the fish (Súras vi. 86; x. 98; xxxvii. 139 ; lxviii. 48.)

The Psalms (الزَّبُور from زبر to write, read, recite) are a writing, a book :
" And to David we gave the Psalms." (Súras iv. 116 ; xvii. 57). " And now
since the exhortation was given have we written in the Psalms that my
servants, the righteous shall inherit the earth" (Súra xxi. 105 ; *see*
Psalms, xxxvii. 29). It may here be mentioned that this is the only
direct quotation from either the Old or New Testament in the whole of
the Qur'án. The history of David is referred to in Súras ii. 252 ; xxxviii.
20-24 ; xxi. 79-80; v. 82 ; xxxiv. 10-12.

unto the prophets from their Lord: and we will not distinguish between any of them, and unto him are we resigned." (Súra ii. 130).

The Gospel is called the Injil (الانجيل). The word انجيل occurs twelve times in the Qur'án, but is only used in the later Súras. "Who follow the apostle, the illiterate prophet, whom they find written down with them in the Thorah and the Injil" (Súra vii. 156). See also Súras iii. 2; iii. 43-58; lvii. 27; xlviii. 29; ix. 112; v. 51-70. Then let the people of the Gospel judge by what is revealed therein "Ye rest on nought until ye observe the Thorah and the Gospel and that which has been sent down from your Lord." Súra v. 72. In Súra lxi. 6, Muhammad refers to the promise of the Lord Jesus that He would send the Paraclete (احمد) mentioned in the New Testament, John xvi. 7. (See Faith of Islám, 13.)

The Qur'án contains far more of the histories of the Old than of the New Testament. It contains, however, the history of the birth of John the Baptist, and of Christ, of the miracles, the death (but not on the cross) and the ascension to heaven. It is to be observed that the references to the Injil as a divine revelation are to be found in the later, i.e., the Madína Súras. (For details see Dictionary of Islám, the article ' Injil' pp. 211-212).

Jews and Christians have been accused by Muhammad and his followers of having changed, and of altering their Scriptures (Súras iv. 48; v. 16; iii. 72). The learned doctors of Islám say that tahríf (تحريف) means the changing or turning aside from the truth, and that it may be effected in two ways: (1) by changing the meaning (تحريف معنوى) or (2) by altering the words of the text (تحريف لفظى). On careful comparison of the passages of the Qur'án which accuse the Jews and Christians of corrupting their scriptures, it becomes clear that Muhammad did not mean to accuse them of having changed and corrupted the text of their holy books, but of having misunderstood, and misinterpreted and concealed (كتموا) certain passages, which he thought contained prophecies confirming his divine mission. This is also the opinion of men of high authority on Muslim lore. Bukhári records that Ibn 'Abbás said that "there is no man who could corrupt a single word of what proceeded from God," so that the Jews and Christians could corrupt only by misrepresenting the meaning of the words of God.

The Qur'án given to Muhammad is considered to be the most excellent and complete of all divinely inspired books. The essential word of God (الكلام النفسى) contained therein is held by the orthodox school to be

As human reason is not sufficient to guide man to the knowledge of the Truth, God has, from time to time, sent his servants, the Prophets (نَبِيٌّ pl. أَنْبِيَاءُ) and Apostles[1]

---

eternal, uncreated (غير مخلوق); the letters and words, however, written down or read by men (الكلام اللفظى) are created, but even in this sense it is considered unbecoming to speak of the Qur'án as created. The creation or non-creation of the Qur'án (خلق القرآن) was a highly disputed question chiefly during the reigns of the Khalifs al Mamún and al Mu'tasim (211-227 A. H.) and some of the most famous doctors of Islám were severely persecuted for holding the doctrine of the non-creation of the Qur'án. (*See* Faith of Islám, 189-191). The Mu'tazila, in opposition to the Sunni doctrine, hold the doctrine of the creation of the Qur'án. (Shahrastáni ii. 30).

The Qur'án is believed to have been written (created by God) on the ' Preserved Tablet' (اللوح المحفوظ), then brought down in sheets (صحائف) to the lowest heaven on the night of al Qadr, where they were preserved in a place called the House of Glory (بيت العزّة), whence they were brought to Muhammad according to the requirements of the case. Some think only the meaning was revealed and that Gabriel and Muhammad clothed them in their own words, but the commonly received opinion is that both the meaning and the words were revealed. (المُنَزَّل المعنى واللفظ)

ان الله خلق القرآن أوّلاً فى اللوح المحفوظ ثم انزلهُ فى صحائف فى السماء الدنيا فى محل يقال لهُ بيت العزّة فى ليلة القدر ثم انزلهُ على النبىّ صلعم مفرّقا بحسب الوقائع (Jowh. 89)

With regard to the inimitability (اعجاز) of the Qur'án, the Nozámiyya dissent from the orthodox opinion by saying that the Arabs would certainly have been able to produce a Súra equal to the Súras of the Qur'án in eloquence, style and elegance, if God had not prevented them from attempting it by peculiar circumstances, and that the excellency of the Qur'án consisted in what it relates of the past and the future.

1 The sending of prophets is something that may reasonably be expected, but it is not, as some sects pretend, incumbent on God to send them ; his having sent them is an act of free grace.

(ارسال جميع المرسل من الجائز العقلى فى حقّه تعالى - ارسالهُ الرسل من محض فضله)

Philosophers pretend that this is incumbent on God, as promoting the spiritual and temporal welfare of man.

(رُسُل pl. رَسُل) in order to guide and teach men, and it is the duty of every Muslim firmly to believe in God's having sent such divinely commissioned messengers.

The number of prophets or apostles God has sent is said, according to a saying of Muhammad, to have amounted to one hundred and twenty-four thousand; some say two hundred and forty thousand and others again one hundred thousand; of these three hundred and thirteen are said to have been 'apostles' with special missions and dispensations and Books, while the others were merely prophets, *i.e.*, men divinely guided and inspired, but having only a general commission to teach and guide their fellowmen, for a prophet, according to Muslim divines, is a man inspired by God, but not sent with a special dispensation (شريعة) nor a special Book, while an apostle is one with a distinct message, (رسالة) and a special Book. Such were Moses, Jesus, Muhammad. According to this definition all apostles are at the same time prophets, but not all prophets are apostles. The commentator of the Jowhara gives the following definition of a Prophet:

(النبى انسان ذكر حُرّ من بنى آدم سـليم عن مُنفّر طبعاً اوحى اليه بشرع يعمل به و ان لم يومَر بتبليغه).

The office of a prophet is the free gift of God - (حصيصة من اللّه فضل اللّه). It cannot be acquired by any acts of man however excellent, such as seclusion, or an ascetic life entirely devoted to the worship of God (النبوة لَيَسَتْ مكتسبة). The philosophers pretend that man may reach this high rank, by which the Sunnis say they accuse the Qur'án of telling falsehoods, for it calls Muhammad the last of the prophets and Muhammad said : "There will be no prophet after me (لانبّى بعدى)."

As regards the characteristics of the prophetical office, we must consider

(1) What must necessarily be ascribed to prophets,

(ما يجب فى حق النبى) -

(2) What it is impossible to ascribe to them,

(ما يستحيل فى حق النبى) -

(3) What it is allowable to ascribe to them,

(ما يجوز فى حق النبى) -

The qualifications which must necessarily be ascribed to a prophet and which he must possess are the following four :

Faithfulness (أمانة), *i.e.*, he must outwardly and inwardly be preserved from the commission of any sinful act.

Inwardly a prophet must be free from envy, pride, and hypocrisy.
As to his total freedom from sin before his assumption of the prophetic
office, the majority admit that he may then commit small as well as great
sins (لا يمتنع ان يصدر عنهم كبيرة). The author of the Mawáqif says:
"We Sunnites hold that prophets, after the assumption of the prophetic
character (بعد الوحى), are absolutely preserved from committing great sins
and from committing small sins intentionally (هم معصومون عن الكبائر
مطلقاً و عن الصغائر عمداً). (For further details on the infallibility of prophets see Mawáqif, 568, et seqq. Faith of Islám, 216-19.) The Qur'án
mentions several cases of prophets committing sins, such as of Adam
(Súra ii. 29-37); Noah (Súras xi. 49; lxxi. 29); Abraham (Súra xxvi. 80-82).
Moses (Súras xxviii. 15-16). In Súra xl. 57, Muhammad is commanded to
ask for pardon for his sin (Súra xlviii. 2). God is spoken of as pardoning
his former and later sins. Tradition reports that Muhammad used to say:
"I ask the Almighty for pardon and repent unto him three times a day"
(انى استغفر الله واتوب اليه اليوم سبعين مرة) see Ghazáli i. 190-191). The
biographers of Muhammad also mention acts of his which are sinful.

This contradiction between the teaching of the Qur'án and that of the
theologians is a difficulty. In order to explain it, Muslim divines say that
what would be disobedience and sin in other men is not to be considered as
sin in the prophets; that Adam's disobedience in eating of the forbidden
fruit was a sin but not like other sins (معصية لا كالمعاصى), that what was
forbidden to him outwardly was commanded to him inwardly (منهى ظاهراً
مامور باطناً) and that there was a secret understanding between him and
his Lord which we do not know. All such sinful acts and disobedience
in prophets must, therefore, be explained, so as to leave their character un-
touched by sin; nor is it becoming to mention or refer to their having
committed illicit acts, except when circumstances necessarily require it.
Muhammad's confessing his sins is explained to be an act of humility,
done in order to be an example to his followers.

Truthfulness (صدق), or their speaking the truth, in accordance with
the real state of the case, or, at all events, in accordance with what
they believe to be the truth. - (مدقهم فى دعوى الرسالة والاحكام الشرعية
مطابقة خبرهم للواقع و لو بحسب اعتقادهم) (Jowh. 114-115). For an explanation of Muhammad's having once recited a verse the devil had suggested
to him, viz., the verse of the غرانيق, see Mawáqif, 573.

Intelligence, sagacity (فطانة), enabling them to silence the objections
of the opponents and to defend the truth by sound and convincing
arguments; apostles must possess this quality in a still higher degree
than prophets. (الرسل الواجب لهم كمال الفطنة)

Delivery of the message (تبليغ لما أتوا) (تبليغهم لما) that is, to deliver (تبليغ) to those to whom they are sent the messages God charges them to deliver, and on no account to conceal (كتم) them. This of course does not include messages they are charged to conceal, or, with regard to which, they are at liberty either to publish or withhold.

(ما أُمروا بكتمانه وما خُيروا فيه) Jowh. 115, 116).

It is impossible to ascribe to prophets (ما يستحيل فى حق الانبياء) attributes opposed to those, which have been mentioned as necessarily belonging to the prophetic office, such as unfaithfulness (حيانة), falseness, mendaciousness (كذب), want of intelligence, dullness (غَفلة), concealing the message (كتمان). A prophet, as a rule, must be a male not a female, free not a slave, free from repulsive diseases and defects (سليم عن مُنَفّر), taken from mankind not from angels or Jinn or animals.

(ما كانت نبيًا قط أُنثى ولا عبد وشخص ذو فعال) (Jowh. 9). Mariam, Eve, and Sarah are admitted by some to the list of prophets.

It is permitted to ascribe to prophets the power of eating, fasting, sleeping, walking, marrying, or abstaining from marriage, and the state of health or sickness. "The leprosy of Job was not a repulsive disease, as it did not appear on the surface, but was hidden between the skin and the bone." "The blindness of Jacob consisted merely in a film over the eye, which was removed when he received the glad tidings of his son Joseph" (Jowh. 9, 10, 116, 117).

Neglect, or omission (سَهْو), with regard to the verbal messages they were commissioned to deliver may not be ascribed to prophets before they have delivered them.

Forgetfulness, oblivion (نِسْيان), may not be ascribed to a prophet before he has delivered the message; after it he may forget it. (Jowh. 117-118) God has given the prophets and apostles the power to perform miracles, i.e., the doing of things contrary to custom (أمور خارقة للعادة) in proof of their prophetic mission, and the truthfulness in what they deliver to men as a divine message (الله تعالى أيّدهم بالمعجزات حيث اظهرها على أيديهم تصديقًا فى دعوى النبوّة والرسالة و فيما بلّغوهُ عن الله تعالى لانها نازلة منزلة قوله صَدَّق عبدى فى كل ما يبلّغ عنى) One single miracle is considered sufficient to prove the prophetic character of him who performs it. (المعجزة امر يظهر بخلاف العادة على يد مدّعى النبوّة عند تحدّى المنكرين على وجهٍ يعجِز المنكرين عن الاتيان بمثله)

The characteristics of a true miracle are the following seven :—

(1) It must consist in a word, or a deed, or the relinquishing of an act. (ان تكون قولًا او فعلًا او تركًا). Examples of these are : the Qur'án—the coming forth of water between the fingers—the fire not burning Abraham (*See* Mawáqif, 547).

(2) It must be contrary to custom (ان تكون خارقة للعادة).

(3) It must be performed by a person claiming the prophetic or apostolic office. (ان تكون على يد مدّعى النبوّة او الرسالة) This distinguishes miracles (معجزة) from unusual acts performed by men of uncommon piety (عبد ظاهر الصلاح), which are called كرامة, and from what happens some-times to common men (عوام), in deliverance from great calamities, which extraordinary thing is called معونة, help; and from what may also be produced by a wicked man (فاسق), which is called استدراج, also from what may be wrought by him with the assistance of the devil, which is called اهانة, contempt, shame.

(4) It must be performed during the assumption of the prophetic office, or, at all events, only a short time before the same.

(ان تكون مقرونة بدعوى النبوّة او الرسالة حَقيقةً او حكمًا) Miraculous works performed by, or in favour of a prophet long before he has assumed the prophetic office, are not called معجزة but ارهاص (v. ارهص to lay the foundations). They are signs preceding a prophetic call, laying the found-ation of the same. Such is said to have been the cloud which appeared over the head of Muhammad, years before his assumption of the prophetic office. With regard to the miracles performed by Jesus when he was a child (Súras xix. 30-32; iii. 43), long before his assumption of the prophetic character, the Qádi says that these may nevertheless be consi-dered معجزات, because Jesus was a prophet even when a babe, for he said : "And God made me a prophet" (جعلنى نبيًا), and there is nothing impossible in God's having created in him all the qualifications of a prophet, even when he was yet a child (Mawáqif, 548).

(5) It must be in accordance with what the prophet pretends to do (ان تكون موافقة للدعوى). If he should pretend to divide the sea, and instead of this the mountain were to be divided, this would not be a true miracle.

(6) It must not declare him who assumes the prophetic office to be a deceiver and liar (ان لا تكون مكذّبة لهُ). If he were to declare that a dumb animal should speak, and the animal really spoke, but called him a deceiver this would be a proof of his being a false prophet. If he were to ask a dead man to rise and speak, and the man did so, but

declared him to be a deceiver, this would not be a conclusive proof of his being a false prophet, for the man risen from the dead might be an infidel, and purposely chosen to reject the prophet's divine commission.

(7) It must be such that it is impossible to contradict, deny or imitate it. (ان تتعذّرمعارضتها) Things done by means of sorcery (سِحر) or legerdemain (شعبذة), or conjuring are therefore not miracles. (*See* Mawáqif, chapter كيفية حصول المجزات - and chapter دلالها.)

It is remarkable that, though Muhammad repeatedly and distinctly declared that God had not given him the power to perform miracles, and that he had not performed any miracles (Súras xvii. 16, 92-95; vi. 109-112; xxix. 49, 50; xviii. 110), the learned doctors of Islám insist on ascribing to him a number of miracles and declare that "he who denies the genuineness of such of his miracles as rest on the testimony of an uninterrupted chain of witnesses is an infidel." (اعلم ان ما كان منها (المعجزات)

معلوماً بالقطع منقولاً بالتواتر كالقران كفر منكرهُ ـ فان اشـتهر كـنبع الماء
بين اصابعه صلعم فسـق منكرهُ ـ و ان ثبت بطريق صحيح او حسن عُزّر منكرهُ
(Jowh. 131.

The greatest miracle, mentioned by Muslims as confirming Muhammad's prophetic office, is the Qur'án. It is called "the standing miracle" (الآية الباقية) Súra xvii. 190. Jowh. 33, 134. Mawáqif 557-563). Other miracles, mentioned are the so-called splitting of the moon (انشقاق القمر) Súra lix. 1-2); the pebbles praising God, the night-journey (معراج) Súra xvii. 1). He who denies the truth of this miracle is an infidel. (For more details *see* Jowh. 133-134. Mawáqif, 563. Dictionary of Islám, 351. Faith of Islám, 218). Among the miracles mentioned is also his having been predicted in the Thorah and the Injil as a true prophet. (Mawákif, 565). There are various sects of Muslims which deny the reality of these miracles or the possibility of miracles. (For a detailed account of their opinions and a refutation of the same *see* Mawáqif, 550-557).

The highest in rank among the prophets and apostles is said to be Muhammad, who is considered not only the greatest prophet, but the most excellent among all created things. (افضل الخلق على الاطلاق) Then comes Abraham, then Moses, then Jesus. These four are distinguished by the title أُولُو العزم, possessors of constancy. (Súras xlvi, 34). After these in rank come the apostles (الرُّسل) and then the other prophets. The following six prophets are said to have brought new dispensations and new law (شريعة): Adam (صفىّ اللّه), Noah (نبىّ اللّه), Abraham (خليل اللّه), Moses (كليم اللّه), Jesus (روح اللّه), Muhammad

Immediately in rank after the prophets and apostles
come the Companions[1] of Muhammad (صُحْبُه اصحاب النبي),
who are considered to be the most excellent men after
Muhammad ; after these come the followers (التّابِع pl.
التّابعون)); after these in rank come the followers of the
followers (اتباع التابعين) ; after these the Khalifs (خليفة pl.
خُلَفَاء)

(رسول الله). The dispensation of Muhammad is considered to have
superseded all previous dispensations and to be superseded by none.
Muhammad is considered to have received a general mission to all
nations (شرعه لا يُنسَخ بغيره و نسخه لشرع غيره وقع حتماً - تعميم بعثة محمد).
Muhammad's spirit is said to have been created before all others, and
then sent to them to make them acquainted with his apostleship
and divine mission. He was sent to all men, including himself. Though
Jesus will come down at the last day to judge, it is believed that He
will judge according to the law of Muhammad, and as a follower of
his law. (Jowh. 128). All prophets are believed, in their previous
existence (as spirits), to have declared their submission to Muhammad,
and to have been in this world merely his representatives (نَوَّابُه). It is
difficult to reconcile this classification with the teaching of the Qur'án
and the sayings of Muhammad, which declare that there is no distinction
between the apostles. (لا تفضلونى بين الانبياء -) Súras ii. 285 ; v. 130; iii.
78). Muhammad said : " Do not give me the preference over Moses " ...
(لا تخيّرونى على موسى) - Jowh. 122-123). For a detailed description of
the life of Moses as given in the Qur'án see Dictionary of Islám, pp.
356-366, taken from Lane's selections. (For the Muslim opinion of Jesus,
His sonship and death see Súras xix. 35-36; iii. 52; liii. 57-65; ix. 30;
iii. 72-73; v. 19. 76-79; iv. 169; v. 116-117. For details see Dictionary
of Islám ; 229-235).

1 Muhammad said : " God has chosen my Companions before all the
worlds, with the exception of the prophets and the apostles." The
followers are those who lived, and had intercourse with the Companions
even if but for a short time. The Khalif is a representative, a successor
of the Prophet, a substitute. Muhammad is reported to have said : " The
Khalifate after me will last thirty years, then will come a tyrannical
monarchy " (الخلافة بعدى ثلاثون سنة ثم تصير ملكاً عضوضاً) Jowh. 136).

The Khalifs who were, at the same time Companions, were Abú Bakr, 'Umar, 'Uthmán and 'Ali, who together reigned twenty-nine years, six months and four days. Mu'áwiya is reported to have said : "I am the first king" (Jowh. 137). After these come in rank the following six men to whom Paradise was expressly promised : Talha, Zubair, Abdu'r Rahmán bin 'Auf, Sa'd bin Abi Wakkás, Sa'd bin Zaid, Abú 'Ubaida. To these Muhammad had expressly promised Paradise by saying : " 'Abu Bakr is in Paradise, ' Umar is in Paradise " (Jowh. 138). After these come the men who fought at the battle of Badr, three hundred and seventeen fighting men ; after them those who fought at the battle of Uhud, three hundred men, of whose seventy were martyrs. After these in rank come " the covenanters " (اهل بَيعة الرضوان) *i.e.*, the fourteen hundred men who accompanied Muhammad on his pilgrimage to Mecca, six years after his flight from Mecca to Madína, and made a covenant with him (بايعوه), that they would stand by him against the hostile Meccans. They are praised in the Qur'án (Súra xlviii. 18. Jowh. 140-141 ; 142-143). After these in rank come the four great Imáms, the guides of the Muslim nation (هُداة الأُمّة) ; the Imáms Málik, Sháfi'i, Abú Hanífa, Ahmad ibn Hanbal. To this class of great doctors belong also Sufian ath Thuri, Abú Hasanu'l-Ash'ari (For details *see* Jowh. 143, 144). Málik and the three other Imáms are the teachers and guides of the nation in the branches (فروع, *i.e.*, Fikh, or practical part, jurisprudence) ; the Imám al Ash'ari and those of his kind in the Roots (أُصول) *i.e.*, the articles of faith, the creed (العقائد الدينّية) and al-Zunaid and those like him in Súfiism.

It is the duty of every Muslim who has not reached the degree of knowledge which constitutes him a Mujtahid (المجتهد المطلق) to follow one of the great Imáms in what they have laid down as the law with regard to practice (واجب التقليد فى الاحكام الفروعّية). He who has become a Mujtahid need not do so. (يحرم عليه التقليد) Jowh. 144-145).

A Wali, or saint (ولى pl. أوْليا), is a believer who is distinguished by great piety and asceticism. He is not considered exempt from sin, but if he transgresses, he repents at once. He is called a ولى (from وَلَى to possess, be in charge of a thing) because God takes charge of his concerns (لان الله تولى امَرَه) and also because he himself only cares for the worship of God (يتولّة). He is able to do things contrary to custom, and such acts are called " beneficence." Such miracles do not appear in his lifetime but after his death. Such a saint, if no miracles appear through him, is not a true Wali. (For further details *see* Jowh. 145-146).

Prayer, supplication, intercession, petition, (الدُّعَاءُ لِفُلَانٍ) as well as imprecation, (الدُّعَاءُ عَلَى فُلَانٍ) profit and injure respectively, both the living and the dead, even when proceeding from an infidel[1].

---

[1] Prayer and supplication are said to be of use against all calamities, whether they be decreed by God absolutely (قَضَاء مُبْرَم), or only conditionally (قَضَاء مُعَلَّق). With regard to what God has decreed only conditionally, there is no difficulty in believing that He will in answer to the supplications of His servants not send it down. As regards such calamities which He has irrevocably decreed, it is believed that He may lessen them, so if He has decreed that a large rock shall fall down upon men, He may, in answer to their supplication, cause it to be broken up into small pieces like sand in order that it may not hurt them. The Qur'án commands men to make supplications (Súras xl. 62; ii. 182; Jowh. 147).

Such supplications, however, in order to be efficient, must be in accordance with certain conditions, *i.e.*, the person who offers them must have the following qualifications: (اِنَّ لِلدُّعَاء شُرُوطًا و آدَابًا) (1) he must live on what he has honestly acquired (اَكْل الحَلَال); (2) he must call on God with firm confidence in His help (بِالاِجَابَة); (3) his heart must not be distracted (لَا يَكُون قَلْبُهُ غَافِلًا) (4) he must not ask what is wrong or what may injure his relatives or any Muslim; (5) he must not ask for things impossible (اِن لَا يَدْعُو بِمُحَال).

The following rules are to be observed when offering supplications and intercessions: (1) to choose the proper time (اِن يَتَخَيَّر الاوقَات الفَاضِلَة); (2) before offering such petitions to perform the ablution and canonical prayers, to turn to the Qibla, lift up the hands towards heaven, confess sins, repent, praise God and ask for blessings on the Prophet at the beginning, the middle and the conclusion. (Jowh. 147). God's answer to such petitions may be given in a variety of ways, and at different times; but, under all circumstances, man's obtaining what he asks for is subordinate to His will.

It may be useful here to mention that دُعَاء is used for (Jowh. 148), private prayer, in which a person is allowed to use his own words, while صَلاة is only used of the stated liturgical form of prayer, the appointed prayer-service. (For further details on the subject and specimens of petitions offered by Muhammad for forgiveness of sins, of 'Ayesha, Fátima, Abú Bakr, Abraham, Jesus, Adam, 'Ali and others *see* Ghazali i. 182-199. A specimen of imprecation is found in Súra 111).

The Qur'án, in many passages gives a minute description of Death,[1] the Resurrection, the last Judgment, Paradise, and Hell, (البعث الحشر المَعَاد). It may suffice here to refer to the following Súras: lxxv; lxxxi. 1-19; lxxxii; lxxxiii. 4-20; lxxxiv. 1-19; to a later period belong the following verses: Súra xxii. 1-7. Death (الموت) is the lot of every man. Súra iii. 182.

(كلّ نفس ذائقه الموت)

---

[1] Death takes place when men have reached the age which God has appointed for them (عند فراغ الآجال المقدّرة). He respites them up to a fixed time, and when that is come they cannot put it off one single hour, nor can they bring it on sooner (Súra xvi. 63). Learned men differ as to whether death is a positive or negative thing. Al Ash'ari defends the former opinion arguing that it is a positive, really existing state or qualification (كيفية اوصفة وجوديّة), while others like al-Asfaráini, Zamakhshari hold the second opinion, saying that death is the want of life (عدم الحيوة). Al Ash'ari appeals, in support of his opinion, to the verse of the Qur'án: " God the highest who has created life and death" and to certain traditions, such as " God has created death in the shape of a ram (بصورة كبش): every one before whom it passes will surely die." This doctrine refutes the opinion of the Atheist that man appears and disappears in the course of nature. The word بعث means quickening, or vivifying (يَوم البعث) : The term حَشر is collecting, congregating (يوم الحشر), the day of congregating the dead. The word المعاد means returning from death unto life. These are synonymous terms for the Last Day.

Ghazáli says: " When God Almighty let His hands pass over the back of Adam and gathered men into His two hands, He placed some of them in His right hand and the others in His left; then he opened both His hands before Adam, and Adam looked at them and saw them like imperceptible atoms. Then God said: " These are destined for Paradise and these are destined for hell-fire." He then asked them: " Am I not your Lord?" and they replied: " Certainly, we testify that Thou art our Lord." God then asked Adam and the angels to be witnesses ... after this God replaced them into the loins of Adam (صَلْب). They were at that time purely spiritual beings without bodies. He then caused them

When the hour is come for man to die, ' Izrá'íl, the Angel of death, appears with his assistants (اعوان); these draw out the spirit up to the throat[1] (حنجرة), when it is pierced by a poisonous lance which detaches it completely from the body. ' Izrá'íl then seizes it.

Súra xxxii ; 11. (يتوفا كم ملك الموت الذي وكّل بكم)

Immediately after the burial, two large, black livid angels visit dead men in their grave, whether they were infidels, hypocrites or believers. These angels are called Munkar and Nakír[2] (نكير ـ منكر), hideous, horrid,

to die, but gathered them and kept them in a receptacle near His throne (فى خزانة من خزائن العرش). When the germ of a new being is placed in the womb of the mother, it remains there till its body is sufficiently developed; the soul in the same is then dead yet, when God Almighty breathes into the spirit, He restores to it its most precious part (سرها) of which it had been deprived while preserved in the receptacle near the throne. This is the first death and a second life. Then God places man in this world till he has reached the term fixed for him.

[1] As long as the soul slowly ascends from the heart through the throat, it is exposed to various temptations and doubts, but when it has been pierced by the lance and thus separated from the body these cease. 'Izrá'íl is said to be frightful in appearance and of enormous size; his head in the highest heaven, his feet in the lowest parts of the earth, and his face opposite the preserved Tablet. To a believer, however, he appears in a lovely shape, and his assistants as 'Angels of Mercy, while to the unbelievers they are tormenting angels. The soul, spirit, according to the orthodox school is said to be a subtle body, intimately united with the body of man, like the juice is united with the green branch of a tree. (الروح جسم لطيف مشتبك بالبدن كاشتبان الماء بالعود الاخضر). The angel of death also takes the life of Jinn, of angels and even of animals (Jowh. 158).

[2] Their eyes are said to be like copper cauldrons, their voices like thunder . . . . in their hands they hold enormous iron hammers of such weight that, if they were to let them fall down on a mountain they would grind it to powder. In order that this examination of the dead may take place, God is said to cause the spirit of the dead person to return to its body with its senses and reason and memory.

abominable) who examine the dead as to their belief in
the Unity of God and the divine mission of Muhammad.[1]

---

[1] The spirit of the believer, according to some, is, immediately after his
death, taken up through the seven heavens to the presence of God,
and then returns to the grave, to re-enter the body in order to be
examined. (Ghazali Durr 13-19). The examining angels will say to
the dead person : " Who is thy Lord and what is thy religion and who
is thy prophet?" (مَن نبيّك و من دينك و ما ربّك, من). (See Jowh. 160,
also Dictionary of Islám 79-80. Faith of Islám, 204). If the person so
examined returns a satisfactory answer : " God is my Lord, Islám is my
religion and Muhammad my prophet," a beautiful angel approaches
him and assures him of the mercy of God and the delights of Paradise.
Then orders are given to spread carpets for him in Paradise, to
assign to him a green garden and he is made to shine like the
full moon. His grave is made spacious for him (70 × 70 cubits), and a
window is made in the same, opening into Paradise. (Gházali iv. 312.
314 ; Jowh. 161). If the answer is not satisfactory, the two angels beat
him between his eyes with the iron maces, till he roars for anguish so
loud that his cries will be heard by all creatures except man and genii.
He is then doomed to eternal hell-fire ; orders are given to spread for him
fiery boards and to open for him a door into hell fires. Ninety-nine dragons
sting and scratch and lick and torment him till the day of resurrection.
This grave is made narrow for him by the pressure of the earth upon
him till his ribs are almost crushed. The infidel will suffer such torments
for ever ; the disobedient believer however only for a time, according to
his sins. (جرائمهم بِحسب). See Gházali iv. 312. Jowh. 161. Dictionary
of Islám, 27 and 80). Prophets and Martyrs, it is said, are not subjected
to this examination. Angels are also held to be exempt from it but not
the Jinn.

The inhabitants of the grave are said to be of four kinds, (1) those who
sleep on their backs till their corpses become dust, when they constantly
rove about between earth and the lowest heaven ; (2) those on whom God
causes sleep to descend and who only wake up at the first blast of the
trumpet ; (3) those who remain in their graves only two or three months,
then are carried away into Paradise ; they perch on the trees of Paradise
in the shape of birds. The spirits of martyrs are in the crops of birds. (4)
Prophets and saints who may choose their own habitation. (See Ghazáli
Durr 33-38).

He who dies a violent death at the hand of a murderer, or otherwise,
must nevertheless be considered to have reached the proper term of his

Muhammad taught that, though man's body will be consumed by the earth, yet one part[1] of it will remain uncorrupted till the last day namely the *os sacrum* (عجب الذَنَب the rump-bone), and that from this God will, at the last day, create a new body so that, as it was the first part created, it will remain to the last uncorrupted, to become the seed whence the whole body is to be renewed (Jowh. 155 ليس من الانسان شئ لا يبلي

الَّا عظماً واحداً و هو عجب الذَنَب منه خلق الخلق يوم القيامة)·

---

life; for, if he had not died a violent death, he would have died a natural death at the same hour. (For various other opinions of the Muʻtazila *see* Jowh. 36, 153. Ghazáli Durr).

Though the body becomes dust and perishes after death, the soul, spirit, will continue alive till the first blast of the trumpet at the last day. In this all learned men are agreed. Whether, however, it will die or continue alive after Isráfíl has sounded the first blast of the trumpet is a controverted subject; some hold that it will then die, or vanish (فناء), till made alive again at the second blast; while others believe that it will not die, (حكموا بعدم فنائها). At this second blast God is believed to collect all the souls into the trumpet, in which there are said to be little holes or cells, like those in a bee-hive. They then leave their cells and repair, each to its own body.

[1] Some object to this statement, for God has declared in the Qur'án that everything will perish except His (God's) face (كل شئ هالك الا وجهه). To enquire in what the spirit of man consists and where its seat is in the body is useless; some say forbidden. Súra xvii. 87. It is generally admitted that man has only one soul; but some are of opinion that he has two, one is called the spirit of watchfulness (روح اليقظة) which, while it resides on the body, causes man to be awake and watchful and, when it departs from it, causes him to sleep and to have dreams; the other the spirit of life (روح الحياة) which, while it abides in the body, causes man to live, and when it departs causes him to die. (Jowh. 156).

The spirit after death enters the state, or interval, called al Barzakh (البرزخ = interval, separation), *i.e.*, the intervening state between death and the last day (Súra xxiii. 19).

As regards their abode, the generally accepted opinion is that the prophets are admitted into Paradise immediately after death; that the

The exact time when the Resurrection will take place no one knows but God. The approach of the Last Day, the Hour, (الساعة ـ اليَوم الآخر) may, however, be known from certain signs which are to precede it (أشراط الساعة). These are distinguished into the lesser and the greater signs (العلامات الكُبرى ـ العلامات الصُغرى)[1].

---

martyrs, according to a saying of Muhammad, rest in the crops of green birds, which eat of the fruits and drink of the river of Paradise (ارواحهم فى حواصل طيور خضر), Súra iii. 163. This living in the crops of birds cannot be explained, but must nevertheless be believed. The commentator of the Jowhara says that the birds may be transparent, or the saying may be understood figuratively, as representing the speed with which they are able to move about. The spirits of common believers are usually believed to stay near their graves (Jowh. 181-182 ارواح السعداء بافنيّة القبور على الصحيح); but they enjoy liberty to go wherever they please: others say that they are with Adam in the lowest heaven. The spirits of infidels are said to be cast down into a pit in hell, in the seventh earth called Sijjín (سجّين), where they are to remain to the day of Resurrection (Súra lxxxiii. 7-10). Others fancy that they remain in a certain well called Barhút (بئر برهوت) in Hadrament or, according to a saying of Muhammad "under the devil's jaw", to be tormented till they are called to join their bodies.

As regards the enjoyment of Paradise and the torments of Hell there will be the following classes: believers and infidels. The infidels will, according to a general agreement, be in hell for ever (مخلّد فى النار); the believers are of two kinds: (1) obedient (طائع) who go to Paradise; (2) the disobedient (عاص) who, if penitent (تائب), go to Paradise also, or, if impenitent (غير تائب), they are treated according to God's will (فى المشيئة), that is, He pardons them, or torments them as He pleases. He will not leave them in hell for ever, for, though disobedient, they are Muslims and Believers, and therefore are not to be treated like Infidels.

[1] The lesser signs of the Hour are, according to some authorities, as many as five hundred. Of these we may mention (1) the decay of faith among men (كثرة المظالم و ارتكاب المآثم و قلّة الامانسات وكثرة الخيانات)

(2 the advancing of the meanest persons to eminent dignity ساد القبيلة

فاسـتقهم - رفَع الاسافل) (3) A maid servant becomes the mother of her mistress, *i.e.*, there will be an increase of sensuality. (4) Tumours and seditions. (5) A war with Greeks and Romans. (6) Great distress in the world. (7) The provinces of Irak and Syria shall refuse to pay tribute.

The greater signs are the appearance of the Mahdi (ظهور المهدى), the directed one, who is therefore fit to direct others and concerning whom Muhammad foretold that the world would not come to an end, till one of his own family should govern the Arabians and should fill the earth with righteousness. It is believed that the Mahdi will come from Madína and go to Mecca where the people will make him Imám. He will be a great conqueror, causing the Muslims to become a mighty nation. He will break crosses and kill swine. According to the Shí'ahs, the Mahdi has already appeared in the person of Abú'l-Qásim, the 12th Imám (255 A.H.), who is believed by them to be alive now, but concealed in some secret place until the day of his manifestation before the end of the world (Mashar 185-192. Jowh. 168. Faith of Islám, 99).

The appearance of antichrist is another sign (خروج المسيح الدجّال). He is said to be one-eyed (اعور), and marked on the forehead with the letters K. F. R. which stand for Káfir, or infidel. According to some traditions he is to appear first between Irak and Syria: according to others near Madína. He will ride on an ass and be followed by seventy thousand Jews of Ispahan and continue on earth for forty days; he will lay waste all places, but will not enter either Mecca or Madína or Jerusalem. At last he will be slain by Jesus, who is to encounter him at the gate of Lydda. (For more details *see* Mashar 197-199; Bukhári's Commentary, x. 199-205. Sale, 57. Dictionary of Islám, 328).

The descent of Jesus, son of Maryam, (نزول عيسى بن مريم) will take place near the white minaret to the east of the Mosque at Damascus at the time of the afternoon prayer. The Imám, it is said, will make room for him, and he will lead prayer according to the rite of Muhammad; he will marry a wife, get children, and die after forty years' continuance on earth and be buried at Madína. Under him there will be great security and plenty. . . . lions and camels, bears and sheep, shall live in peace, and a child shall play with serpents unhurt (Mash. 192, 197-199. Sale 57-58. Isaiah xi. 6 *et seqq*).

The appearance of the Beast (خروج الدابّة) fifty cubits high, a compound of various species with the head of a bull, the eyes of a hog, the ear of an elephant, is also a sign. . . It will rise out of the earth in the temple of Mecca and mark the face of believers and of the infidels, so that every person may be known for what he really is. (*See* Mash. 203 *et seqq*. Dictionary of Islám, 64-539. Sale, 57).

The first sign of the immediate coming of the Hour will be the sounding of the Trumpet (نفخ الصور). At the first blast of the Trumpet[1] (نفخة الفزع) all creatures will be struck with terror. This blast will be followed by a second blast, when all creatures in heaven and on earth will die, or be annihilated, except those whom God may exempt from the common fate.

Another sign is the appearance of Gog and Magog (خروج ياجوج و ماجوج). These barbarian nations of whom many things are related in the Qur'án and the Traditions, will make inroads into the Holy Land, cross the lake of Tiberias, which the vanguard of their vast army will drink dry, proceed to Jerusalem and there greatly distress Jesus and his companions, till, at his request, God will destroy them. Their carcases will fill the earth, and the burning of their bows, arrows and quivers will last for seven years. God will at last, send a rain to cleanse the earth and make it fertile; (Súras xxi. 96; xviii. 93-97: Revelation xvi. 14; xx. 8: Ezekiel xxxviii. 2; xxxix. 1-9. Sale 58; Geiger 74. Bukhári's Commentary x. 205.)

The rising of the sun from the west (طلوع الشمس من مغربها), and the appearance of a mighty smoke (الدخان) which will remain on earth for forty days (Jowh. 168) and the destruction of the Ka'ba by the Abyssinians (خراب الكعبة) and the removal of the Qur'án from books and the memory of people. (رفع القرآن من المصاحف والصدور), and the inhabitants of the earth becoming infidels (رجوع اهل الارض كلهم كفارا) are all signs which indicate the near approach of the Hour; but the exact time will still remain uncertain.

[1] At the first blast of the Trumpet the earth will be shaken, and all buildings and mountains will be levelled; the heavens shall melt, the sun be darkened, the stars fall and the sea be troubled and dried up. Women who suck shall abandon their infants and even the she-camels which have gone ten months with young shall be utterly neglected. (Súra lxxxi.) This first blast shall be followed by the second blast, when nothing shall survive except God alone, with Paradise and hell and the inhabitants of these two places and the throne of glory. The last who will die is the Angel of death.

There is a difference of opinion as to the number of blasts. Some say they are three: (1) نفخة الفزع the blast of consternation; (2) نفخة الصعق

All creatures are said to remain for the space of forty years in the intermediate state (البرزخ) of insensibility and death, between the first and the last blast of the Trumpet. During this interval God is said to cause a rain, or dew supplied from the water under the throne of God, to fall upon the earth. It is called the water of life (ماء الحيوة) and will penetrate the earth to the depth of twelve feet. By the efficacy and virtue of this water, the dead bodies will spring forth from the graves, (the *os sacrum* being the germ) as they did in their mothers' womb, or as corn sprouts forth from common rain, and grow till they become perfect.

Immediatley at the sound of the blast of Resurrection (نفخة البعث ـ نفخة الأحياء) the souls of men will repair to their several bodies[1].

---

the blast of dying; (3) نفخة الاحياء the blast of resurrection. The truth is that there are only two blasts, that of consternation, and that of the resurrection.

[1] Isráfil, who with Gabriel and Míká'íl, has been restored to life, standing on the rock of the temple of Jerusalem, will at the command of God, call together the souls from all parts, those of believers from Paradise and the unbelievers from hell and throw them into his trumpet. There they will be ranged in little holes, like bees in a hive, and will, on his giving the last sound, be thrust out and fly like bees, filling the whole space between earth and heaven. Then they will repair to their respective bodies. (Mashar 212-213. Ghazáli iv. 320. Sale 59. Dictionary of Islám 540-541). The earth will then be an immense plain without hills or villages (الساهرة Súra lxxix. 13-14), and the dead, after they have risen, will sit down, each one on his tomb, anxiously waiting for what is to come. (Ghazáli Durr 43).

The first to rise will be Isráfil, then the other archangels, then Muhammad will mount the Buráq (البراق), a wonderful animal, between the size of a mule and an ass, having two wings and moving with remarkable swiftness, and repair to the presence of God. The dead will arise from

All mankind will then have to repair to the place of assembling[1] (الموقف - المَحشر) for judgment.

In consequence of the heat, and the press of people a copious sweat (العَرَق) will come out of every pore of the skin, forming a deep sea of sweat covering the whole place into which all will be immersed according to their works.

---

their graves in the same shape and with the same qualities (اعراض) in which they lived on earth. Even the still-born child (السقط) will rise in this condition. As the glorious change of the bodies of believers will only take place in Paradise, when Muhammad stated that men would rise barefooted, naked, and uncircumcised, 'Ayesha objected that it would be indecent for men and women to look at each other. The Prophet replied that people would then have weightier matters to care for than to look at each other.

Men will then, according to Muhammad, be distinguished into three classes : (1) those who go on foot are those who have performed few good works ; (2) those who ride are true believers who have been obedient servants of God ; (3) those who creep, grovelling with their faces to the ground, dragged along by angels, are the infidels. The various classes of evil-doers will be distinguished by their outward appearance : adulterers as apes, usurers as swine, etc., etc.

1 As to the place of assembling the Qur'án and the Traditions agree that it will be on earth, but as to the exact place opinions differ. Some say it will be Jerusalem. Ghazáli says it will be an extensive plain without any hills, valleys or trees where one might find a hiding place. (Súra xiv. 49). On this place of judgment, angels, men, genii, devils, animals will be gathered and kept standing, some say, for seventy, others for one hundred years, anxiously looking up to heaven and waiting for their sentence, but God will not speak to them. The sun will be very near the earth and the heads of the infidels will almost be burned (Ghazáli iv. 322).

This sea is said to be seventy feet deep ; some will stand in it up to their ankles, others up to their knees or loins, others to their ears, and some will be almost drowned in it. Prophets, saints and pious Muslims will not suffer from these troubles, for they will be protected by the shade of the throne of God. (Súras iii. 102-103, 182, 192 ; iv. 89 ; vi. 12 ; xvii. 54, 99 ; xviii. 99-101 ; xix. 69, 95, 96 ; xlv. 25 ; xxxii. 11.)

Then God will appear in the clouds, surrounded by angels, to judge those who have risen from their graves. This judgment will consist of the following :[1] the presentation before God (العَرْض), and the taking of the books of account (اخذ الصّحف), then the questioning (السّوَال), the account (الحساب), and then the weighing in the balance (الوزن - الميزان).

Muhammad, according to tradition, will be the first man to rise on the day of resurrection and will stand on the right of the throne of God. All other prophets will then range themselves under his flag. Men on rising will in their fright flee for refuge to Adam and entreat him to intercede (يشفع) for them, but he will

---

[1] The presentation means that all men will have to present themselves before God in their true character. The books in which all good and bad acts of man are recorded will be blown by the wind from a repository under the throne of God, where they have been preserved, and will then be fixed to the necks of those to whom they belong (Súra xvii. 14). The angels will then come and place these books in the right hand of those who will be saved (ان كان سعيداً) and in the left hand, behind the back, of those who go to hell. Angels and prophets will enter Paradise, without having to render an account and so receive no book (Súras lxxxiv. 8-12 ; lxix. 19, 20).

The first whom God will question will be the angels, then the prophets. Men will be questioned concerning their outward actions as well as their inward thoughts (عن سرّه و علانيته Súras lxxv. 5 ; v. 108, 116). All creatures, that is, men, angels and genii also will then be clearly made acquainted with the account of their works, good and bad (الحساب هو توقيف الله عبادَهُ). All wrongs and differences between men and beast will then be settled satisfactorily. God will then also judge wild beasts, and reduce them to dust. (Súras iv. 45 ; lxxviii. 41).

decline,[1] so with Abraham, Moses and Jesus. At last
Muhammad will undertake the office of Intercessor.[2]

After all creatures have been questioned and received
their account, then, in order still further to show the
justice of the account, a balance (ميزان) will be set up,
in which the books of actions, bad and good, will be
weighed[3].

---

[1] Adam will decline on the score of having disobeyed God. Jesus, it
is said, will also decline for the reason that he had been made the object
of worship due to God only.

[2] Jesus will send them to Muhammad who at once will accept the office
of intercessor. There is said to be an interval of one thousand years
between this going from one prophet to another for aid. Muhammad will intercede for his people. Súra xvii. 81, is said to refer to
this circumstance (المقام المحمود). After this general intercession of
Muhammad (الشفاعة العامّة), the door of intercession will be opened to
others and prophets and also to other pious men. Numbers will thus be
saved from hell-fire.

Besides this general intercession, Muhammad is believed to exercise
several other kinds of intercession for a number of people, some of whom
never performed a good work : also for such as have committed mortal
sins and for Muslims who are already in Hell-fire, for people in paradise
to raise them to a higher degree (رفع الدرجات فى الجنّة), for lightening
the torments of some people in Hell, for alleviating the torments of
the grave. (For further details see Jowh. 178-179 ; Mashar. 255, 259-264 ;
Ghazáli iv. 329-340. Súras ii. 256 ; xix. 90 ; see also Súras ii. 45 ; xx.
108 ; xxxiv. 22 ; xxxix. 45 ; lxxiv. 49 ; lxxviii. 38). Every sin may be
forgiven except idolatry (Súra iv. 51-116).

[3] There will then, according to Ghazáli, be three classes : (1) those
who have done no good works and who will go to hell-fire at once ; (2) those
who have committed no evil action (prophets) and those who have performed many excellent works, who will go to Paradise at once ; (8) those
who have done both good and bad works. These constitute the majority.
For this class chiefly are the balances set up. Their books of actions,
some say the actions themselves, which will assume a bodily shape, will
be thrown into the scales and weighed (توزن الكتب او الاعيان). This
balance is referred to in the Qur'án (Súras xxi. 48 ; xviii. 105). The
orthodox opinion is that it is to be understood literally, not allegorically.

After the account has been rendered and every man's works weighed, and sentence pronounced accordingly, a bridge[1] (صراط) will be spread over the midst of hell and all believers and unbelievers will have to pass over it.

After having passed over the bridge, a pond[2] (حوض) will be given to Muhammad. It will be full of sweet and refreshing water. It is said to come from the river Kauthar (كوثر), which flows from under the throne of God.

Hell (دار العذاب ـ نار ـ جهنم) is the place of punishment, and torment. All men, without exemption, believers as well as infidels, will have to enter it. "There is not one of you that shall not go down to it." (Súra xix. 72.)[3] The

---

(For further details *see* Jowh. 170-171; Ghazáli iv. 325; Ghazáli Durr 69; Mash. 264. Faith of Islám, p. 225.)

[1] صراط means a road. Those who enter Paradise will take the right hand way, and those who are doomed to Hell-fire will take the left, but both of them will have to pass over the bridge spread over the midst of hell, finer than a hair and sharper than the edge of a sword and beset on each side with briars and thorns. The righteous cross it with the swiftness of lightning, others like the wind; the wicked will soon miss their footing and fall into the fire of Hell.

[2] Muhammad and his people will drink from it. Every prophet also is to be given such a pond, but of inferior quality. Súra cviii. 1 is said to refer to this delicious water. The throne of God (العرش Súra ix. 130) is a large body, or cupola, spread over the world, made of fire or green emerald, or red ruby, resting on four columns which are borne at present by four angels; but at last by eight. The seat (الكرسى) also is a body of light (جسم نورانى), attached to the throne from beneath. The Pen (القلم) is a large shining reed (قصب), which God is said to have created and commanded to write down everything that was and shall be to the day of the resurrection. (Bukhári's Commentary ix. 331). The Preserved Tablet (اللوح المحفوظ) is said to be a large shining slab, on which the Pen writes down, with the permission of God, everything that has happened and will happen.

[3] Some commentators make Súra xix. 72 refer to the believers' passing the bridge spread over hell; but the majority hold that believers also

believers will scarcely, if at all, feel its heat, and will pass through it quickly ; infidels will remain in it for ever.

Hell is said to be divided into seven stories (طَبَقَة) or apartments, one below the other, designed for as many distinct classes of the damned. They are given below[1] :

---

will enter Hell but pass through it quickly and that the heat will be cooled down for them (*see* Baidáwi Commentary). Hell, according to the Sunni doctrine, has been created by God in past times and exists now. Hell is described as an awful place, terribly hot, its fuel are men and stones, its drink matter mixed with blood, the clothes of its inhabitants are made of ever-burning pitch (قَطْرَان) ; serpents and scorpions will sting and torment its victims.

1 1. Jahannam (جَهَنَّم), in which the wicked believers will be punished, according to their works or demerits, till they are, at last, released. It is a purgatorial hell for Muslims and will be destroyed after they have come out of it.

2. Laza (لَظَى), a blazing fire for Jews.

3. Hutama (حُطَمَة), an intense fire for Christians (Súra civ. 4).

4. Satír (سَعِير), a flaming fire for the Sabians (Súra iv. 11).

5. Saqar (سَقَر), for the Magi (Súras, liv. 47 ; lxxiv. 44).

6. Jahím (جَحِيم), for idolaters (Súra ii. 113).

7. Háwía (هَاوِية the abyss), the lowest hell, the bottomless pit for hypocrites (مُنَافِقِين), *i.e.*, those who outwardly professed Islám, and inwardly were infidels (Súra ci. 7).

Over each of the gates of these stories is set a guard of Angels (خَزَنَة Súras xxxix. 71 ; lxvii. 8), whom the damned will beg in vain to intercede for them with God that they may be relieved from their torments or annihilated (Súra xl. 52). Over these guards is set as chief, Málik (مَالك). The food of the damned is a bitter fruit called Zaqqúm (شَجَرة الزَّقُّوم Súras xxxvii. 60-64 ; xliv. 43-44 ; lvi. 51-53), their drink is hot, stinking water (حَمِيم), mixed with matter (غَسَّاق Súra xxxviii. 57, مَاء صَدِيد Súra xiv. 19).

The unbeliever who dies as such, though he had been a believer all his lifetime, will remain in Hell for ever (النَّار دار خلود للشقي Ghazáli iv.

The abode of the blessed is believed to be a kind of
partition wall, called the A'aráf[1] (الأَعْرَاف), between heaven
and hell. Those who have not yet entered Paradise,
although they desire it, rest on this wall. From this
place they see both those who enter Paradise and those
in Hell. (Súra vii. 44).

The righteous having safely passed the bridge and
having refreshed themselves at the pond, will at last
enter Paradise,[2] and in the heavenly garden (الجنّة) will
enjoy all kinds of delights, bodily as well as spiritual. The
Qur'án gives a detailed description of these delights in a
number of passages ; among others in Súras lxxvi. 12-22 ;

---

331 *et seqq*). The children of infidels are, according to the best authorities, admitted into Paradise ; some place them in the A'aráf (الأعراف) ;
a kind of Hades ; some few pretend that they are in Hell-fire. No Muslim
will be doomed to eternal fire, all will be released from it after a shorter
or longer period. Even during their stay in Hell, Muslims will not be
made to feel the torments like infidels, as they are believed very soon
after they enter it, to undergo a kind of death, and to become
insensible to pain. (يفصدون احساس الم العذاب)   Jowh. 175. Mashar, 276.
Dictionary of Islám, 171-172).

[1] Baidáwi says that the term اعراف is derived from عرف pl. أعراف
and is the mane of a horse, or the most elevated part of a thing; other
commentators say that the place is so called because it 'distinguishes'
between heaven and hell, or because those who stand on it know and
distinguish the blessed from the damned by their respective marks
(عرف, to know, distinguish). Some consider this place a kind of limbo
for the patriarchs and prophets and saints; some also place the children
of infidels on the A'aráf.

[2] Paradise, according to the orthodox doctrine, was created of old, is
in existence now, and will last for ever (دار الخلود) and will not, as the
Mu'tazila pretend, be created on the day of resurrection and eventually
cease to exist. As to the number of Paradises, some believe that there is
only one, some two, others four, seven or eight. Those who adopt only
one say that the various names mentioned in the Qur'án only designate the various delights to be found in the one Paradise. Those who

lvi. 12-39 ; lv. 54-56 ; xlvii. 16 ; xviii. 30 ; xxii. 23 ; xxxvi.
55 ; xxxvii. 39-59 ; xxxix. 21, 73-75 ; lii. 17-18 ; lxxxiii.
22-36 ; x. 9-11 ; xxiii. 8-113 ; xxxviii. 49-55.

---

admit more than one mention the following: جنّة الخلود garden of immor-
tality (Súra xxv. 16) ; دار السلام dwelling of peace (Súra vi. 127) ; دار القرار
lasting habitation (Súra xl. 42) ; جنّات عدن gardens of Eden (Súra ix. 73);
جنّات الماوى gardens of refuge (Súra xxxii. 19) ; جنّات النعيم gardens of
delight (Súra v. 70) ; علّيون the highest place in heaven (Súra lxxxiii. 18) ;
and جنّات الفردوس the gardens of Paradise (Súra xiii. 107).

The highest and most excellent of these eight Paradises is said to be
the Firdaus, above which is the 'throne of the Merciful' (عرش الرحمن)
from which flow the rivers (انهار) of Paradise. Muhammad is believed
to occupy the highest place in Paradise, called the Maqámu'l-wasíla
(مقام الوسيلة), the place of relationship, of influence. Paradise is also
said to have eight gates: gate of fasting, of prayer, of alms and so on.
(For details see Ghazáli iv. 335-336 ; Mash. 227-279). In Paradise there are
upper apartments (عرف), palaces (قصور), consisting of one single pearl,
in every palace seventy houses (دار), in every house seventy rooms (بيت),
bedsteads, beds, on every bed a Houri, tables, dishes, girls to serve (وصيفة)
and the believer will have power given to enjoy all these delights. (Mash.
280 يعطى المومن فى كل غداة من القوّة ما ياتى على ذلك كلّه اجمع).
Paradise is a shady place (Súra iv. 60) full of sweet perfumes and no
one there suffers from fatigue (Súra xxxv. 32). In it there is a tree called
سدرة المنتهى, Sidratu-l-Muntaha, also delicious fruits and other kinds of
food. The occupants of the lowest place in Paradise will be feasted on
the liver of the great fish (كبد الحوت) and the ox of Paradise
(ثور الجنّة) (Ghazáli iv ; 386. Mashar 281-284). Rivers of sweet smelling
water, milk, wine and clarified honey flow from the mountains of musk.
One of these is the Kauthar (الكوثر) Súra xlvii. 16 ; Mashar 285). There
are said to be in Paradise four springs (عيون), the two issuing from
under the throne of God are the Zanjabíl (زنجبيل), and the Salsabíl
(سلسبيل) Súra lxxvi. 18). As so much eating and drinking necessarily
requires proper evacuations, God is said to have so arranged that all
superfluities will be discharged, and carried off by perspiration as odori-
ferous as musk. (See Ghazáli iv. 336).

The blessed in Paradise are dressed in clothes of the finest silk and brocade (سُنْدس - استبرق), with silver and gold bracelets on their arms, and crowns of inlaid jewels and shining pearls on their heads (Súras xviii. 30; xliv. 53; lxxvi. 21-22, 33; xxxv. 30-32; Mashar 285-287); they will rest on beds of silk (ارائك) Súras lxxxviii. 13; xv. 47; xxxvii. 43; lii. 20; lvi. 15). The tents in which they live are each made of one large pearl.

They have wives (أهل), whom no stranger ever sees and who never look at any man but their own husbands (قاصرات الطرف), and who are pure (ازواج مطهرة), that is free from the ordinary habits of women (الحَيْض - الغائط - البَوْل - البَصَاق - النُخَامة) Súra ii. 23; iii. 13; iv. 60; Ghazáli iv. 337; Mashar 287; Nazha'l Arwáh 37). Every believer (none of them will be unmarried) will have, besides other wives and houries, two wives so beautiful and transparent that he will see the marrow of their bones behind the seventy magnificent dresses which they wear, and will see his face in their cheeks as in a mirror. Besides these he will have four thousand virgins (بِكر), and eight thousand women who have already been married (ثَيّب) and five hundred houries (حُور العَين) having the white of the eye intensely white; and the black intensely black (Súra lv. 72). These are the finest damsels of Paradise. According to Ghazáli (iv. 337) Muhammad said "The believer in Paradise will marry five hundred houries, four thousand virgins, and eight thousand married women; their occupation will be the enjoyment of the sensual delights provided for them (فى شغل فاكهون) Súra xxxvi. 55; which commentators explain to mean (افتضاض الأبكار). It is a controverted question whether women will conceive and bear children in Paradise. The best authorities are of opinion that children, being the chief pleasure of man, will be born to those who desire it, but their conception, birth, weaning and growth into youthful age will all take place within the space of one hour. Music will be provided for those who like it; horses for those who wish to ride, camels, fields and, in short, "things which eye saw not and which did not enter into the heart of man." (Ghazáli iv. 338 (ما لا عينى رأت ولا اذن سمعت ولا خطر على قلب بشر). Among these there is also said to be a tree called Túba (طُوبِى), not mentioned in the Qur'án, on which grow precious jewels, and fine clothes. On entering Paradise believers will be youthful-looking creatures, beard less, thirty-six years of age and they will grow neither older nor younger. The statements mentioned in the chapter on the resurrection are to be firmly believed by the Muslim, as they rest, if not all on the Qur'án itself, on Tradition and the agreement (اجماع) of the learned doctors. On

The delights of Paradise are not, however, considered to consist solely in bodily and sensual pleasures and enjoyments, but to include spiritual[1] enjoyments also. The highest spiritual delight (اللذة الكبري), the blessed in Paradise will enjoy, consists in seeing the face of God (النظر الي وجه الله).

---

certain details of minor importance the Muslim is, however, at liberty to adopt what commends itself to his own mind. (For further details *see* Ghazáli iv. 337 بيان جمل متفرقة من اوصاف اهل الجنّة وردت بها الاخبار).

The orthodox and general opinion concerning the above described delights of Paradise is that they are to be understood in their literal and obvious sense, and not in the figurative sense to designate spiritual pleasures and enjoyments.

[1] This spiritual delight is said to be referred to in Súra x. 27 " to those who do good will be given goodness and increase " (زيادة). This 'increase being the seeing of the face of God. Muhammad one fine moonlight night is reported to have said to his disciples : " You will see your Lord as you see this moon "—the curtain will be lifted, and they will look into the face of God and nothing of all that has been bestowed upon them will delight them more than the seeing of His face. Some are said to see him for the space of a whole year, others for a week, others morning and evening ; others will be privileged to see him without ceasing. Another of the spiritual delights the believer will enjoy in Paradise is to behold Muhammad. Ghazáli, at the conclusion of his description of the delights of Paradise, says : ' Nothing of the delights of Paradise can be compared to the delight of meeting God (لذّة اللقاء), for the other bodily enjoyment of Paradise dumb animals share with the believer, but this is reserved to him alone. The possibility and reality of God's being seen (رؤية الله) by his faithful servants in Paradise—men, angels, genii, is an article of faith which must be believed by every Muslim, as it is supported by the Qur'án, Traditions and the Ijmá'. There are some sects which pretend that it is impossible that God should be seen with the eye.

The sources from whence Muhammad and his disciples derived most of the statements on the resurrection, the last judgment, Paradise and Hell are explained by Sale in his Introductory Discourse and by Geiger in his book : Was hat Mohammed aus dem Judenthume auf genommen, now translated into English under the name of " Judaism and Islám," Simpkin Marshall & Co. *See* also Tisdall's Yanábí'u'l-Islám in Persian, and in English on " The Original Sources of the Qurán. S. P. C. K.

The sixth article of faith is that of Predestination[1]
(القضاء والقدر - تقدير - قدر) Every Muslim must believe in
God's absolute decree and predestination both of good and
evil, and that God has from eternity predetermined and
decreed everything, good as well as bad, belief and unbelief and that everything that has been or will be depends

---

[1] The Qur'án speaks in many passages of this all-important subject
"All things we have created after a fixed decree" (Súra liv. 49). "No one
can die except by God's permission according to the Book that fixeth the
term of life" (Súra iii. 139). "All sovereignty is in the hands of God. He
whom God guideth is the guided, and they whom He misleadeth shall be
the lost" (Súras liv. 49; iii. 139; xiii. 30; vii. 278). The Sunni doctrine
on the subject is that whatever happens in this world, good or evil, faith
or unbelief, obedience to God and disobedience, proceeds entirely from
the will and decree of God and is irrevocably written down and fixed on
the 'Preserved Tablet.' Not a worm creeps on earth, not a leaf falls from
the tree, except by the decree and will of God.

As regards man, God has from eternity (من الازل) fixed his adverse or
prosperous fortune in this world, his faith or infidelity and consequently
his happiness or misery in the next world. Muhammad said 'Every man
is joined together in the womb of his mother forty days, then he becomes
coagulated blood for the same time, then a bit of flesh for the same time,
then God sends an angel (ملك الأرحام = the angel of the wombs) whom
he commands to write down for the embryo four things: its portion of
prosperity; food, much or little; its life, short or long, miserable, damned
or happy in the future world." He also said السعيد من سعد فى بطن أمّه
والشقى من شقى فى بطن أمّه واللذان احدكم يعمل بعمل اهل النار حتى
ما يكون بينه و بينها غير باع او ذراع فيسبق عليه الكتاب فيعمل بعمل اهل الجنّة
فيدخلها - و ان الرجل ليعمل بعمل اهل الجنّة حتى ما يكون بينه و بينها غير
ذراع او ذراعين فيسبق عليه الكتاب فيعمل بعمل اهل النار فيدخلها (Jowh. 97.
Muhammad taught the fore-knowledge of God, but he did not lay down
precisely the doctrine of predestination. It perplexed him and he spoke
of it, but often contradicted himself and he would become angry if the
subject were mooted in his presence. "Sit not down with a disputer
about fate" he used to say. Bukhári mentions that the Prophet once
came out of his house when the Companions were debating concerning fate
(predestination). He became angry and red in the face and said: "Has God
ordered you to debate on fate? Was I sent to you for this?... I adjure

entirely on His fore-knowledge and sovereign will (Jowh.
93-106 ; Mawáqif 515-538 ; Bukhári's Commentary ix.
328-338.)

As regards the exact meaning of the قضاء and the قَدَر ¹,
which both designate the act of God's predetermining and

---

you do not argue on these points." Among other sayings of Muhammad
on the subject Bukhári mentions the following : "God created Adam
and touched his back with his right hand and brought from it a family,
and God said to Adam : 'I have created this family for Paradise, and
their actions will be like those of the people of Paradise.' Then God
touched the back of Adam and brought forth another family and said :
'I have created this for Hell ! ' "

Then a man said to the Prophet : "Of what use will deeds of any kind
be ? He replied when God createth his servant for Paradise, his actions
will be deserving of it till he dies, when he will enter therein ; and when
God createth one for fire, his actions will be like those of the people of
hell till he die, when he will enter therein.—'There is not one amongst
you whose place is not written by God whether in the fire or in Paradise.'
Thereupon the Companions said : 'O prophet ! since God has appointed
our places, may we confide in this and abandon our religious and moral
duties'? "He said : 'No, because the righteous will do good works, and
the wicked will do bad works, "'.... (See Jowh. 93, 105 ; Bukhári's Commentary ix. 232). Though good and evil are predetermined and decreed by
God, yet man may not use this doctrine as an encouragement to commit
sin ; for example, he must not encourage himself to commit adultery by
saying : "God has decreed that I should commit this sin, and therefore I
will commit it," nor may he use it as an excuse when he has committed it
in order to escape punishment. Then again the doctrine of predestination
must not prevent man from asking God in prayer and supplication what
he is in need of, for his praying and obtaining in answer to prayer what
he wants are also predetermined. As to the lot of children who die young
Muhammad replied : "God knows best what they have been doing." The
learned Nawawi says that the majority of learned men are of opinion that
the children of Muslims go to Paradise ; as to the children of infidels
some say that they go to hell-fire, some that their lot is undecided ;
(توقّف طائفة) others that they enter Paradise, which, Nawawi says, is the
true opinion (انهم من اهل الجنّة) (Bukhári ix. 333.)

1 As regards the meaning of the term قدر those of the Ash'ariyya
School say that it designates God's creating things in certain proportions

decreeing everything, and the difference between the two terms there are various opinions :

---

and in a special manner in the strictest accordance with His will (ايجاد الله الاشيا على قدر مخصوص ووجه معيّن ارادة الله تعالى). The term according to this opinion refers to the attribute of God's works يرجع لصفة فعل لانّه عبارة عن الايجاد وهو من صفات الافعال. The Máturídiyya (الماتريديه) say that the قدر refers to God's defining and knowing from eternity the limits which every man should reach as regards beauty or ugliness, wealth or poverty, success or misfortune, and has reference to God's knowledge, which is an attribute of His essence.

As to the meaning of the term قضاء, the Ash'ariyya say that it means the will of God that wills things from eternity as they are. ارادة الله الاشياء من الازل على ما هى عليه فيما لا يزال فهو من صفات الذات عندهم The Máturídiyya say that it means God's creating things with additional finishing and perfection ايجاد الله الاشياء مع زيادة الاحكام والاتقان فهو صفة فعل عدهم. With the Ash'ariyya the قدر is recent (حادث) and the قضاء (eternal (قديم) in opposition to the Máturídiyya. The difference between these two terms has been summed up thus :

ارادة الله مع التعلق – فى الازل قضاؤه محقق

والقدر الايجاد للاشيا على – وجه معيّن ارادة على

و بعضهم قد قال معنى الاوّل – العلم مع التعلّق فى الازل

والقدر الايجاد للامور – على و فاق علمه المذكور

The قضاء is eternal, and the قدر recent, and both terms have reference to God's knowledge and will and power. Some say that the قضاء designates what is decreed in a general manner (مجتمعة), while the قدر designates the things decreed in particular (متفرقة). The following definition is given in the كتاب الفتوح هو التفصيل :—

القدر هو التقدير - والقضاء والقطع . فالقضاء اخصّ من القدر لانّه الفصل بين التقدير . فالقدر كالاساس والقضا هو التفصيل والقطع . مذكر بعضهم ان القدر بمنزلة المعدّ للكيل والقضاء بمنزلة الكيل .

قدر has been compared to the thing to be measured, the قضاء to the measuring itself. When the Khalif 'Umar intended to flee from the plague which had broken out at Damascus, 'Ubaid said to him : "Dost thou think thou canst flee from the decree (قضاء) of God ?" 'Umar

Man's acts are of two kinds : voluntary (افعال اختیاریة)
and involuntary (افعال اضطراریة). As regards voluntary
acts of man there are different opinions, as that things
operate by means of their nature or the power inherent
in them (ان سیئاً یوثر بطبعه اوبقوة فیه), just as fire burns, the
knife cuts by reason of its nature or the power inherent
in it.   Those who hold this view are, by common consent,
considered infidels.   Those who say that things operate
by reason of the power God has created in them are
considered to be either infidels, or impious or sectarians
(مبتدع ـ فاسق ـ کفار).   Thus, the Mu'tazila believe that
it is God who operates, but that he has ordered a
necessary connection between (الله فیه) causes and effects
which can never be revoked.   They are ignorant (جاهل)
and their opinion may ultimately lead to infidelity by
denying the miracles of prophets, as being contrary to
the usual course of nature.   The only true and orthodox
opinion on the subject is that it is God who operates,
and has ordered a certain connection between causes
and effects, which can however be revoked :—

(الموثر هوالله وجعل بین الاسـباب والمسبـبات ملازماً عادتاً
بحدیث یصح تخلفها)

As regards involuntary acts of man such as the
movements of him who trembles (حرکة المرتعش), they

---

said : "I take my refuge from the قضاء of God to the قدر of God,"
(افوض قضاء الله الی قدرالله) implying that one may hope what God has
determined to do (قدر) may be averted, if it is not absolutely irrevocably decreed.   The learned Commentator of the Jowhara says : "God is
the Creator of man, and his actions (الله تعالی خالق العبد و ما عمل) ;
this is called the oneness of works (وَحْدة الافعال) and refutes the opinion
that things can operate by the nature or power inherent in them."

are, by common consent, created and produced by God.
(هي مخلوقة كله).

As regards God's and man's parts in producing men's
voluntary actions, the orthodox opinion is that man has
no influence whatever on his voluntary actions, but that
they are the result of God's power alone, that God causes
power and choice, to exist in man and, if there be no impediment, He causes his action to exist also, subject to His
power and joint with that and His choice ; which action
as created is to be ascribed to God, but as produced, em-
ployed or acquired, is to be ascribed to man.   This acquisition (كَسْبٌ) of an action by man, therefore, properly means his joining or connecting the same with his
power and will, yet allowing herein no impression or
influence on the existence thereof save only that it is
subject to his will,[1] (افعال العباد واقعة بقدرة الله تعالى وحدها

وليس لقدرتم تأثير فيها بل الله سبحانه اجرى عادته بانه يوجد في
العبد قدرة واختياراً و اذا لم يكن هناك مانع اوجد فيه فعله
المقدور ومقارناً لهما فيكون فعل العبد مخلوقاً لله ابداعاً واحداثاً
و مكسوباً للعبد . والمراد بكسبه اياه مقارنته لقدرته وارادته من
غير ان يكون هناك تأثيراً او مدخلاً في وجوده سوى كونه
محلاً له . و هذا مذهب الشيخ ابي الحسن الاشعري Jowh.

97-98 ; Mawáqif 515-229)

---

[1] Though God has created all acts of man, good as well as evil, still man
has no right to say : " How can God punish me for bad actions I have
committed since it is He who has created them, for no man has a right to
enquire concerning the doings of God (لا يُسْأَل عمّا يفعل) and his duty is to
acknowledge God's absolute sovereignty in everything (لا يسعنا الا التسليم

المحض) and to ascribe to Him all that is good, and to ourselves all evil

As regards the promises (وعد ـ ميعاد) God has made
to believers by the mouth of His prophets and in His
Book that He will cause them to enter Paradise, He will
certainly fulfil them.[1] As regards the threats (وعيد) with
which God has threatened the wicked, He may choose
not to carry them into execution.

As the eternal happiness of him who is saved is pre-
ordained from eternity in God's fore-knowledge (عِلم), so
is the eternal misery of him who is damned also decreed
from eternity in God's fore-knowledge.[2]

(فوزالسعيد مقدر من الازل كذا الشقي)

---

works, out of respect (تأدّباً), created it is true by God, but acquired
(كَسْب) by ourselves according to the words of the Qur'án: Súra iv. 81
'What happens to thee of good things is from God, and what happens
to thee of evil is of thyself' and Súra xlii. 29: 'What happens to you of
calamities is by what your hands have acquired.' 'Say: Everything is
from God!'"

God has created in the man who is to be accepted and saved the power
of obedience, together with the disposition and the will to obey, and provided him with the means to walk in the right path, or, as others say,
He creates in him the power of obedience itself (قدرة الطاعة). Even
the disobedient believer is included in this class.

God has created in those whom he has decreed to reject and doom to
hell, some say disobedience (المعصية) as others say the power of disobedience (قدرة المعصية).

[1] "Verily God will not fail the promise" (Súra iii. 7), for if He did so
He would have told an untruth which cannot be admitted. God may, if
He wills, not carry out threats, for not carrying them out is not a defect;
but, on the contrary, a characteristic of generosity and perfection
(الوعيد يجوز الخلف فيه ـ لان الخلف فى الوعيد). Muhammad is reported
to have said: "God will surely fulfil His promise to reward certain
actions, but as to the punishment He has threatened, He is at liberty to
choose, if He wills, He will punish, and if He wills, He will pardon."
There are, however, other opinions opposed to this Sunni doctrine on
the subject. (See Jowh. 95-96, 100).

[2] This divine decree cannot be changed, otherwise God's knowledge
would be changed into ignorance. The happiness of man or his misery

Besides the Sunni doctrine on predestination there are two Schools which differ from it. One is, the Jabariyya[1] (الجبرية from جَبَر to compel). Their opinion is that man is necessarily and inevitably compelled and forced to act as he does by the force of God's immutable degree.

The other is the Mu'tazila (المعتزلة) also called the Qadariyya[2] (القَدَرية from قَدَر to have power, to decree).

---

depends, according to the opinion of the Ash'aríyya, entirely on the state in which he is at his death. If at the moment of his death man is a believer, he will inherit eternal bliss, in accordance with God's fore-know-ledge, if, on the contrary, he dies in a state of infidelity, his lot will be eternal misery, in accordance with God's fore-knowledge.

(السعادة هى الموت على الايمان باعتبار تعلق علم الله ازلاً بذلك – الشقاوة هى الموت على الكفر بذلك الاعتبار).

The end, therefore, clearly indicates what has been pre-ordained (الخاتمة تدل على السابقة). If a man dies a believer, though he has spent his whole life as an infidel, he will enter Paradise. The Máturídiyya, in opposition to the Ash'aríyya School, are of opinion that man's going to Paradise or Hell depends on his life of faith or infidelity, and that should he, who has lived as a believer, die as an infidel we must admit that he has been changed from one destined to eternal happiness into one destined to eternal misery... (السعادة الايمان فى الحال – والشقاوة هى الكفر فى الحال – فالسعيد هو المومن فى الحال و اذا مات على الكفر فقد انقلب شقياً بعد ان كان سعيداً – والشقى هوالكافر فى الحال . واذا مات على الايمان فقد انقلب سعيداً بعد ان كان شقيا). (Jowh. 96-97.)

[1] Man, according to their view, is forced to act as he does like a feather in the air which the wind moves about at will, and that he has neither power, nor will, nor choice any more than an inanimate agent and there-fore no acquisition (العبد ليس له كسب بل هو مجبور مقهور) (كسب) (For details see Sharastáni 59 ; Mawáqif 633 ; Jowh. 97-99.)

[2] They are called Qadariyya, either because they deny the قَدَر or predestination, or as others say, more correctly, because they assert man's power (قدرة) to act freely. They consequently believe that he deserves either reward or punishment (ثواب او عقاب) in the next world in accordance with his actions. (العبد قادر خالق لافعاله الاختيارية خيرها و شـرها مستحق على ما يفعله ثواباً و عقاباً فى دار الآخرة)

They deny God's eternal predestination and say that man produces his voluntary actions, good as well as bad, by the power which God has created in him ; in fact, that man is a free agent.

Wásil Ibn 'Atá, the founder of the Mu'tazila sect, says that God, being wise and just, it is impossible to ascribe to Him evil and injustice, or that He should compel a man to do a thing, and then requite him for it. It is impossible to believe that God should command man to act, if He had not given him the power to do so.

The author of the Jowhara says that the Jabariyya and the Qadariyya entertain on the subject extreme opinions, but that the men of the Sunni school have chosen the safe middle road between the two, by asserting that man is neither absolutely compelled, nor an absolutely free agent; but that, though God is the creator of his actions, still man shares in producing his voluntary actions, so that they are the result of two different powers, viz., of God's creation and man's acquisition. He further explains the orthodox view by saying : man has no power or influence (تأثير) over his actions but he is inwardly forced, outwardly free (مجبور باطناً مختار ظاهراً). Man is a compelled being in the shape of one enjoying free will.

(الله خالق للفعل لكن للعبد فى الاختيارى منه كسب والمقدور الواحد يدخل تحت قدرتين فيدخل تحت قدرة الله تعالى بجهة الخلق و تحت قدرة العبد بجهة الكسب) (Jowh. 98-99). " He who considers man from the point of view of his real condition excuses him, but he who considers him from the point of view of the Law hates him."- (من نظر للخلق بعين الحقيقة عذرهم و من نظر لهم بعين الشريعة مقتوهم) (Jowh. 99). The objection of the Jabari and the reply of the Sunni contained in the following verses is very characteristic :

ما حيلة العبد والاقدار جارية - عليه فى كل حال أيها الرامى

القاه فى اليم مكتوفاً وقال له - اياك اياك تبتل بالماه

ان حقة اللطف لم يمسة من بلل - ولم يبالى بتكتيف والقاه

وان يكن قدر المولى بغرقه - فهو الغريق و لم ألفى بصحراه

Jabari :—" What can man do since everything has been decreed and pre-ordained concerning him ? This is as if God threw him into the sea with hands and feet bound and told him : ' Be careful not to make thyself wet with water' ".

As regards reward (ثواب) and punishment (عقاب),
man neither deserves reward for his good actions, nor
punishment for his bad actions, since God has created
them both (لم يحصل منهم خير يستحقون به ثواباً ولا شر
يستحقون به عقاباً); but, though man does not deserve either
the one or the other, still it is generally agreed, among
the orthodox, that God does reward or punish. When He
rewards He does so by an act of His free will and sovereign
grace; (اثابة الله تعالي لذا انما هي بفضله المحض و ان يعذب
فبمص العدل). When He punishes He does so as an act
of pure justice.

On the much discussed question whether it is incumbent on God in His dealings with man to do and promote
what is good (صلاح), or best (الاصلح), the orthodox doctrine is that it is not incumbent on God to provide for
a man either the one or the other, for God is not bound
to do anything, but does everything according to His
free will and pleasure.[1]

Sunni:—If the favour of God encompass him, water will not make him
wet, nor will he care about being bound and cast into the sea. If God
decreed that he shall be drowned, he will be drowned, even if he were
thrown into the midst of dry land. (For further details on the controversy between both parties *see* Dictionary of Islám, 473 ; Faith of Islám,
234-289).

The Mu'tazila, in opposition to the orthodox dogma, teach that it is
incumbent on God, according to His justice, to reward those who obey Him
and to punish the evil-doers. Reward and punishment are merely signs
pointing to the reward of him who obeys, or to the punishment of him who
disobeys. Even if God reversed the meaning of these signs by saying :
"Him who obeys me I will punish, and him who disobeys me I will
reward," this would be good and just as coming from God (Jowh. 100-101 ;
Mawáqif, 584-586).

[1] The Mu'tazila, on the contrary, say that it is incumbent on God in His
dealings with man to provide for him what is good or best. Some of them
say that this is the duty of God both with regard to worldly and religious

God gives every creature (man and beast) its due portion[1] (الرِّزق), material as well as spiritual, such as food
and raiment for the body, learning, sciences and so on for
the understanding and the heart.

Sins, (ذَنْب) pl. ذنوب ; سَيِّئَة pl. سَيِّئَات ; فاحشه pl.
(خطايا pl. خطيئَة ; آثام pl. اثم ; فواحش) according to the orthodox teaching, are of two kinds:[2] (1) little, venial sins,

---

concerns, others say that only with regard to religion is He bound to
consider what is best for man. They also hold that God can and will
only create what is good and not what is evil for their own sake. To this
the Sunnis reply that reason is not competent to judge what is good or
bad, that this can only be decided by the Law; that, on the whole,
nothing is bad (قبيح) in the sight of God:—

(الحسن ما حسَّنه الشرع والقبيح ما قبحه الشرع ـ انه لا يقبح من الله شئ ـ
غاية الامر انه يخفى علينا وجه حَسَنه .)

God has good reasons for creating evil also in the world.

[1] By this portion is meant, however, not what man possesses, but only
that part of it of which he makes use or derives benefit from. What he possesses, but does not make use of nor derives benefit from, is not his portion.
(من ملك شيئاً و تمكَّن من الانتفاع به و لم ينتفع به بالفعل فليس ذلك
الشئ رزقاً له .)

وانما يكون رزقاً لمن ينتفع به ـ كل احد يستوفى رزقَه . ولا يا كل احدُ
رزق غيره ولا ياكل غيرة رزقه

The Mu'tazíla believe that all that man possesses is his portion,
whether he makes use of it or not, and all that which is blameable or
positively forbidden, such as wine, etc., cannot be the portion of man
ordered for him by God.

It is a matter of controversy between learned men whether man's
acquiring by personal exertion what he is in want of, or his expecting
it from simple reliance on God without personal exertion is the more
excellent way. (افضلية الاكتساب او افضلية التوكّل For details see Ghazáli
and Jowh. 182-185).

[2] Muhammad made the following statements on the subject: "He is
not a believer who commits adultery, or steals or drinks liquor or plunders

(صغيرة pl. صغائر) and (2) great, capital sins (كبيرة pl.
كبائر) The Qur'án says on the subject : " Who avoid the
heinous things of crime and filthiness..... forgive ". (Súra
xlii. 35) " Those who avoid great sins and scandals but
commit only lighter faults, verily thy Lord will be diffuse
of mercy." Súra liii. 33.

---

or embezzles when intrusted with the plunder of the infidel. Beware,
beware !—the greatest sin is to associate with God, or to vex your father
and mother, or to murder your own species, or to commit suicide or to
swear or to lie.—Abstain ye from the seven ruinous and destructive things
namely : (1) Associating anything with God. (2) Magic. (3) Killing anyone without reason. (4) Taking interest on money. (5) Taking the property
of the orphan. (6) Running away on the day of battle. (7) Accusing an innocent woman of adultery.—Verily everyone who performs the five prayers
and fasts in Ramadán and avoids committing the seven great sins, God
will open for him eight gates by which he will enter Paradise on the day
of resurrection." The seven sins are called the الهوبقات السبع

The sect of the Murjia, on the contrary, hold that all sins are little, and
do not harm man, as long as he is a Muslim. One of their doctors has
embodied this opinion in the following verses :

مُت مسلماً و من الذنوب لا تخف – حاشا المهيمن ان يرى تنكيداً

لو ارام ان يَملِّيك نار جهنم – ما كان الهم قلبك التوحيدا

The Khawárij, on the other hand, pretend that all sins are great sins,
and that every great sin is infidelity. Others again hold that, though all
sins are great in consideration of the majesty of Him against whom they
are committed, yet that they do not amount to infidelity, and that he
who commits them, does not thereby become an infidel, except he commit
sins which imply infidelity, such as worshipping an idol, or casting the
Qur'án into a dirty place (Jowh. 186).

As to the number of the great sins the learned doctors are not agreed.
The Companions and the Followers differed on this point. Some said
they were four, others said seven and others eleven or more. Ibn 'Abbás
used to say that they are nearer to seventy than to seven. Ghazáli and the
doctors of the Sunni School are of opinion that it is not possible to de-
termine the exact number of capital sins and that the Law has purposely
left them indefinite in order to frighten men from committing sin.
The capital sins may be distinguished from the smaller ones by certain
signs (امارات), their deserving the punishment of حَدّ, and by their being

threatened with torments, or by the circumstance that he who commits them deserves to be called impious (فاسق), or to be cursed by God (اللعن).

The most grievous of the capital sins are :

Polytheism, idolatry, associating anyone with God (الشرك بالله).

Murder without reason. (قتل النفس انى حرّم الله قتلها الا بالحق).

Adultery (زناه), sodomy (لواط), disobedience to parents (عقوق الوالدَين), sorcery (سُحر), false accusation of adultery (قذف), fleeing on the day of battle (الفرار يوم الزحف), usury (اكل الربا). As regards the capital sins, enumerated after the two first ones, the degree of their grievousness depends on the circumstances under which they are committed and the consequences which result from the same.

To the class of the greater sins, belongs also the sin of intentionally deceiving the Prophet by lies (الكذب عليه ملعم). A Muslim, though he commits small and great sins, unless be become an idolater (مشرك), or declares lawful what God has forbidden, can never remain in hell-fire for ever. (على تقدير عذابه لا يُخلّد فى النار) Jowh. 166, 167, 186.)

Some give the following list of great sins : infidelity (كُفر), perseverance in committing little sins (الاصرار على الصغائر), despairing of God's mercy (القنوط من رحمة الله), considering oneself safe from the wrath of God, false witness (شهادة الزور), falsely charging a Muslim with adultery (القذف), swearing a false oath (اليمين الغموس), sorcery (سُحر), drinking wine (شرب الخمرة), appropriation of the property of orphans, usury (اكل الربا), adultery (زنا), unnatural crime, sodomy (لِواط), theft (سَرقة), murder (قتل النفس), fleeing in battle before the face of an infidel enemy (الفرار يوم الزحف), disobedience to parents (عقوق الوالدين).

Every sin which has not the abovementioned characteristics belongs to the class of little sins. Small sins may become great sins by being repeatedly committed with intention or persevered in, or when committed by a learned man, who thereby misleads those who take him as a guide on the right way. (الصغيرة تعطي حكم الكبيرة بالاصرار عليها و هو معاودة) (الذنب مع نيّة العود اليه عندا لفعل) If a man commits small sins repeatedly but without intention, they do not become great sins. Small sins are forgiven if great sins are avoided (باجتناب الكبائر).

Forgiveness of sin (تكفير - غفر الذنب) consists either in God's pardoning it and not punishing man for it (العفو اى عدم المواخذة به), or in concealing it from the eyes of angels, or in wiping it out from the book of

It is the duty of the Muslim to show repentance[1] (فوراً ـ علي الفور) for sins at once (متابة ـ متاب ـ تَوبة), immediately after the sin has been committed, for delay constitutes in itself a sin. The degree of the guilt of such delay, however, depends on the length of the time which elapses before repentance.

---

account. According to a Tradition small sins are also atoned for by Wadú, the legal ablution before prayer. (الوضو يكفّر عن الذنوب).

The orthodox belief is that the prophets do not commit sin, and are sinless (مَعصوم), but this dogma contradicts various statements of the Qur'án and of Muhammad as recorded in the Traditions (Súras xxvi. 82; xl. 57; xlvii. 21; xlviii. 2.)

التوبة من جميع المعاصى واجبة على الفور ولا يجوز تاخيرها سواء كانت [1]
معصية صغيرة او كبيرة ـ والمتاب واجب عيناً فى حال التلبّس بالمعصية فوراً

(Jowh. 187; Maw. 189; Ghazáli iv. 3 et seqq.)

Repentance is enjoined in the Qur'án "Those who, after they have done a base deed or committed a wrong against their own selves, remember God and implore forgiveness of their sins—and who will forgive sin but God only?—and persevere not in what they have willingly done amiss. As for them! Pardon from their Lord shall be their reward," (Súra iii. 129) See also Súras iv. 21; ii. 155; iv. 22; v. 43; ix. 113; xxv. 70; lxvi. 8). Muhammad said: "The greater wailing of the inhabitants of hell-fire comes from those who have delayed repentance."

(اكثر صياح اهل النار من التَسويف)

True repentance comprises the following:

(1) Forsaking sin (الاقلاع عن الذنب).
(2) Sorrow for having committed sin against God.

(الندم على المعصية لوجه الله)

(3) Firm purpose never to return to sin.

(ان لا تتعلّق المعصية ـ العزم على ان لا يعود الى المعصية ابداً بالآدمى)

(4) Making amends or obtaining forgiveness, if the sin has been committed against man whom he has injured thereby.

(ردّ الظلامة الى صاحبها او تحصيل البراءة منهُ ـ ان تعلّقت المعصية بالآدمى)

Another condition of true repentance is that it should take place before the pangs of death come on (صدور التوبة قبل الغرغرة). At this time repentance is considered of no avail. Some, however, hold that repentance is accepted (Jowh. 187; Ghazáli iv. 34) from a Muslim even at this time; but not from an infidel.

When a man, after having repented, returns to sin, this does not invalidate his former repentance and its beneficial effects; the sins of which he has repented are not placed to his account, but remain blotted out (لا انتفا من لتوبة التائب). The Mu'tazila hold that, in this case, his former sins are again placed to his account (Jowh. 188).

As regards the certainty of God's accepting repentance (قبول التوبة), the learned doctors are not quite agreed. The Imám Abú Hasanu'l-Ash'ari and those of his School believe that there can be no doubt with regard to God's accepting repentance, and that this is according to undeniable proof from the Qur'án: Súra xlii. 24 : ‘ It is He who accepts repentance from his servants.’ See also Súras ix. 105; vii. 152. The Imámu'-l-Haramain is of opinion that the acceptance of repentance with God is not a matter of absolute certainty, but rests on probability, which amounts almost to certainty. (ان التوبة تقبل ظنًا بدليل ظنى لكنه قريب من القطع)

As regards the repentance of the infidel, all are agreed that it is accepted according to the verse : " Say to the infidels, if they cease from their unbelief the sins they have formerly committed will be forgiven them." (Súra viii. 39.)

There is some difference of opinion with regard to the infidel's embracing Islám, as to whether this act may be considered as equivalent to repentance for his former infidelity, or whether, besides the embracing of Islám, it is his duty to repent of his former infidelity.

(هل توبة الكافر نفس اسلامه اوابّد مع ذلك من الندم على كفره)

Some consider that the embracing of Islám is equivalent to his repentance of his former infidelity, while others are of opinion that, besides this embracing of Islám, he must repent of his former infidelity.

Whoso commits a capital sin and dies unrepentant, God will deal with him according to His will (اجرة و سانة مفومس و موكّل الى ربّه). If He sees fit He will pardon him, for He can forgive all sins, except polytheism. The Máturídiyya hold that, if God does not punish all Muslims who have committed capital sins, He must, at least, punish some of them, because He has threatened to punish them, and he cannot contradict Himself. The Ash'ariyya, however, believe that, if He chooses, He need not carry His threats into execution (Jowh. 180-181).

CHAPTER III.

THE IMÁMATE.

The Imámate[1] (الخلافة ـ الامَامَة) is the general leadership in religious and worldly affairs over the Muslim nation (الامامة رياسة عامة في امورالدين والدنيا), or, as others define it, the succession of the Prophet for the purpose of upholding Islám, and the interests of the Muslim nation. (الامامة او الخلافة هي نيابة عن صاحب الشـريعة و حفظ الدين و سـياسـة الدنيا به ٠ والقائم به خليفة و امام وامّا تسـميته اماماً فتشبيهاً بامام الصلاة و اتّباعه والاقتداء به ولهذا تقال الامامة الكُبرى ٠ و امّا تسميته خليفة فلكونه يخلف النبي في أمّته و يقال خليفة باطلاق و خليفة رسول الله ٠)

---

1 Imám comes from أُمّ to proceed, have precedence, to lead. Khalífa from خلف to succeed, to become a substitute.

It is the duty of the Muslim nation to appoint a duly qualified Imám to be the vice-regent of the Prophet and leader of the nation, when no person has been specially appointed to take this office, either by divine command or by order of the Prophet, or when the late Khalif has not himself designated the individual who is to succeed him in the Imámate.

The author of the Sharhu'l Mawáqif says: "The Imámate is valid when resting (1) on a command of the Prophet, or (2) on a command of the preceding Imám, or (3) on the appointment of those who have the right to elect the Imám" (تثبت الامامة بالنصّ من الرسـول و من الامام السـابق بالاجماع و تثبت ببيعة اهل الحلّ والعقد٠)

Adam and David are mentioned in the Qur'án (Súras ii. 29; xxxviii. 25), as having been appointed vice-regents of God on earth. Muhammad died without having appointed his successor. The people chose Abú Bakr, who appointed 'Umar to be his successor in the Khalifate.

The Imám must, according to the opinion of the Ash'ariyya (orthodox) school, possess the following qualifications (شروط): (1) Islám, (2) be of full age and of sound mind, (3) freedom, (4) not impious, (5) just, (6) be of the tribe of the Quraish.[1]

In proof of the necessity of appointing an Imám it is mentioned that the Imámate was established after the death of Muhammad by general consent on the election of Abú Bakr. In his first sermon, after the death of the Prophet, Abú Bakr said: "Muhammad certainly is dead, and it is necessary for this religion that some one should be appointed for its protection." And all the Muslims agreed with this saying (ان محمداً قدمات ولابدّ لهذا الدين ممّن يقوم به - فبادر الكل الى قوله). The appointment of an Imám is said to be necessary both in time of peace and in time of war and rebellion. This is the opinion of the Sunnis and most of the Mu'tazila, while others pretend that it is only necessary in times of rebellion and of internecine wars. Others, again are of opinion that he is only to be appointed in times of peace, while others again deny the necessity of the appointment of an Imám at all. (For further details *see* Mawáqif 603; Jowh. 191; Ibn Khaldún i. 159 *et seqq.*)

The appointment of the Imám is, according to the orthodox opinion, dictated by the Law (نصب الامام واجب سمعاً - ان وجوب نصب الامام بالشرع). The Mu'tazila and the Zaidiyya consider it merely expedient, in accordance with the dictates of reason; while the Ismá'íliyya and the Imámiyya say that it belongs to God only to appoint an Imám and the Khawárij are of opinion that there is no necessity for the appointment of an Imám at all. (Jowh. 191-192 ; Mawáqif 603).

[1] شرط الاسلام, A non-Muslim cannot care for the true interests of Islám. He must be of full age (شرط البلوغ والعقل), for children or insane persons are not able to manage their own affairs, much less those of Islám. He must be a free man (شرط الحرّيّة), not a slave (رقيق) whose mind is taken up with the concerns of his master and who enjoys not sufficient respect. He must not be impious (شرط عدم الفسق), for no one would have sufficient confidence in him. He must be just, (شرط العدل), if only outwardly. He must be a Quraish (ان يكون قُرَيْشياً), for Muhammad is reported to have said : "The Imáms must be from the Quraish." The Shí'ahs pretend that, being a Quraish, he ought to be of the family of the Háshimites also. (ان يكون هاشـمياً).

The author of the Sharhu'l-Mawáqif, says that with regard to the first five qualifications, they are by common consent necessary qualifications but, as regards the sixth qualification, *i.e.*, his being a Quraish, there are different opinions, the Khawárij and the Mu'tazila being of opinion that it is not a qualification required of necessity, the Prophet having said : " Obey the Imám, even if he be an Abyssinian slave." He explains, however, that the Prophet in giving such advice could not have meant the Khalíf; but he must have referred to an Amír (أمير), or Commander appointed by, and under the order of the Khalif, for such an explanation, he says, is required in order to reconcile the two contradictory sayings of the Prophet.

According to some authorities the Imám, in addition to the qualifications just enumerated, must possess the following also :

(1) He must be a man of learning in the roots and branches of the science of religion (مجتهد فى الاصول والفروع) *i.e.*, in theology and jurisprudence.

(2) He must understand the art of war, leading an army, concluding peace, etc. (ذو رأى و بصارة بتدبير الحرب والسلم و ترتيب الجيوش و حفظ الثغور)

(3) He must be courageous (شجاع).

But as these three qualifications are rarely found united in the same individual, it is said they cannot be required as necessary qualifications of the Imám, and the majority, therefore, agree that the six qualifications (p. 112) suffice to make a man eligible for the Imámate. (Mawáqif 605.)

These qualifications the Imám must possess at the time of his election and appointment (هذه الشروط انما هى فى الابتداء او حالة الاختيار). Should he afterwards become defective concerning them, or should he have assumed the office by force, when once appointed, he is to be considered the rightful Imám and obeyed in whatever he commands or forbids, even though he should be unfit and unworthy.

The belief in the necessity of the appointment of an Imám is not an article of faith, so that he who does not accept it is not to be considered an infidel (ليس ركنًا يعتقد فى قواعد الدين) Jowh. 190 *et seqq*). With the orthodox school it belongs to the secondary doctrines (فروع), while with the Shí'ahs it is an article of faith and of the first importance (من أصول الديانات والعقائد Mawáqif 606).

It is the duty of every Muslim to obey the Imám inwardly and outwardly (تجب طاعة الامام على جميع الرعايا ظاهرًا و باطنًا), so long as his commands and prohibitions are in harmony with the doctrines of Islám. Should he give orders contrary to the same, *i.e.*, positively wrong (حرام), or objectionable (مكروه), he is not to be obeyed. When he commands

The first four Khalifs[1] Abú Bakr, 'Umar, 'Uthmán and 'Ali are called by the Sunnis the ' rightly directed Khalifs' (الخُلَفَاءُالرَاشدين), and are considered to have possessed the perfect Khalifate (الخِلَافَة الكَامِلَة), in distinction from their successors who are not considered as such.

The Imámate is one of the four points on which many and angry controversies have arisen among Muslims, and which have given rise to the formation of a number of sects, the chief of which are the Khawárij and the Shí'ah[2].

---

what is allowable (مُبَاح), if his orders are such as tend to promote the interests of the Muslim nation, they are to be obeyed ; if not, there is no obligation on the Muslim to obey them.

If he should command a thing which implies infidelity, Muslims are to give up their allegiance to him ; if possible, publicly, if not then, at least, secretly. This is the only reason for which the allegiance may be given up, or for which he may be deposed.

(اذا امر بكفر فاطرحنّ بَيْعَتَهُ جهراً فان لم تقدر على الجهور بذلك فاطرحوها سرّاً ـ

و بغير هذ لا يُبَاح صرفهُ اى خلعهُ من الامامة .)

Even if he should lose the qualification of justice (العدالة) and become an impious, unjust or cruel tyrant, this would not be a sufficient reason for his deposition (لا يُعزَل ان أزيل وصف العدالة) ; some, however, allow it under these circumstances (Jowh. 192.)

[1] The first rightful Imám after Muhammad was Abú Bakr. The Shí'ahs, on the contrary, regard 'Ali as the first or rightful Imám, and are of opinion that he, and not Abú Bakr, ought to have been appointed the first Khalif. According to their traditions Muhammad had distinctly nominated 'Ali as his successor. (For details on the subject see Mawáqif 606-616). Muhammad is also reported to have said : "The Khalifate after me will last for thirty years, then it will become a kingdom " (Mawáqif 613-614. الخلافة بعدى ثلاثون سنة ثم ملكاً عَضوُضاً)

[2] خَوَارِج pl. خارجى. The first of this sect were the twelve thousand men who revolted from 'Ali, after they had fought under him at the battle of Siffin, taking offence at his submitting the decision of his right to the Khalifate, which Mu'áwiya disputed with him, to arbitration, though

If several Imáms have been chosen and appointed in the same country, the one who has been first appointed is to be considered the rightful Imám, and the others are to be opposed, and, if they refuse to abdicate, they are to be considered rebels (من البغاة) and ought to be fought against, till they be overcome.

---

they had first obliged him to do it. They blamed ʻAli for referring a matter concerning the religion of God to the judgment of man. They held the opinion that a man may be made Khalif, though he was not of the tribe of the Quraish, nor even a free man, provided he possessed the other necessary qualities . . . that there was no absolute necessity for any Imámate in the world. They charged ʻAli with sin, and went so far as to declare him guilty of infidelity and to curse him. They also reject ʻUthmán.

الشيعة, followers, companions, from شائع, to follow, to accompany. They, in opposition to the Khawárij, maintain that ʻAli was the first legitimate Imám, and that he ought to have been appointed as the first successor of the Prophet, and not Abú Bakr. They therefore reject Abú Bakr, ʻUmar and ʻUthmán as usurpers, and say that the Imámate belongs of right to ʻAli and his descendants. They are also of opinion that the office of Imám is a fundamental affair of religion and one of the foundations of faith, and does not depend on the will of the vulgar. Though widely differing among themselves on certain points connected with the subject, they all agree on the following : (1) the necessity of appointing an Imám, of his being specially designated and appointed by the proper authority (وجوب التعيين والتنصيص) ; (2) that the Imám is, as a matter of necessity, exempt from committing great as well as small sins (ثبوت عصمة الائمة) ; (3) that every one ought publicly to declare whom (وجوباً عن الكبائر والصغائر) he adheres to and from whom he separates himself, by word, deed or engagement, except in time of great fear. Many of the Shíʻahs carried their veneration for ʻAli and his descendants so far that they transgressed all bounds of reason and decency, though some of them were less extravagant than others. The branch of the ʻ Ghália ʼ (غالية, extravagant, fanatic) raised their Imáms (descendants of ʻAli) above the degrees of created beings and attributed to them divine properties. Some affirmed that ʻAli was not dead, but would return again in the clouds and fill the earth with justice. They held the doctrine of metempsychosis, and what they call the immanency, the indwelling of God in man (الحلول). . . . . . (*See* Ibn Khaldún i. 159 ff ; Sharastáni ii. 132. Sale 125.)

Should it be difficult to decide who was first appointed, they are all to be deposed and a new choice is to take place. Should the country, however, be so extensive that it would be impossible for one man to direct the affairs of the property of the Muslims, it will be a question for the consideration of learned men (المجتهدين) to decide whether another Imám may be appointed or not. The sect of the Jarúdiyya, in opposition to the Sunni doctrine, believe that there may exist several rightful Imáms even in a small country, and that every descendant of Fátima, if he draws the sword with the intention of calling people to embrace Islám, and is learned and courageous, is an Imám and may be appointed as such, and is to be obeyed.

The Muslim nation, as they have the right to elect and appoint an Imám, so they have the right to depose him for any cause justifying their doing so. Such a cause would be, if he commits acts which tend to bring ruin on the Muslim nation or endanger the religion of Islám. If such a deposition should become the cause of internal war and rebellion, the smaller evil (war, rebellion) will have to be borne with submission.

CHAPTER IV.

FIQH.

Fiqh (فقه) includes religious, ceremonial, civil and moral laws and regulations. It properly means knowledge, science in general, but has been adopted as the technical term to designate the science of the Law of Islám. The preceding chapters of this book deal only with the theoretical part (dogmatics), this one treats of the practical part. Fiqh is also called the علمُ الفُروع or knowledge of the branches, as distinguished from علمُ الاصول or knowledge of the roots.[1] The dogmas, articles of faith, are considered the roots, and the laws and regulations concerning worship, religious practice, civil transactions and jurisprudence are considered the branches springing out of and derived from the roots. The regulations, ordinances and decisions are (الاحكام) derived from the Qur'án, the Sunna, the Ijmá' and Qíás.

These then are the sources from which Fiqh is derived. It is, however, necessary that the Muslim should rightly understand and interpret the same, and certain principles

---

[1] (الفقه هوالعلم بالاحكام الشرعيّة الفرعيّة المكتسب من ادلتها التفصيليّة)
Some say that a man is a فقيه, a Lawyer, a Jurist, when he knows the laws and regulations, together with the proofs in support of the same from the Qur'án, Sunna, Ijmá' and Qíás ; the majority, however, agree that a man may be considered a Faqíh, if he knows the laws and regulations and without being able to produce the proofs in support of the same ; that he need not even know them all. Some take a higher view of the Faqíh and say that, if he combines good works with the knowledge of the Law, he deserves to be called a Faqíh.
(الفقه الجمع بين العلم والعمل) Ibn 'Ábidín i. 28. Ghazáli i. 21).

and rules have, therefore, been laid down according to which the Qur'án and the Hadíth must be interpreted. It must also be known how the Ijmá' and the Qíás are to be understood, and how questions are to be decided and deductions to be made by means of the same. To deal with these questions is the object of the اُصوُل الفِقه[1].

From early times great differences existed on a variety of questions connected with Fiqh and everyone adopted the opinion which recommended itself to his own mind. This state of things continued for some time until the differences greatly increased. When the systems of the four great Imáms became generally adopted, their decisions were received on all controverted questions, and all other opinions of minor authority rejected. The students then began to examine and compare the decisions of the four Imáms and to discuss the relative value of the same,

---

[1] The early Muslims, says Ibn Khaldún, were not in want of this branch of religious science, as their exact knowledge of the Arabic language enabled them to find out the various meanings conveyed by the text not did they require the study of the Isnád, or the chain of narrators of a Tradition, for they personally knew and conversed with the men who first reported the Traditions. When the first generation of Muslims had disappeared, the necessity made itself felt of acquiring by artificial means and special exertion the knowledge which their predecessors had naturally possessed. A code of rules and principles was therefore laid down. (*See* Faith of Islám pp. 23-30).

The Imám Sháff'i was the first who composed a work on this subject, by dictating to his disciples his famous treatise on " what is commanded by the Law, and what is forbidden, on abrogation and the manner of analogical deduction." After his time jurists of the Hanafi School and the men of scholastic theology wrote many treatises on the subject and considerably developed the new branch of theological science. The best works written by earlier divines on the subject are the بُرهان of the Imámu'l Haramain, the مُنتَصفى by Ghazáli, the كتاب المحصول by Fakhru'd-dín and the كتاب الاحكام by Saifu'd-dínu'l Ámadi and the جمع الجوامع of Ibnu's-Sabki with a commentary by Bannáni.

each endeavouring to defend the opinion of the Imám whose system he follow-d, and thus sprang up a special branch of learning called علم الخلافيات.

Among the best works on this subject may be mentioned the كتاب المأخذ of Ghazáli. The science of disputing on these controverted points, called علم الجدل, dialectics, lays down the laws and rules to be observed in carrying on controversy with an opponent, whether to refute the opinion of the opponent or to defend one's own. (هو معرفة آداب المناظرة التي تجري بين اهل المذاهب الفقهية و غيرهم) For details *see* Ibn Khaldún i. 278-381[1].

---

[1] It may be useful, at this stage, to explain the meaning of several technical terms which are of frequent occurrence.

فَرْض (from فرض, to order, to command, to make incumbent) designates a duty absolutely obligatory, according to a command of the Qur'án or the Hadíth.

فرض عين is an absolute duty incumbent on every individual believer, male or female, free or slave, such as prayer, fasting, etc.

فرض كفاية is a duty which is not incumbent on every Muslim, but which, if fulfilled by some members of the community, (some say one in eight or ten suffices) is considered to be as good, as if the whole community had fulfilled it. Such duties are the attending a funeral, visiting the sick, accepting an invitation to dinner.

واجب, a duty obligatory on the Muslim, but not in the same degree as فرض

سُنَّة, a duty in so far as it was practised by the Prophet. It is laudable to imitate his example.

مُستحَبّ a praiseworthy act. It is desirable to conform to this.

مُباح, allowed, licit, desirable, but it is a duty which may be omitted without fear of committing a sin.

حَلال, a thing lawful, licit, honestly acquired.

حرام, something unlawful, illicit, forbidden, dishonestly acquired.

مكروه, a thing not exactly forbidden, but disliked; it is to be avoided.

The subjects treated of in the Science of Fiqh are, according to Ibn 'Ábidín (i. 58) :

(1)   The عِبَادات, or laws concerning worship, religious duties, rites and ceremonies.

(2)   The معاملات, or laws concerning dealings between man and man.

(3)   The عُقُوبات, or laws concerning the punishments to be inflicted on transgressors of the law.

The duties to be treated of under عبادات are :

(1)   Prayer, (صلاة) including purification, ablutions (تطهير ـ طَهَارَة)·

(2)   Alms, tithes, poor-rates, (زَكَاة)·

(3)   Fasting, (صَوْم)·

(4)   Pilgrimage, (حج)·

(5)   To these some add Holy War, (جِهَاد)·

The first fundamental point of religious practice, as required by the Qur'án, is prayer. In order to be able properly and acceptably to perform his prayers, the Muslim must first purify himself, i.e., he must be clean from

---

مَنْدوب, a duty recommended.

محْظور, a duty prohibited, forbidden.

حَسَن good and lawful duty, performed by the responsible Muslim, comprising what is obligatory, and laudable.

(الحَسَن فعل المكلَّف المادون فيه واجباً و مندوباً و مُباحاً)

قبيح, is something bad, hideous, forbidden.

The learned Bairáni says that فرض and واجب are synonymous (مترادف), and also سنَّة, تطوّع, مستحبّ, مندوب. Some like Abú Hanifa differ from him, but Bairáni says they are differences in words only. (i. 50 et seqq.)

from all material and all legal or ceremonial impurities, so that he may present his prayers whilst he is in a state of purity (علی طهارة) Before treating of prayer, we must treat of purification, as the preliminary preparation for the same.

PURIFICATION.[1]—The purity required of the Muslim, as a necessary preparation for prayer is, according to the Qur'án and Traditions, the purity from outward, material, as well as from legal, ceremonial uncleanness.

(التنزّه عن الادناي ـ الطهارة عن حَدَث و خَبَث)

Before we proceed to describe the various kinds of purification, ablutions, and washings and the manner of performing the same, it will be necessary to show what, according to Muslim law, is considered unclean and polluting, and what, therefore, are the things from which a Muslim must cleanse and purify himself in order to

---

[1] The Qur'án gives the following general precepts on this duty: "O ye believers; when you rise up to prayer, wash your faces, and your hands as far as the elbows and wipe your heads and your feet to the ankles, and if you are polluted (جُنُبّا) then purify yourselves" (Súra v. 8-9). See also Súras iv. 46; ix. 109; lvi. 78. "He sent you down water from heaven that he might thereby cleanse you and cause the pollution of Satan to pass from you." (Súra viii. 11.)

Muhammad used to say: "Purification, that is, ablution, washing, bathing is the key of prayer" (مفتاح الصلاة الطهور) : "Religion is built on cleanliness" (بُنَى الدين على النظافة) and "Purity is one-half of faith" (الطهارة نصف الايمان). Ibn 'Abidín says: "The state of impurity prevents prayer, puts a lock to the door of prayer; purification is the key which removes the lock."

Ghazáli quotes the following sayings of the Prophet on the necessity of purification: "God accepts no prayer without previous ablution" "He who performs the Wudú (وضو) in the proper manner . . . . . will be cleansed of his sins."—"He who performs the ablution when he is already clean (على طُهْرٍ) God will account it for ten good actions." (Bukhári i. 24-51; Kashf i. 42-98).

be clean, or in a state of purity (طَاهِرٌ ـ طَهَارَةٌ عَلَى). There
are three kinds[1] of things which defile a Muslim, and
from which it is consequently his duty to purify himself :
(1) Filth, ordure (خَبَثٌ) (2) Legal, ceremonial impurity
(حَدَثٌ) (3) Superfluities of the body (فَضَلَاتٌ).
The only means by which impurities can be removed
is water.[2]

---

[1] خَبَثٌ, dross, excrement, ordure, filth ; حَدَثٌ, impurities contracted
by voiding of ordure ; فَضَلَاتٌ superfluities such as long nails, hair, etc.
Impurities are also divided into (1) real, material, substantial impurities
(نِجَاسَةٌ حَقِيقِيَّةٌ), which may be either greater (نِجَاسَةٌ مُغَلَّظَةٌ) or smaller
(نِجَاسَةٌ مُخَفَّفَةٌ). (2) legal, ceremonial impurity (نِجَاسَةٌ حُكْمِيَّةٌ), which may
consist in a greater (حَدَثٌ اكبر) or smaller defilement. (Ghazáli i. 83).

Substantial, material impurities (الْمُزَال أَعْيَان) may be either inanimate things (جمادات), or animals (حيوانات), or parts of animals
(اجزاء حيوانات)

Inanimate things are all clean and do not defile, except wine (خمر) and
all intoxicating drinks. Animals are all clean, except the dog and pig
(خنزير). When dead, however, all animals are unclean, except man, fish,
locusts, worms in apples; insects like the fly and the beetle. Of parts of
animals, some are clean, some unclean. . . . Of some of the defiling substances, a small quantity does not defile, e.g., a small quantity of dirt of
the street, a little blood caused by lice or fleas. (For more details see
Ghazáli i. 83.)

[2] There are various and conflicting opinions on the subject of the
cleanness or uncleanness of water, and the most minute, difficult and
puzzling distinctions are made by the learned doctors of the four Orthodox Schools on the most important subject of finding out whether a
certain kind of water is clean or unclean. On the whole, however, the
rule generally accepted is that water, the taste, colour or smell of which
has not been changed, is to be considered as clean. Muhammad said :
"عَلَى الْمَاءِ طَهُورًا لَا يُنَجِّسُهُ شَيْءٌ الَّا مَا غَيَّرَ طَعْمَهُ اولونهُ اورا رِيحَتَهُ". Ghazáli (i. 88)
deplores the importance attached to this subject and the scruples and
doubts it causes to many pious Muslims, and mentions that, at the time

The purification from any legal, or ceremonial impurity (طهارة الأحداث) is made, according to circumstances, in one or more of the following ways[1] :

(1)   Abstersion, called Istinjá (إِسْتِنْجَاء).

---

of the Prophet to the end of the period of the Companions, no such importance was attached to the subject.   Indeed, 'Umar once performed his ablutions from water in the jar of a Christian woman.   Muhammad said : "When water amounts to two large jars (قلّة), it does not admit impurity" (Kashf i. 44-50; Ghazáli i. 83-84.)

In order to remove substantial impurities (كـيفية الازالة), it is not sufficient to pour water over them; it is necessary to remove the unclean substance itself by rubbing and scratching and wringing, till the smell, taste and colour of the impure substance have been removed.

(ان كـانت النجـاسة عينّية فلابّد من ازالة العين).

[1] Before explaining the manner of performing the above operations, Ghazáli considers it necessary to mention a number of regulations to be observed during natural evacuations (فى آداب قفاء الحاجة Ihyá i. 85.) "When the Muslim goes to ease himself, he must remove to a distance and, if possible, hide himself behind some object, so that he may not be seen by men.   He must not turn his face or his back to the sun, or the moon or the Ka'ba, except he be within a building, nor use his right hand for washing or removing impurities.   On entering, he is to put forward the left foot, on coming out the right.   Certain prayers are to be said on entering : "I take my refuge to God from the devil"

(اعوذ بالله من الحمد لله الذى اذهب عنّى مايوذدينى و ابقى) on leaving :

الرجس النجس الخبيث المُخبت الشـيطان الرجيم علىّ ما ينفعنى)

Istinjá (إستنجا), abstersion, (from نجا to escape), means to deliver oneself from impurity, or to clean oneself with pebbles and water (هو ازالة نجس من احد السبلين الغائط والبول) i.e., by wiping it off by means of three, four or, if necessary, five pebbles taken with the left hand, and then washing the parts of the body with water.   When finished, the following ejaculation is said : اللهم طهّر قلبى من النفاق و حصّ فرجى

من الفواحش. When Súra ix. 109 was revealed : "Therein are men who aspire to purity for God loveth the purified?" the Prophet asked the people of Kufa : "What is meant by this cleanliness (طهارة) for which God praises you," to which they replied : "We used (in our lustration)

(2)   Partial ablution, called Wudú (وُضُوء).

(3)   Total ablution, immersion, bathing, called Ghusl (غُسل).

---

both water and stone " كنا نجمع بين الماء والحجر الاستنجاء وآداب
دخول الخلاء والخروج منه (Ghazáli i. 85. Ibn 'Abidín, i. 245-256).

Muhammad affirmed that Gabriel taught him how to perform the Istinjá by performing it before him. (Kashf i. 54-55.)

Wudú, وضوء from وَضَاء to wash, perform ablutions, is a partial ablution, the performance of which rests on the command of the Qur'án: 'O ye who believe! when ye rise up to prayer wash your faces, and your hands as far as the elbow, and wipe your heads, and your feet to the ankles.' (Súra v. 8.)

Muhammad, before performing the Wudú, used to clean his teeth with the miswák (مِسْواك), a kind of tooth brush made of fibrous wood, about a span long and ordered his followers to do the same, for he said: "Your mouths are the paths of the Qur'án, make them sweet-smelling with the siwák." The use of the siwák is therefore considered a Sunna duty (سُنّة مُوَّكَدة). On using it, the believer must propose to himself to cleanse his mouth for the reading of the Qur'án and for mentioning God's name in prayer. (ينوى تطهير فمه لقرواة القران وذكر الله تعالى فى الصلاة) Muhammad used to say: "One prayer after the use of the siwák is more excellent than seventy-five without it." (For further details on the importance and benefits derived from the use of the siwák *see* (Ghazáli i. 86. Ibn 'Ábidín i. 83-85).

After having done with the siwák, the believer makes the Wudú. He sits down facing the Qibla and says: "In the name of the Gracious, the Merciful, I take my refuge unto Thee from the instigations of the devils. I take my refuge unto Thee, O Lord, lest they approach me "—

"باسـم الله الرحمن الرحيم اعوذ بك من همزات الشياطين و اعوذ بك ربّ
ان يحضرون"

Then he washes his hands three times before dipping them into the vessel used for his ablutions, saying: "O God, I ask Thee for prosperity and blessing, and flee to Thee from misfortune and ruin."

(اللهمّ اسالك اليمُن والبَرَكة و اعود بك من الشوٌم والهلكة)

Then he proposes in his mind the removal of all impurity and thereby makes the performance of prayer legal for himself.

(4) Ablution with fine sand, called Tayammum (تَيَمُّم).

(ثم ينوى رفع الحدث و استباحة الصلاة). In this state of inward proposal and intention he must remain, till he comes to the washing of the face.

Then he rinses his mouth (يَتَمَضْمَض) three times and gargles (يَغُرر) saying: " O God, help me to read Thy Book and to multiply the mention of Thy name " (اللهم أعنّى على تلاوة كتابك و كثرة الذكر لك).

Then he takes a handful of water and snuffs it up thrice into his nostrils, saying, while doing so: "O God, create in me the smell of Paradise, and be pleased with me"; then he blows out the water again three times by compressing his nostrils with the thumbs and the forefingers of the left-hand, saying while he does so: "I take refuge unto Thee from the smell of hell-fire and from the evil of that abode."

(اللهم اعوذ بك من روائح النار و من سوء الدار)

He then throws the water into his face three times, from the top of the forehead downward to the chin, and from one ear to the other, not forgetting to wash the roots of all hairy parts of the face and body and letting the water flow from his beard, and combing it thrice with the fingers of his right-hand, passing the fingers through the beard from the throat upwards. The eye-holes also (محاجر العَيْنَين) must be carefully washed.

While performing these operations, he repeats, at every part which he washes, the following petition: "O God, make white my face with Thy light on the day when the faces of Thy saints become white (i.e., pale from fright), and do not cause my face to become black, on the day the faces of thy enemies become black."

اللهم بيّض وجهى بنورك يوم تبيض وجوه اوليائك ولا تسوّد وجهى بظلماتك يوم تسوّد وجوه اعدائك. 86 .i Ghazáli)

He next washes his hands and arms (يديه الى مرفقيه) up to the elbows three times, causing the water to run along his arm from the palm of the hand to the elbow. Beginning with the right arm, he says: "O God, give me my book (of account) in my right-hand, and make a small account with me" (اللهم اعطنى كتابى بيمين و حاسبنى حسابًا يسيرًا). On washing the left arm, he says "O God I take my refuge unto Thee that I may not have my book given into my left-hand, or behind my back."

(اللهم الى اعوذ بك ان تعطينى كتابى بشمالى او من وراء ظهرى) He then washes his whole head, rubbing it all over with both hands from the front to the back thrice (one rubbing backward and forward being counted

When the Wudú has been properly performed, it is valid for the five daily prayers, and need not be repeated;

---

as one rubbing (مسحة واحدة) ; so doing he says : "O God, cover me with Thy mercy, and send down upon me Thy blessing and shade me with the shade of Thy Throne on the day there is no shade but Thy shade."

(اللّهمّ غشّنى برحمتك و أنزل علىّ من بركتك و اظلّنى تحت ظل عرشك يوم لا ظلّ الّا ظلك) He then takes a fresh handful of water and washes the outer, as well as the inner parts of his ears, by putting the tips of his forefingers into his ears and twisting them round, passing his thumbs at the same time the back of the ears from the bottom upwards. While doing so he says : "O God, let me be of the number of those who hear the words and follow the best of it. O God, let me hear the call of Paradise with the righteous." (اللّهمّ اجعلنى من الذين يستمعون القول

و يتبعون احسنه - اللّهمّ أسمعنى منادى الجنّة مع الابرار)
Then he takes fresh water and washes the neck with both hands, making the ends of the fingers meet behind the neck. While so doing he says : "Deliver my neck from hell-fire. I take my refuge unto Thee from chains and bonds." (اللّهمّ فك رقبتى من النار و اعوذ بك من السلاسل والاغلال).
Lastly, he washes his feet as high up as the middle between the feet and the knees thrice. Beginning with the right foot he says : "O God cause my feet to stand firm on the straight path on the day when the feet slip into hell-fire." (اللّهمّ ثبّت قدمى على الصراط المستقيم يوم تزلّ الاقدام فى النار)
Then, washing the left foot he says : "I take my refuge unto Thee, lest my foot slip on the path on the day when the wicked slip into hell-fire." He (أعوذ بك ان تزلّ قدمى على الصراط يوم تزلّ اقدام المنافقين فى النار). must also be careful to pass the wet fingers of his lef-thand between the toes, and the water must reach the middle between the foot and the knee (الى انصاف الساقين) The Qur'án says : "الى الكعبين " (Súra v. 8).
When all this is done, he lifts up his head towards heaven and says : "I testify that there is no God but God and that there is no partner to Him and that Muhammad is the servant and Messenger " (اشهد ان لا الّه

الّا الله وحدَهُ لا شريك لهُ و اشهد ان محمداً عبدُهُ و رسولهُ - سبحانك اللّهمّ و بحمدك لا اله الّا انت - عملت سوّاً و ظلمت نفسى - استغفرك اللّهمّ واتوب اليك - فاغفرلى و تب علىّ انّك انت التوّاب الرحيم . اللّهمّ اجعلنى من التوّابين و اجعلنى من المتطهرين . و اجعلنى من عبادك الصالحين . و اجعلنى عبداً صبوراً شكوراً - و اجعلنى اذكرك ذكراً كثيراً و أسبحك بكرةً و اصيلاً.

unless it has been rendered invalid by the person's having contracted one of the lesser impurities [1] (حدث أَصغر), in which case he has to repeat it.

The petitions to be repeated during the abovementioned manipulations are not obligatory (فَرْض); but only laudable (مُسْتَحَبّ) and various other petitions may be used instead. This mode of performing the Wudú has been given from Ghazáli's Ihyá (i. 87).

[1] The defilements which render Wudú invalid (ما ينقض الوضو), and therefore require a new ablution before prayer can be performed are (1) ordinary natural evacuations of the body, (2) extraordinary secretions, (3) worms, gravel, stones, (4) blood, matter, coming in contact with parts which must be washed in Wudú, (5) vomiting food, blood, bile, (6) insanity, (7) drunkenness, (8) swoon or temporary absence of mind, (9) laughter at the time of prayer, (10) voluptuous embraces, (11) sleep. (Ibn 'Ábidín i. 98-104.)

Wudú is absolutely obligatory (فَرْض) before performing prayer, canonical as well as supererogatory (فرضها و نفلها). It is desirable, laudable (واجب), but not obligatory before touching the Qur'án, or on performing the procession round the Ka'ba at the time of the pilgrimage (طواف) (Ibn Ábidín i. 66.) It is a laudable custom also (سنة) before going to sleep.

Ibn 'Abbás said that the command (فريضة الوضو) was given at Mecca; but the revelation concerning the same in the Qur'án was only given at Madína. As regards the blessings of the Wudú Muhammad said : " When the Muslim performs his ablutions......all his sins will be forgiven him.) (Kashf i. 60-64. As regards the necessity of performing the Wudú, he said : " God accepts no prayer without ablution." (ان الله لا يقبل صلاة) (بغير طهور) Abú Huraira mentioned to a man from Hadramant the necessity of ablution after having defiled himself; (حَدَث) whereupon the Hadramanti enquired : " What is حدث," to which Abú Huraira replied : "فسا او ضراط." (Bukhári i. 25). Intention must be combined with Wudú (not as فرض but as سُنة). The Sunna of Wudú, i.e., things it is a duty to observe in imitation of the custom of the Prophet, though they are not an absolutely obligatory duty, are (1) the use of the siwák (سواك), (2) washing of hands (غسل اليدين), (3) rinsing of the mouth, snuffing up and blowing out the water (الاستنشار – الاستنشاف – المضمضة), (4) disjoining the hair of the beard and the fingers (تخليل اللحية والأصابع), (5) the rubbing of the

A greater defilement,[1] (حَدَثٌ أَكْبَرُ) cannot be removed by partial ablution (Wudú) but requires a total immersion in water. This washing or bathing of the whole
body is called Ghusl (غُسْل). It is founded on the express injunction of the Qur'án: 'If you are polluted
(جُنُبَاً), then purify yourselves (Súra v. 9).

The Muslim intending to perform the Ghusl[1] places
the vessel containing the water for his ablution on the

---

ears (مَسْح الأُذُن), (6) the pouring out of the water over all the parts of
the body (اسَاغ الوضو), (7) the quantity of water to be used (مقدار الماء)
(8) the towel (المندِيل) used for drying after the Wudú, (9) mention of
the name of God and supplication (الدعاء والتسمية), (10) consecutiveness
(الموالاة), that is, observing the consecutive order in performing the
Wudú (Kashf i. 65-70).

A Muslim in the Mosque who fears that something renders his Wudú
invalid, is not to leave it in order to peform a new ablution, till he has
clear proof of it and that he has become مُحدَث or impure. Muhammad
said : "فلا يخرج حتى يسمع صوتًا او يجدريحًا" (Kashf i. 71); he also said :
"لا يقبل الله صلاة من احدث حتى يتوضاه." 'Umar said : " He who has touched
the cross of a Christian, let him perform the ablution " (Kashf i. 73-77).

Muhammad often merely touched his boots instead of washing his feet.
(المسح على الخُفين) Kashf. i. 77 ; Bukhári i. 33). It is admitted by the
Muslim doctors that Wudú was practiced by other people before Islám.
(Ibn Ábidín i. 67, Sale 74-75.)

[1] A Muslim man or woman is in a state of greater defilement (جنابة) *i.e.*,
greater defilement by (1) pollutio nocturna (خروج المنى – اِحْتِلام) (2) coitus
(التقاء الختانين جماع), (3) menses (المَحيض – الحَيض), (4) puerpurium
(النفاس). On these occasions Ghusl is absolutely obligatory (فَرض), on
other occasions such as before Friday prayer, on the two great Festivals,
on entering Mecca, after having washed the dead, after blood-letting,
Ghusl is only Sunna (غُسل مَسنون), or a praiseworthy and meritorious act
(Ibn Ábidín i. 124 ; Ghazáli i. 87-88). A woman is considered unclean
for the space of twenty-five to forty days after childbirth (نفاس) and
for three to ten days at the time of her menstruation. (*See* Súra ii. 222.)

right hand, then mentions the name of God, then washes his hands thrice,¹ then performs the Instinjá, then removes any impurity that may cleave to his body, then performs the Wudú in the manner before described, except that the washing of the feet is delayed. After this, he pours out the water three times over his head, and on the right and left side and then rubs the front and back part of his body and combs the hair of his head and beard with his fingers. A woman need not undo her hair, except she fears the water may not penetrate sufficiently.

When the Muslim does not find water, or is prevented by some weighty reason, as illness or extreme scarcity of water, etc., from performing his ablutions with water, he may perform the same with fine clean sand or earth (تُراب ـ صَعِيد) This is called Tayammum² (التَّيَمُّم)

---

¹ The chief points (أَرْكَان) to be observed in Ghusl are (1) the proposal, intention, (2) that the water should touch all parts of the body (استيعاب البدن بالغسل). Ibn 'Ábidín says that a person (male or female) in a state of جنابة may not enter or walk through a mosque, nor read or even touch the Qur'án, nor read the Taurat or the Psalms or the Injil, these also being the Word of God. " Christians are not allowed to touch the Qur'án but there is no harm in instructing them in the same in the hope that they may be guided aright." (For further details on the subject of Ghusl see Ibn 'Ábidín i. 111-131).

Ibn 'Umar says: Prayers were at first fifty and Ghusl from janaba (الغسل من الجنابة) seven times and Ghusl from urine from the coat (غسل البول من الثوب) seven times; the apostle of God did not, however, cease to entreat his Lord, on the day of the heavenly journey (ليلة الاسراء), till he reduced the daily prayers to five and the Ghusl from janaba to one only. For a detailed account of the sexual intercourse which requires Ghusl, and that which does not require it, and the manner in which Muhammad used to perform the Ghusl see Ibn 'Abidín s. l., Bukhári i. 40, 42; Kashf i. 79-83. Muhammad ordered those who wished to embrace Islám to perform the Ghusl, to have their heads shaved and to be circumcised (القى عنك شعر الكفر و اختتن).

² This practice rests on the command of the Qur'án: "If you are ill, or on a journey, or any of you come from easing himself, or you have touched

Purification from superfluities is very necessary.[1]

(التنظيف عن الفضلات الظاهرة وهي نوعان اوساخ و اجزاء)

women and do not find water, then wipe yourselves with clean sand, and wipe with it your faces and your hands." تيمّموا صعيداً Súra v. 9). In order to perform the Tayammum, the Muslim places both his hands, the fingers being joined together, on the ground covered with clean sand or dust and then carefully wipes with it his face once, proposing to himself the lawfulness of prayer after this kind of ablution; then, if he has any ring on his finger, he takes it off, places the palms of his hands on the dust again, this time with his fingers spread out, and then rubs his arms up to his elbows. The chief points of this operation (الأركان the Arkán), are الفرضتان and the استيعاب; the conditions (شروط) are (1) النيّة (2) المسح (3) كونه بثلاث اصابع او اكثر (4) المعيد (5) كون المعيد مطهراً (6) فقد الماء. The Sunan are (1) اقبالهما (2) الضرب بباطن كفّيه (3) ادبارهما (4) نفضهما (5) تسميّة (6) تفريج اصابعه (7) ترتيب (8) ولاه con- secutiveness. Ibn ʿÁbidín i. 168. Kashf i. 188-92).

1 The following impurities all of which come out of the body (الاوساخ والرطوبات المترشحة) must all be removed: filth and lice gather- ing on the hair (الوسخ من معاطف), dirt cleaving to the ear, (الدَّرَن والقَمل), mucous matter collecting in the nose, to be removed by snuffing (الأُذن) up and blowing out (استنشار - استنشاق); impurities attaching to the teeth and the tongue (قلح) to be removed by the siwák and rinsing, or gargling; filth gathering in the beard, to be removed by washing and the use of the comb; (مدرى - مشط), iron instrument used to scratch with; dirt at the fingers' joints (البراجم) and at the fingers' ends (رواحب) and under the nails; impurities collecting on the body in consequence of perspiration to be removed by the use of the bath (الحَمّام). (For details as to the manner of bathing and the proper behaviour in public baths see Ghazáli i. 89).

There are also many impurities which form themselves on the body. (ما يحدث فى البدن من الاجزاء) These must be removed. They are the hair of the head which must be occasionally shaved off; mustachios (شارب) plural (شوارب) which must be clipped; the hair under the arm- pit (الابط) at least every forty days; the hair of the 'regis pubis' (عانة) which is to be removed at least every forty days by shaving or a depila- tory (نُورة); the nails of the hands and feet which are to be trimmed

Ghazáli and some other doctors of Islám, of the more spiritual-minded and idealizing sort, pretend that the purification here meant is not merely or chiefly outward purification by water and sand, but inward purification of the heart and mind. Ghazáli distinguishes four kinds or

---

(تقليم الاظفار) ; superfluity of the navel (زيادة السّرة) which is removed at the birth of the child ; the foreskin (قلفة الحشفة) which is to be removed by circumcision (التطهير بالختان). The circumcision should be delayed until the child has shed its teeth, when it is said to be less dangerous. Muhammad said : "Circumcision is Sunna for males, an honorable act for females (الختان سنة للرجال مكرمة للنساء) He said to Umm Atiyya who used to circumcise females (the act of circumcising a female is خفض) : " Do not exceed the bounds in circumcision." The beard, if too long, is to be cut off. The normal length of the beard is, however, a matter of dispute. Ghazáli gives a detailed description of ten bad methods of dealing with the same, among them the customs of dyeing or tearing out of gray hair, which the Muslim ought to avoid. (Ghazáli i. 90-92).

It is a remarkable fact that circumcision is neither commanded, nor even once alluded to in the Qur'án, though it is now considered incumbent on every Muslim. There is also no authentic account of Muhammad's having been circumcised. Some writers pretend that he was born circumcised (وُلد معدوراً اى مختوناً), but this is denied by the most eminent scholars.

Those who deny that he was born circumcised say that, even if this were the case, it would not be a special privilege of the Prophet, as many children are born with a kind of circumcision (لان العرب تزعم ان الغلام اذا وُلد فى القمر فُسِخت قلفته اى اتّسعت فيصير كالمختون.) It is generally admitted that circumcision is not a duty involving the degree of absolute obligation (فرض) ; some are of opinion that it is of the degree called واجب that is, a duty incumbent on the believer, though not absolutely obligatory ; the majority are in favour of its being only Sunna (سُنّة) that is a degree lower than واجب. In the case of a convert to Islám from some other creed, to whom the operation may be an occasion of great suffering, it can be dispensed with, although it is considered expedient and proper for all new converts to be circumcised. (For details on the subject and arguments in favour and against, see Mawáhíb i. 149-156 ; see also Dictionary of Islám, 57 ; Sale 76.)

degrees of purifications which, he says, are implied in the purification commanded in the Qur'án.

(الطهارة لها اربع مراتب)

1. Cleansing the body from all pollution, filth and superfluities (تطهير الظاهر عن الاحداث والاخباث والفضلات).

2. Cleansing the members of the body from sins and transgressions (تطهير الجوارح عن الجرائم والاثام).

3. Cleansing the heart from blameable inclinations and odious vices (تطهير القلب عن الاخلاق المذمومة).

4. Cleansing the secret thoughts from everything except God (تطهير السرّ عما سوي الله).

Outward cleanliness, he says, is in comparison with inward purity as the shell compared with the kernel . . . . . If, however, we carefully compare all the passages of the Qur'án which speak of purification, and purity it becomes evident to every unprejudiced reader that in none of them is there any reference to inward, moral or spiritual purity of the heart, but that what is required in them is the outward, bodily cleansing by means of ablutions and washings. The celebrated collections of Traditions also, as well as the standard works on Fiqh, contain pages and pages of most minute and often obscene and disgusting explanations on what constitutes impurity and defilement, which cannot be given here. In practice they do not allude to moral purity as a preparation for prayer. We see also to this day the most pious Muslims far more anxious concerning the outward and ceremonial than about inward and moral purity.

PRAYER[1] (صلاة) is the second of the five foundations or pillars on which Islám is built up. This most important

---

[1] Muhammad used to call prayer "the pillar of Religion" and "the key of Paradise"..."and that which caused man to be a true believer" and

duty (فرض) of every Muslim is frequently enjoined in the Qur'án : " Glorify God when it is evening and morning, and to him be praise in the heavens and the earth, and at afternoon and at noontide." (Súras xxx. 17; xi. 116; xx. 130; xvii. 80; ii. 40; iv. 104).

---

also : وَسُئِل اىّ الاعمال افئل فقال الصلاة لمواقيها – الصلاة عماد الدين فمن ترکها هدم الدين (Ghazáli i. 93-94).

At the beginning of Islám Muhammad and his followers performed only two prayers: the morning prayer before sunrise, and the evening prayer after sunset. Besides these they used regularly to spend a great part of the night in praying and reading the Qur'án. When their health began to suffer in consequence of these night exercises, this practice was given up and, after it had been obligatory (فرض), it became optional (تطوّع), and was left to the choice of every individual. 'Áyesha says that " God at first commanded the spending of the night (قيام الليل) in pious exercises mentioned in the Súratu'l Muzammil (lxxiii), which the Apostle and his companions observed for a whole year, till their feet became swollen, then God revealed the alleviation (التخفيف) mentioned at the end of the Súra" (Kashf i. 98 ; see Súra lxxii. 1-8 and 20).

These two prayer times were observed till the famous night journey of Muhammad (ليلة الاسراء) when the five prayers (الصلوات الخمس) are said to have been appointed, and this command holds good to the present day. The change is not mentioned in the Qur'án, but rests entirely on the sayings of the Prophet, transmitted by Tradition. Of the appointment of the five prayer times Muhammad gives the following account : " The divine injunctions for prayer were originally fifty times a day, and as I passed Moses (in heaven during the night journey), he said to me: 'What hast thou been ordered?' I replied 'fifty times!' Then he said : 'Verily thy people will never be able to bear it.' I then returned to my Lord and asked for some remission, and ten prayers were taken off then I pleaded again, and ten more were remitted and so until at last they were reduced to five times. Then I went to Moses, and he said : ' How many prayers hast thou been ordered'? and I replied : ' Five ' and Moses said 'return to thy Lord and ask for a farther remittance,' but I said : 'I have asked until I am quite ashamed. I cannot ask him again.'" (Bukhári i. 51-52).

Muhammad used to say : " Five prayers has God prescribed for his servants. God has promised that he will cause him who performs them to enter Paradise " (خمس صلوات كتبهنّ الله على العباد) ; they are therefore called

134 THE RELIGION OF ISLÁM.

The five obligatory prayers[1] (or rather prayer-services) are (1) Morning prayer, (2) Noon prayer, (3) Afternoon prayer, (4) Evening prayer, (5) Night prayer.

---

the stated, the obligatory prayers (الصلاة المفروضة – الصلاة المكتوبة) (On the meritoriousness of observing these five prayer times punctually *see* Ghazáli i. 93-94).

It is worth noticing that the term صلاة is now used by Muslims only of the stated five prayer-services or liturgical prayer hours, while private prayer is called دُعَاء (pl. أَدْعِيَة from دعا, = to call, to supplicate, to intercede).

[1] Morning prayer صلاة الصبح, also called صلاة الفجر, may be performed at any time between dawn and sunrise. When the sun has risen, the time for morning prayer has passed. It is a prayer of two obligatory and two Sunna rak‘as (رَكْعَة pl. رَكَعَات Bowings).

Noon prayer صلاة الظهر begins from the inclination of the sun towards the west (من زوال الشمس), and closes at the time when the shadow of a person shall be the length of his own stature, which time makes the beginning of the afternoon prayer. This noon prayer consists of four obligatory and two Sunna rak‘as after the obligatory rak‘as.

Afternoon prayer may be said at the expiration of the time for noon prayer and then at any time the sun assumes a yellow appearance. It consists of four obligatory and four Sunna rak‘as before the obligatory ones.

Evening prayer (صلاة المغرب) may be said after sunset and until the red appearance on the horizon disappears. It consists of three obligatory rak‘as and two Sunna ones after them.

Night prayer (العشا الآخرة – صلاة العشا), may be performed at any time between the time when the night has closed in and the beginning of dawn when morning prayer is due; it consists of four obligatory and four Sunna rak‘as after them. (Ghazáli i. 122; Bukhári i. 73-82).

Though these prayers may be said at any time of the respective intervals mentioned, and do not cease to be valid, even when delayed till the latest portion of the appointed hour, yet it is considered preferable and more meritorious not to delay, but to recite them at as early a part of the prayer time as possible. Muhammad used to say on this subject: "The worst thing I fear for my nation is their delaying prayer till after the appointed time, or their hastening to perform it before the appointed time" (Kashf i. 100).

Besides these five obligatory prayers (or prayer-services) there are other kinds of prayers, which it is desirable and meritorious to perform also, but on the character of which, whether they are Sunna or only Wájib there is difference of opinion. These are: The Witr prayer, the Duha prayer, the Tahajjud prayer.[1]

The manner of performing prayer is as follows:

(كيفيّة الاعمال الظاهرة من الصّلاة)

When the time of public prayer is come, the Mu'azzin (المؤذّن), standing near the Mosque, or on the minaret, (منارة) calls to prayer by reciting the Azán (الأذان) with a

---

It has been calculated that a Muslim, conscientiously performing his obligatory devotions (including three other prayer-services تهجّد, ضُحَى اشراق, mentioned hereafter), recites the same form of prayer at least seventy-five times in the day.

[1] Witr prayer (صلاة الوتر = odd prayers, from وِتر, odd,) is so called because it consists of an odd number of rak'as (3, 5, 7,) or of one single rak'a (فَرْدَة). It is to be performed after the night-prayer (بعد صلاة العشا), and to be the last prayer before the dawn of day.

The Duha prayer (صلاة الضُّحَى) is a forenoon prayer. (ضُحَى is the time before noon when the sun is already high above the horizon). Muhammad used to make it a prayer of four or more, but at the utmost of eight rak'as.

The Tahajjud prayer (صلاة التّهجّد, from تهجّد, to sit up at night vigils) is also called the prayer between the 'Ishá'ín (احياء ما بين العشاءين), said to be between the evening prayer (صلاة المغرب) and the night prayer (صلاة العشاء). It is considered incumbent on the Muslim and highly meritorious (سنّة موكّدة). Muhammad used to make it a prayer of six rak'as.

Besides these, Ghazáli mentions special prayers for every day and night of the week which he recommends as most profitable and meritorious. The obligatory prayers are فريضة; the supererogatory, voluntary prayers نفل (For traditions on the above statements and further explanations see Bukhári's Sahíh i. 73-80).

loud voice thus : " God is most great, God is most great
......I testify that there is no God but God......I testify
that Muhammad is the Apostle of God......come to prayer
......come to prosperity......God is great. There is no
God but God."

الله اكبر ـ الله اكبر ـ الله اكبر ـ الله اكبر ـ اشهد ان لا اله
الا الله ـ اشهد ان لا اله الا الله ـ اشهد ان محمداً رسول الله ـ اشهد
ان محمداً رسول الله ـ حيّ علي الصلاة ـ حيّ علي الصلاة ـ حيّ
علي الفلاح ـ حيّ علي الفلاح ـ الله اكبر ـ الله اكبر ـ لا اله الا الله

This call to prayer takes place before every one of the
five prayer services. In the call to morning prayer after
the words : " Come to prosperity," the following sentence is added twice : " Prayer is better than sleep."

.(الصلاة خير من النوم)

When the believer hears this call to prayer it is desirable that he should repeat what the Mu'azzin says, except
that instead of saying : " Come to prayer," he says :
" There is no strength and no power except with God."

(لا حولَ ولا قوّةَ الا بالله). Should he, however, already be in
the mosque when he hears the Azán, he need not repeat it.[1]

---

[1] Having already performed his ablutions, and removed all impurities
from his body and his clothes, he repairs to the place of worship where-
ever that may be (the mosque, which is more meritorious, a private room,
court or an open place), and there stands upright, with his face turned
towards the Qibla (القبلة, that is, the direction of the Ka'ba at Mecca),
having carefully covered his nakedness (عورة) from the navel to the
knees, and placed his feet together, yet not too closely.

Muhammad especially warned his followers against two false posi-
tions (1) joining the feet too closely together, called صفد, and (2) raising
one foot somewhat above the other, called صفن ; his legs and waist must
stand quite erect, and his arms down at the sides ; as to his head he
is at liberty to hold it up, or to bend it a little forward (اطراف) in sign

of humility, the eyes are to be directed fixedly to the place which indi-cates the direction of the Qibla which is, as a rule, the Mihráb (مِحْراب).
If there is no Mihráb or prayer-niche, it is good for the worshipper to draw a line on the opposite wall, in order to prevent the eyes from wander-ing and the thoughts from being distracted. This upright position is called the Qiám (قيام).

In this position the worshipper recites the verse: "I take my refuge to the Lord of the nations," (اعوذ برب الناس) If prayers are said in a mosque, or there is at least a congregation, large or small, the call to prayer is repeated, except that at the end are added the words "Prayer, has begun." This is called the Iqáma (اقامة, the beginning of prayer).

The worshipper, still standing with his hands close to his sides, proposes (ينوى) to perform morning or evening, obligatory or supererogatory, prayer, as the case may be, by saying in a low voice: "I have purposed to offer to God with a sincere heart this morning, or as the case may be, with my face qibla-wards, two, or as the case may be, rak'a prayers Fard, Sunna or Nafl. This purpose he must constantly keep before his mind to the end of the Takbíra (تكبيرة). This is called the Niyya (النيّة).

He then raises his hands to the height of his shoulders, with the thumbs touching the lobules of the ears, the fingers somewhat separated from each other, and the palms of the hands toward the Qibla. In this position he recites the Takbír, praising God thus: "God is most high......There is no God but God ... to God be praise."

الله اكبر - الله اكبر - لا اله الا الله - والله اكبر - الله اكبر ولله الحمد

This Takbír is called تكبيرة التحريم a prayer of prohibition, consecra-tion, because it prohibits the worshipper from saying or doing anything extraneous to prayer. It is also called the تكبيرة الافتتاح, the opening, beginning of praise, because this is the first time in the prayer-service in which it is recited. Later on it occurs several times.

Then he places his hands between the chest and the navel, putting the palm of the right hand on the back of the left, stretching out the fore and the middle finger, and seizing the wrist of the left hand with the thumb and little finger. While so standing he recites the opening invo-cation (دعاء الافتتاح) consisting of the تسبيح or تحميد and the تعوّذ or taking refuge in God. The Tasbih is:

سبحانك اللّهم و بحمدك و تبارك اسمك و تعالى جدّك و جلّ ثناؤك ولا اله غيرك

"Holiness to Thee, O God! and praise be to Thee! Great is Thy name, great is Thy greatness, there is no God but Thee." The Ta'awwuz is

اعوذ بالله من الشيطان الرجيم, "I take my refuge from the cursed Satan."
Then follows the Fátiha or the 1st chapter of the Qur'án.

After the Fátiha the worshipper recites a Súra, or any portion of the Qur'án, consisting at least, of three verses. The worshipper is recommended to read from the long Súras in the morning and from the short ones in the evening. A Súra which is most commonly recited is the سورة الاخلاص (Súra 112) which says: "He is God alone, God the Eternal! He begetteth not, and is not begotten; and there is none like unto Him."

After having recited the portion of the Qur'án the worshipper performs the Ruqú' (رکوع, bowing) in the following manner: standing upon his feet, as before, he inclines the upper part of his body so as to bring it in a horizontal position and places his hands upon his knees, separating the fingers a little. He then repeats three times (or more up to seven times when there is no Imám who leads in prayer): "Praised be my Lord, the exalted One and glory be to Him!" (سبحان ربى العظيم و بحمده) This is called the تکبيرة الرکوع the praise of Bowing.

He then raises himself up, places the hands on either side, and says: "May God hear him who praises him!" (سمع الله لمن حمده) This is called the تسميع to which he adds: "Praise be to Thee the fulness of the heaven and earth." (ربنا لك الحمد ملأ السموات و ملأ الارض) This standing position must not be made too long, except in a service of praise. (ملاة التسميح)

After the bowing the worshipper drops on his knees, saying: "God is Great" and prostrates himself in such a manner that his knees, the toes of his feet, the palms of his hands, the fingers close to each other, the nose and the forehead touch the ground. In thus prostrating himself, he must be careful to touch the ground first with his knees, then with his hands, then with the nose and the forehead, taking care that the thumbs just touch the lobe of the ears. The elbow must not touch the side, nor the stomach the thigh, nor the thigh the calf of the leg. (The woman on the contrary keeps all the limbs of the body together). In this position, called the سجود Sujúd, or prostration, he says: "Praise be to thee, O my Lord, the most High!" three times or more, if he chooses. This Takbíra is called تکبيرة السجدة Takbíru-'s Sajda, or "praise of the prostration."

Then he raises his head and body, sinks backwards on his heels, and thus, half sitting, half kneeling on his thighs, he repeats the Takbíra: "God is Great." While in this posture, called the جلسة (or sitting), he says: "O Lord, forgive me and have mercy upon me, and grant me my portion and guide me." (رب اغفرلى و ارحمنى و ارزقنى واهدنى .)

He must not lengthen this sitting, except in the prostration of praise.

After this he sits up to rest a moment, and then rises and stands erect, repeating, while doing so, the takbíra: "God is Great!" This is called

The total of these various postures with their respective prayers and praises constitutes what is called a rak'a (رَكْعَة). Each full prayer-service consists of a number of such rak'as.

The worshipper having completed the first rak'a, now performs the second in the same manner as the first, beginning however with the Fátíha. At the end of every two rak'as, as also after the last one, instead of rising from his half kneeling, half sitting posture, he remains sitting on his left foot, and placing his hands above his knees he says : "Praise be to God and prayers and good works. Peace be on thee, O Prophet, with the mercy of God and His blessing." This is called the Salutation, or greeting, (التَّحِيَّة). Then raising the first finger of the right hand he recites the Tashahhud (التَّشَهُّد, the confession) : "I testify that there is no God but God, and I testify that Muhammad is the apostle of God." At the end of all the rak'as, that is, at the end of the respective prayer-service, he asks for blessings on Muhammad and his descendants, saying : "O God have mercy on Muhammad and his descendants. Thou art to be praised, and Thou art great. O God bless Muhammad and his descendants, as Thou didst have mercy on Abraham and his descendants ; Thou art to be praised and Thou art great. O God bless Muhammad and his descendants. Thou art to be praised and Thou art great." This is called the Blessings (الصلوات). Then the Salutation (السلام) is said : "Peace be on you and the Mercy of God,"[1] (Ghazáli i. 98).

---

the تكبيرة القيام the "praise of standing up." (For further details see Ghazáli i. 97-98. See also Faith of Islám, pp. 257-263.)

[1] The two recording angels are supposed to be standing, the one recording the good actions on the right, the one recording the bad actions on

At the close of the prayer-service the worshipper raises his hands as high as his chest, with the palms towards heaven and offers up a Supplication[1] (دعاء القنوت), and when this is done he draws his hands over his face (مسح) as if to convey the blessing received from above to every part of the body.

---

the left shoulder of the Muslim. Then the Muslim is to salute by turning to the right and left. By so doing, Ghazáli says, he is to have in view not only the two angels but also the congregation of Muslims.

[1] قنوت (from قنت, to adore, to worship God) is adoration, supplication. In these supplications the worshipper is not bound to certain prescribed forms but may use his own words. When prayer is ended, the men remain standing at their places for a short time in order to allow the women, who may have been standing behind, to retire first.

Women who are bound to perform the prescribed prayers, as well as men, have to observe some slight alterations in the postures. For instance, they are not to raise their hands as high as the men at the takbíru't-tahrím; and at the tashahhud they are to place both their legs bent under them, instead of stretching out one, like the men.

All these rites and ceremonies are partly obligatory, partly in a less degree incumbent on the worshipper, partly praise-worthy, and optional.

The obligatory things are, according to Ghazáli (i. 99), the following twelve : الاعتدال عنه قائماً – الانحاء فى الركوع – الفاتحه – التكبير – النيّة

– التشهّد الاخير – الجلوس للتشهّد الاخير – الاعتدال عنه قاعداً – السجود

. السلام الاول – الصلاة على النبى

Things which are Sunna are the following four : رفع الدين فى تكبيرة

والجلسة للتشهّد – وعند الارتفاع للقيام – وعند الهوى للركوع – الاحرام .

The following are also considered Sunna التعوّذ – دعاء الاستفتاح

الذكر فى الركوع والسجود – تكبيرات الانتقالات – قراءة السورة – قوله آمين

– الدعاء فى آخر التشهّد – التشهّد الاول والصلاة فيه على النبى – والاعتدال عنهما

. التسليمة الثانية

The omission, purposely or by forgetfulness, of an obligatory part of prayer, makes that prayer invalid and it must be performed again. The omission what is merely Sunna has not this bad effect (Ghazáli i. 99-100).

Friday (يوم الجمعة ـ الجمعة) is the day appointed by
Muhammad as the day of solemn, public and united
prayer for Muslims. It rests on a direct command,
(Súra lxii. 9). It is the bounden duty (فرض عين) of
every Muslim personally to attend public noon prayer
with the congregation at the mosque.[1]

Under things prohibited (المنهيّات) in prayer may be mentioned the
following which Muhammad commanded his followers to avoid :

صفن and صفد, wrong position by either joining the feet too closely or
raising the one a little above the other ; اقعاء wrong position in sitting
on the ground ; سدل, wrapping oneself up in a coat, shirt and putting
the hands inside ; كفّ, raising the dress in front or behind when going
to kneel down ; صلب ـ اختصار, the placing the hands on the waists ;
مواصلة, joining those parts of prayer between which there is to be a short
pause ; حازق ـ حاقب ـ حاقن having small shoes which incommode the
worshipper. A Muslim is also to avoid saying his prayers when hungry
or angry or sleepy (Ghazáli i. 98-99).

Muhammad and his followers while at Mecca used to worship with
their faces towards the Ka'ba, that is, the Ka'ba was their Qibla; after
the flight to Madína, however, Muhammad, in order to conciliate the
Jews, adopted their Qibla, and ordered prayers to be said with faces turned
towards Jerusalem. When, after the space of about sixteen months, he de-
spaired of winning over the Jews to Islám, he changed it back to the Qa'ba
again. When one day he performed noon prayer in the new mosque of
Madína, with a large congregation behind him, he suddenly in the midst
of prayer turned round and completed prayer with his face towards the
Ka'ba, and all the congregation followed his example. The mosque was
therefore called the mosque of the two Qiblas (مسجد القبلتين) (See
Súra ii. 136-145).

The origin of the Azan was as follows: 'Umar relates that after the
flight to Madína, the Muslims used to assemble to prayer, without anyone
to call them. When they consulted together about the way of calling the
believers to prayer, some proposed the use of an instrument like the Christians, others said : ' No, let us take horns like the Jews,' but 'Umar
said : " Would it not be better to let a man call to prayer ; " whereupon
Muhammad ordered Bilál to call to prayer.

1 Muhammad said that God had originally appointed Friday as the
solemn day of worship both for the Jews and the Christians, but that they

had acted contrary to God's command, the Jews by choosing Saturday
and the Christians Sunday, and that it was reserved to the Muslim to
keep it as the appointed festival day (Ghazáli i. 112).

Every other prayer-service may be held by the Muslim alone, in his
house or any place he may be at the time, but Friday noon prayer must
necessarily be performed by him in common with the other believers and
in a special place of worship, whatever that may be, mosque, prayer place
or chapel.

The conditions (شُروط) of Friday prayer are the following six :

(1) It may not be performed in the open air, or in tents or outside the
town (المُصَر) ; but inside the town or village, in a mosque or a decent
prayer house.

(2) The Sultan, or his locum tenens, must be present. The Imám is
considered to be the lawful representative of the Sultan.

(3) In order to be valid, it must be performed at noon (الظُهر)

(4) The Khatíb (خطيب preacher) must deliver a sermon (الخُطبَة) at the
Friday service ; this sermon consists of two distinct parts, so it is also
called خطبتين, or the two sermons. Between the two parts of the sermon
he sits down for a short time of rest. The first part is called خطبة الوعظ,
the sermon of admonition, consisting of the praise of God, invocation of
blessings on Muhammad and his family and companions, and admoni-
tions and exhortations to the congregation. The second part is called
خطبة النَعت, the sermon of the mention of God's glorious attributes.
(For specimens of such Khutbas see Faith of Islám p. 268, 269.)

The Khutba is said in the following manner : the Khatíb, after the four
Sunna rak'as have been performed, seats himself on the pulpit, while the
Mu'azzin recites the Azan, after which he stands up on the second step
and delivers the Khutba leaning, while so doing, on a wooden staff or
sword. After he has delivered the first part, he descends from the pulpit,
and sitting on the floor of the mosque offers up a silent prayer ; he then
again ascends the pulpit as before and delivers the second part. The
Khutba being ended, the Khatíb descends from the pulpit and the obligatory prayer of two rak'as begins.

(5) In order that Friday service may be held in a mosque it is necessary
that a congregation (الجماعة) of at least three Muslims besides the Imám
should be present according to the Hanafi rite. The Shafi'í School requires
the presence of, at least, forty male worshippers, besides the Imám.

Every Muslim must have full liberty (الإذن العام) to enter the mosque
and join in the service.

The Muslim, while on a journey, especially when he is in haste, is excused from performing the full prayer-service. He says the صلاة السافر and need say only two rak'as instead of four at the noon, afternoon and night prayers (صلّي الفرض الرباعي ركعتين), nor is it required that he should recite a portion of the Qur'án after the Fátiha. He is also excused from attending the public prayer on Friday and the prayers at the great festivals. He need not fast. When performing the Wudú, instead of washing his feet, he is allowed only to wet the stockings and shoes.[1]

If any of these conditions be wanting, the Friday prayer service cannot be held. Ibn 'Ábidín mentions the following conditions – صحّة – اقامة بمصر

حرّية – ذكورة – بلوغ – عقل – وجود بصر – قدرة على المشى – عدم حبس و خوف و مطر شديد (i. 596-600)

Ghazáli (i. 113-116) devotes a long chapter to observations on the due preparation for the Friday service and the behaviour during the same. Another chapter is devoted to the subject of the best way of spending Friday (Ghazáli i. 116-117). In another chapter (i. 118-120) he treats of a number of general questions connected with prayer such as: killing a scorpion, louse or a flea, yawning during prayer, praying with shoes on, spitting and so on.

1 A Muslim is considered a traveller, enjoying the above mentioned mitigations from the time he leaves his home to undertake a journey of at least three days. Should he, however, on arriving at the village or town propose to himself to stay a fortnight or more, he ceases to be a traveller, and becomes a resident (مُقيم). If he stays at a village or town without intending to take up his abode there, he may put off his departure from day to day and thus enjoy the privileges of a traveller for years (Ibn 'Ábidín i. 576-588). On these mitigations Muhammad used to say: "They are a gift of God, accept them." He forbade the traveller to perform more than two rak'as instead of four. Some persons once said to 'Umar: "We find the prayer of fear and the prayer of residence (صلاة الخوف و صلاة الحضر) written in the Qur'án, but not the prayer of the traveller", to which 'Umar replied: "O my cousin, God sent to us Muhammad when we did not know anything of religion, we do what we saw him do." (Kashf i. 197-202).

There are two great feasts of Islám, and the prayer connected with them is called the prayer of the two feasts[1] (صلاة العيدين).

The feast of breaking the fast of Ramadán is called the عيد الفطر and also عيد رمضان, which is kept immediately on the conclusion of the thirty days' fast of Ramadán, that is, on the first day of the month of Shawwál. It is also called the minor festival (العيد الصغير) or the feast of almsgiving (عيد الصدقة).

The feast of the sacrifices, 'Ídu'l-Adha عيد الاضحي (from أضحي pl. اضحاة an animal offered as sacrifice) is also called the great feast (العيد الكبير) which is celebrated on the 10th of the month of Zu'l-Hijja (ذوالحجة), seventy days after the former (Súra xxii. 28-33).

The prayer Taráwíh[2] (صلاة التراويح prayer of pauses) is so called because he who performs it rests awhile after each tarwiha prayer, which consists of four rak'as, and

---

[1] The prayer of the two feasts is a special prayer service to be held on the first day of each of these feasts. The conditions are the same as for the public Friday prayer, with the exception that the Khutba follows instead of preceding it. It is a prayer of two rak'as. The time at which this service is to be held is from the time, when the sun, after rising, has apparently reached the height of a lance above the horizon to the time when noon prayer is to begin. When this time is passed, it is not lawful to hold it and it must be deferred to the next day; if for some reason or other it should again be omitted, it cannot be held on the third day, nor can it be replaced by a ' redeeming prayer.' (For further details see Ghazáli i. 125).

[2] ترويحة pl. تراويح a rest, pause. Whether it is to be performed in private or in public with the congregation, is a controverted question. During the five pauses the worshipper may, resting on his knees, recite the tasbíh, or tahlíl, or verses from the Qur'án, or supererogatory prayers, or sit still in deep devotion. The pause should be as long as it would require

because worshippers used to rest after each two pairs of salutations. It is a prayer-service of twenty rak‘as. Every Muslim must, in imitation of the Prophet, perform it at night, after the five obligatory prayers during the thirty days of the fast of Ramadán.

The Prayer of Fear (صلاة الخَوْف) is said, in imitation of the Prophet, during the time of war when there is imminent danger from the approach of an enemy. The Imám, under such circumstances, divides the army into two bodies, one of which is placed in a position towards the enemy so as to observe and keep him in check ; with the other he recites, if they are on the march, one rak‘a; if stationary in a place two rak‘as. This division will then march towards the enemy and the first division will recite as many rak‘as as may be required to complete the prayer. The Salám is said by the Imám alone.[1]

---

to say four rak‘as. It is meritorious during these prayers and the nights of Ramadán to repeat the whole of the Qur'án. (Ibn ‘Ábidín i. 519-523 ; Kashf i. 166 ; Ghazáli i. 125). As regards the importance of private prayer Muhammad is reported to have said : " A prayer in this my mosque (Madína) is worth more than a hundred thousand prayers in other mosques and a prayer in the Holy Mosque (مسجد الحرام at Mecca) is worth more than a thousand prayers in my mosque ; of greater worth than all these is the prayer of two rak‘as a man performs in the corner of his room : of which nobody knows anything but God Almighty." This prayer is not obligatory. The Shí‘ahs do not observe these prayers. (Faith of Islám 272). Muhammad used to make it a private prayer of twenty rak‘as and the witr ; after every four rak‘as he used to rest awhile (ترويح), after this he stood up and performed the regular obligatory prayer.

1 The first division will not recite the Fátiha and the verses of the Qur'án usually required, but the second division will supply the omission. If the enemy are so near that the cavalry dare not dismount, then each man will pray a rak‘a for himself and make the bowing and prostration by means of signs. Should the danger be very imminent this prayer may be altogether dispensed with ; so also in case of other imminent dangers such as, the being attacked by a lion, or a large serpent, etc., etc.....This prayer rests on the command of the Qur'án (Súra iv. 102-103 ; Ibn ‘Ábidín i. 624-626 ; Kashf i. 219-221. Dictionary of Islám, 561).

The Prayer at the time of an eclipse of the sun, or an eclipse of the moon is also called صلاة الكسوفين, the prayer of the two eclipses. This is a prayer said by the congregation and performed in the mosque, headed by the Imám; it consists of two rak'as and the reading of long portions of the Qur'án such as the Súra of the cow, the Family of 'Imrán or some other appropriate portion.[1]

When there is a scarcity of water from want of rain the prayer in time of drought (صلاة الاستسقاء) is used. It is a time when rivers become dry and wells and springs do not yield sufficient water for men, animals and fields. It is desirable that the Imám should order the people to fast, to give alms for three days and to repent of their sins. Supplications (دعاء), and confession of sins and prayer for pardon are to be offered to God by each private individual; it requires neither congregation in the mosque nor sermon, though both are allowed.[2] (Ibn 'Ábidín i. 622-624; Ghazáli i. 126 or 189; Kashf i. 233-236).

---

[1] The Azan and Ikáma are omitted and there is no Khutba. According to the Shaff'ite rite there are to be two Khutbas. The bowings and prostrations and reading of the Qur'án are to be lengthened so that the service does not cease till the sun has fully regained its light. If there is no Imám, united prayer cannot take place and each Muslim performs the prayer separately. Women also perform their prayer each separately. The prayer during an eclipse of the moon is not necessarily a service of the congregation but is recited by every Muslim privately at home, or wherever he may be at the time; it may, however, be made a prayer of the congregation. This prayer may also be performed at any time of great calamities: violent storm, inundations, earthquakes, etc., etc. (Ghazáli 126; Kashf 232; Faith of Islám, 272.)

[2] For three consecutive days the Imám goes out with the people, rich and poor, high and low, on foot in a procession to some public place, all being dressed in old, well-worn or patched clothes with their heads bent to the earth and showing in every possible way their sorrow, repentance and humiliation. Arrived at the place of prayer, the Imám stands up, his

Within the Ka'ba any kind of prayer prescribed, redeeming, supererogatory, single or in a body may be
offered, without regard to position, place or time. It is
even allowed to turn one's back to the Imám. It is called
the (الصلاة في الكعبة).[1]

The Prayers used for a burial service are called the
صلاة الجنازة. When a person is about to die, the attendants
place him on his back or on his right side, with his face
and feet towards the Qibla, unless circumstances prevent
it. He is then made to repeat the words of the confession
of faith. His last words ought to be : "There is no God
but God!"[2]

---

face turned towards the Qibla, and lifting up his hands offers up supplications, the people sitting with their faces also turned towards the Qibla confirming those petitions by saying : "O God grant us a bountiful, refreshing
rain."......While thus imploring divine help, the Imám turns his coat
inside out or upside down in sign of their anxiety to see a change of
weather.

Care must be taken that no non-Muslims join in this procession and
supplication. They may, however, go out by themselves and offer up their
supplications and prayers. Whether God answers the supplications of
unbelievers is a controverted question, some learned men denying, others
affirming it.

1 Turning one's face towards the Imám is not allowed, as this might
be misunderstood as if the prayers were addressed to him. In support of
this, the example of Muhammad is cited, who, on the day of the conquest
of Mecca, performed a prayer in the midst of the Ka'ba at a non-canonical
hour. (Ibn 'Abidín i. 673-674.)

2 On this occasion it is desirable to read the Súra Yá Sín and the Súra
of Thunder. After death has taken place, some say the corpse is to be
addressed thus : "O. N. N, remember what was thy condition in this world
and say : 'I am pleased to accept God as my Lord, and Islám as my religion and Muhammad as my prophet.'" The jaws are then tied up, the
eyes closed with a prayer for his acceptance with God, the members
stretched, and a sword or piece of iron placed on the belly to prevent its
becoming swollen. It is then laid on a bed or plank, which has been
perfumed all round an odd number of times, and washed, whether it be the
corpse of a man, a woman or a child. It is stripped naked except the
part between the navel and the knees, and the Wudú is performed with

special care. If the dead person was ' junub,' a woman in her courses or
in childbirth, the washing is done with a decoction of aromatic plants
and then rubbed with camphor. The corpse is carefully dried, and the
head and beard are covered with aromatic substances, whereupon it is
wrapped up and tied in a shroud of white cloth called the kafan (الكَفَن).
The kafan of a man consists of three pieces : the shirt (قَمِيص), the izár
(الإزار), a piece of cloth reaching from the navel to the knees or ankle
joint and the sheet (لفافة) covering the whole body. The kafan of a
woman consists of five parts : the chemise (دِرْع), the khirka (خِرقة),
a small piece of cloth to cover the bosom, the khimár (خِمَار), a piece of
cloth to cover the head the izár and the sheet to cover the whole body.

After the corpse has thus been duly washed, wrapped up and placed
on the bier (الجِنازة), the prayer for the dead is recited. These operations and the attendance at the funeral is a duty, called فَرْض كفاية, or a
duty which is not obligatory on every individual of the Muslim community ; if only a few fulfil it it is sufficient ; but if none fulfil it, the whole
community are guilty of sin. The burial service takes place in some open
space near the dwelling of the deceased person, or near the grave-yard.

The following is the order of the service. Some one present calls out :
"Here begin the prayers for the dead." Those present arrange them
selves in three, five or seven rows opposite the corpse, with their faces
towards the Qibla. The Imám stands in front of the ranks near the
chest (صَدْر) of the corpse, this being the seat of faith ; if the Sultán be
present, he is the person to lead in prayers, otherwise his representative,
the Qádi, Imám, or nearest relative of the dead person (الولّي). The
whole company, having assumed the Qiám, recite the niyya : "I purpose
to perform prayers to God for this dead person, consisting of four takbirs."
Then placing the hands to the lobes of the ear they say the first takbír :
" God is great," then folding the hands, the right over the left, below the
navel, they recite the "Praise."

Then comes the petition (الدُّعَام) : "O God have mercy on Muhammad
and his descendants, as thou didst bestow mercy and peace and blessings
on Abraham and his descendants—Thou art praised "....Then follows the
third takbír, after which the following petition (دُعام) is recited : " O God
forgive our living and our dead, those of us who are present, and those
who are absent." (اللَّهمَّ اغفر لِحيِّنا و ميِّتنا و شاهدنا و غائبنا و صغيرنا و كبيرنا
و ذكرنا و أنثانا ـ اللهم من احيتَه منا فاحيه على الاسـلام و من توَّفيتَه منا
فتوفَّه على الايمان)

The صلاة المعذور - صلاة المريض is the Prayer of the
Sick. A man who is sick and cannot stand erect or
bow down without injuring himself is allowed to recite
his prayers in any posture that is convenient for him. He
is to face the Qibla, or at all events to have his feet towards the same. Instead of observing the various postures, if he is not able to do so, it suffices for him to make
a sign with his head (ايماع). It is desirable, that on his
recovery he should make up the neglected prayers by so
many redeeming prayers; should his illness, however, last
longer than a day and a night, he is not obliged to perform
these redeeming prayers. (For more details *see* Kashf
i. 197.)

The Redeeming Prayer is called قضاءُ الفوائت. When
the Muslim has for some weighty reason been hindered

Then follows the fourth takbír and the Salám right and left. The
burial service being now over, the people seat themselves on the ground
and raise their hands in silent prayer in behalf of the deceased soul,
after which the chief mourner gives permission to the people to retire
saying: "There is permission to depart;" this is the اذن العامّ, or general
permission. The corpse is then placed in its grave (اللَّحد), head and feet
towards Mecca; those who place it saying: "We commit thee to the
earth in the name of God and in the religion of the Prophet." Those who
have stayed behind them recite the Fátiha in the name of the deceased,
and again, when they have proceeded about forty paces from the grave
they recite another Fátiha, for at this juncture, it is said, the two Angels
Munkar and Nakír examine the deceased as to his faith (Faith of Islám,
204-276).

Muhammad said: "Hasten to bury the dead, for it is not becoming
that the corpse (جيفة) of a Muslim be long kept in the midst of his
family," and also: "Any Muslim to whom four individuals (Muslims) bear
good testimony, God will make him enter Paradise." (Kashf i. 242-243)
"He who dies in the early morning ought not to rest at midday anywhere
but in his grave." Muhammad at first prohibited visiting the tombs, but
later on he first allowed it to men and then to women also.

in performing one or more of the obligatory prayers, it is his duty to perform what he has omitted at the earliest opportunity, before he performs the next obligatory prayer.

The Prostration of Forgetfulness, سجدتا السهو - سجود السهو, consists of two prostrations which the Muslim is bound to perform at the conclusion of the prayer, after the first salutation (which is towards the right), in order to make amends for any mistakes committed in prayer from forgetfulness or inattention, such as praying one rak'a instead of two, bowing twice instead of once. This prostration is obligatory only when more than one mistake has been made in one and the same prayer. If the Imám commits such mistakes, the whole congregation, which has joined him in prayer, should make such amends together with him. (Kashf i. 179-180).

(1) The Salutation of the mosque is called Tahiyyahu'l Musjid (تحيّة المسجد). Muhammad said: "Give the mosques their due." On being asked what that was, he replied: "When you enter a mosque pray two rak'as; (according to another tradition) make two prostrations before you sit down." (Kashf i. 171-172).

(2) The Prayer after the Wudú is called الصلاة عقب الطهارة. Muhammad recommended his followers to say a prayer, if it be but of two rak'as after every Wudú. (Kashf i. 172).

(3) The Prayer of Need is صلاة الحاجة. Muhammad used to say: "If any of you be in special need of anything whether from God or man, let him perform the Wudú carefully, then let him say a prayer of two rak'as, then praise God, invoke a blessing on the Prophet, then say: 'There is no God but God, the gracious, the bountiful. I pray for the blessing of thy mercy and pardon ... forgive all my sins," ... (Kashf. i. 172).

(4) The Prayer of Repentance is صلاة التوبة. Muhammad said : " If a man have committed a sin, let him go and perform the Wudú, then let him pray and ask God for pardon : verily God will forgive him, then recite Súra iii. 129-130, then let him say a prayer of two rak'as, obligatory or optional."

(5) The Prayer for an object lost is صلاة رد الضالة. When Muslims had lost anything they used to pray two rak'as, after which they said : " O God, the Restorer of lost things, the guide of what is gone astray, restore to us what we have lost, by Thy power and might, for it was of Thy bounty and gift."

(6) The Prayer for Guidance in making a good choice is صلاة الاستخارة. Muhammad used to say : " If any one desires to undertake a thing, let him pray two rak'as in addition to the obligatory prayer, then let him say the following petition (دعاء). " O God, I ask Thee to guide me in my choice by Thy omniscience, and to assist me with Thy omniscience, and I pray Thee to be gracious to me, for Thou art mighty and I am helpless, Thou art omniscient and I am ignorant. Thou knowest hidden things ; if Thou knowest, O God, that this thing is for my benefit as regards my religion and my subsistence and my latter end, then make straight the way and let it succeed and let it be blessed to me ; but if Thou knowest that it will be injurious to me, as regards my religion and my subsistence and my latter end, then remove it from me, and give me what is good for me and let me be content with it." Then let him mention the object of his choice. He also said : " Let a man thus pray for God's guidance seven times ; then let him consider what is nearest to his heart (الذي يسبق اليه قلبه); this will be best for him."

(7) The Prayer of Praise is صلاة التسبيح. The Prophet is reported to have exhorted his followers to observe the prayer of praise saying : " whosoever of you is able to do it, let him say it once a day; if he cannot, then once a week; if he cannot, then once a month ; if he cannot once a month, then once a year ; if he cannot, then once in his life." This is a prayer of four rak'as, at each of which is to be said, after the reading of the Qu'rán fifteen times : " Praise be to God, and glory be to God, there is no God but God."

(سبحان الله والحمد لله ولا اله الا الله والله اكبر). The same is to be repeated ten times at the 'bowing,' and at rising from it, and at each of the two prostrations and during the ' sitting ' between them, and at the tashahhud, making altogether seventy-five praises for each of the four rak'as.

On reading certain verses of the Qur'án a prostration should be made (عزائم السجود ـ سجدة التلاوة).[1]

Besides the aforementioned prayers, prostrations and petitions, the Muslim, who would reach a high degree of perfection and acceptance with God, is recommended to engage in certain additional devotional exercises called Wird (ورد) plural (أوراد), reading of a portion of the Qur'án, chiefly in the hours of night.[2]

---

[1] 'Ali says: "The عزائم السجود, that is, the verses of the Qur'án at which the believer is to prostrate himself are four : ـ حم ـ اقراء باسم ربّك ـ والنجم ـ السجدة ـ آلم السجدة" 'Umar says : "The Prophet taught me fifteen Sijdas in the Qur'án." (See Faith of Islám, 389.)

At the giving of thanks, a prostration should be made.

When any one brought good news to Muhammad he used to prostrate himself and thank God. Abú Bakr did the same. (خرّ ساجداً هكراً لله)

[2] Ghazáli (i. 199 et seqq) devotes several chapters to this subject from which it will suffice to give the following abstract : "From many verses of the Qur'án it appears that the only way of becoming united with

God is constant intercourse with him '' (دوام ذِكرِ المحبوب). This is the object of the devotional services called اوراد, in which the believer can engage at all times of the day as well as the night. The Wirds to be observed during the day are seven :

1st wird (من طلوع الصبح الى طلوع الشمس الورد الاوّل). The Muslim on rising up early mentions the name of God and praises Him and recites certain petitions (ادعيه) ; while dressing, he recites the appointed petitions, cleans his teeth with the siwák, performs the Wudú, then prays two Sunna rak‘as of dawn. After these rak‘as he repeats a petition, then he goes to the mosque with a collected mind. In a solemn and respectful manner he enters the mosque with the right foot first, saying the appointed petitions on entering and on leaving. He enters the first rank of worshippers if there be room and prays the two rak‘as of dawn, if he has not done so already at home ; then two rak‘as of ‘ Saluting the Mosque ’ (التحيّة), then sits down, repeating petitions and praises, waiting for the assembling of the congregation. After having performed the obligatory prayer of dawn, he remains sitting in the mosque till sunrise, meditating and repeating certain petitions and praises a certain number of times (3, 7, 10, 70, 100 times), counting them by the rosary (سبحة) and reciting portions of the Qur'án. (For the formulas to be repeated see Ghazáli i. 200-203).

2nd Wird. Between sunrise and an advanced forenoon hour, the worshipper says a prayer of two rak‘as, and when the sun has risen the length of a lance above the horizon (الضحى الاعلى) more rak‘as. This is the time when the believer may perform good works, such as visiting the sick, and accompanying funeral processions. When nothing of the kind requires his attention, he spends his time in repeating petitions, in zikr, meditation and reading of the Qur'án.

3rd Wird. Between morning (ضحوة) and the declining (زوال) of the sun, the believer, after taking care of his worldly affairs, engages in the devotional exercises as before mentioned.

4th Wird. Between the time when the sun has become somewhat high (زوال) and the noon prayer, four rak‘as between the Azán and the Ikámᵉ are said and portions of the Qur'án are recited.

5th Wird. Between noon and afternoon prayer (العصر), it is laudable to spend the time in the mosque in acts of devotion

6th Wird. This begins at the ‘Asr.

7th Wird. It begins at the time when the sun is near setting and its light begins to grow pale.

The Wirds of the night are five.

There are fifteen special nights in the year which are said to be specially favorable to devotional exercises and which the believer ought therefore scrupulously to observe, as special favors and mercies and blessings may be obtained on the same.   These are six nights in the month of Ramadán, *viz.*, five in the last part of the month, one of which will be the night of the Qadr (ليلةالقدر) and the seventeenth of Ramadán, on the morning of which the battle of Badr occurred.   The other nine most noble nights are : the first night of Muharram ; the night of 'Áshúrá' (عاشـوراء),

---

First night Wird.   After sunset, when the prayer of sunset has been performed to the time when darkness (عَتَمَة) has set in the worshipper says two rak'as, in which certain portions of the Qur'án are recited, then four long rak'as and as much of the Qur'án as time allows.   This Wird may be performed at home ; but it is preferable to do so in the mosque (Ghazáli i. 205).

The second night Wird.   This is from the darkness of the last 'Isha' (العشاالآخرة) to the time when people retire to sleep.   This consists of three things : (1) the obligatory 'Isha' prayer : ten rak'as *viz.*, four before it and six after it ; (2) performing a prayer of thirteen rak'as, the last of which is the Witr prayer.   In this about three hundred verses of the Qur'án are to be recited ; (3) the Witr prayer before going to sleep, unless one is accustomed to rise in the night, when it may be performed later on which is more meritorious (Ghazáli i. 205-206).

The third night Wird.   This consists of sleep, and sleep may well be considered a devotional act (عبادة), if enjoyed in the proper way.

The fourth night Wird.   This is from the time when the first half of the night is spent to when only one-sixth of it still remains.   At this time the believer ought to rise from sleep and perform the prayer of tahajjud.   This prayer is also called the Hujúd (الهُجُود sleep).   Muhammad mostly made it a prayer of thirteen rak'as.

The fifth night Wird.   This begins with the last sixth of the night called the Sahar (وقت السَّحَر), the early morning before dawn to the appearing of dawn (واذا طلع الفجر نقصت أوراد الليل(الفجر)).   To these devotional exercises it was considered meritorious to add four additional good actions : fasting, almsgiving, visiting the sick, attending funerals.

the famous fast day of the Jews, and for some time of the Muslims also ; the nights of the first and the middle and the twenty-seventh of the month of Rajab ; the night of the 15th of the month of Sh'abán ; the night of 'Arafa (عَرَفَة) and of the two festivals (لِيلَتَا العِيدَيْن). The days most favorable to prayer are said to be nineteen (الايَّام الفَاضلَة) *viz.* ; the day of 'Arafa ; the day of 'Áshúra' ; the twenty-seventh day of Rajab, on which Gabriel is said to have been sent to Muhammad with the divine mission ; (بالرِسالة) the seventeenth of Ramadan ; the middle of Sha'ban ; Friday ; the two days of the two great Festivals, and the appointed days of the month of Zú'l-Hijja (الايَّام المعلومات) and the days of Tashríq (نشريق). The most excellent days of the week are said to be Thursday and Monday, on which the account of men's actions are taken up and presented to God. (Ghazáli i. 216-217.)

There are special prayers for every day in the week.

Sunday (day time). Muhammad said : " He who on Sunday says a prayer of four rak'as, reciting the Fátiha in each rak'a, will find that God records these in His account book as so many good actions (حسنات) as there are Christian males and females in the world."

Monday. When the day is somewhat advanced towards noon, he who says a prayer of two rak'as and recites in each rak'a the Fátiha and the verse of the throne, two taawwuz, and asks for pardon ten times, and prays for blessings on the Prophet ten times, God will forgive him all his sins.

Tuesday. Ten rak'as at noon, and the reading of the Fátiha, will gain remission of sins for seventy days.

Wednesday. Twelve rak'as before noon, and Qur'án reading and certain formulas will get remission of all past sins, deliverance from the tribulations of the grave and the reward of a prophet in the future world.

Thursday. A prayer of two rak'as said between noon and afternoon and the reading of portions of the Qur'án get a reward, such as he who fasts during the months of Rajab, Sha'bán and Ramadán and performs the pilgrimage to Mecca obtains.

Friday. He who, after having carefully made his ablutions, says a prayer of two, four, eight or twelve rak'as, will find that God will raise him in Paradise 200, 400, 800 or 1,200 degrees respectively and wipe out 200, 400, 800 or 1,200 sins, respectively.

Sunday night. Twenty rak'as, reciting the Fátiha in each, repeating: " Say God is one " (قل هو الله احد) fifty times, and : "I ask for pardon" (استغفر الله عز و جل) one hundred times, bring a rich reward.

ALMS.—The giving of the duly appointed Alms (tithes, poor rate, taxes, tenth, زكاة)[1] is another of the five foundations of Islám, next in importance to prayer. It rests on a distinct command of the Qur'án. "Perform the prayer and give the alms." Súra ii. 40: (Súras ii. 77, 104; iv. 79; ix. 5, 11; xxii. 42, 78; xxiv. 55; lviii. 14; lxxiii. 20) and is therefore absolutely obligatory.

---

[1] It is called زكاة augmentation, purification, (from زكي to increase, augment; to be, to become pure), because the portion a man gives of his property in alms is considered to purify and sanctify that property and cause it to increase by drawing down a blessing on it. This legal tax is to be paid annually by every Muslim subject towards the support of the poor, the carrying on of holy war against infidels, the spread of Islám and the maintenance of Muslim institutions. It is mentioned in eighty-two passages of the Qur'án in close connection with prayer. Voluntary alms (صدقة) are also meritorious acts strongly recommended in the Qur'án and the Hadíth (Súra ii. 274-275); but are left to the free choice of every believer. The term صدقة is occasionally also used to designate the obligatory alms,

but زكاة is the proper technical term for the latter and is never used to designate voluntary alms-giving. Muhammad used to say : "He who pays the Zakát of his property, evil will be removed from him. Make your wealth sure and heal your sick by giving alms."

(حصّنوا اموالكم بالزكاة و داووا مَرْضاكم بالصدقة)

The Zakát is incumbent on every Muslim who is free (حرّية), sane (عَقْل), adult (بُلُوغ), provided he possesses, in full, property the amount or value of such estate or effects as is termed in the law the Nisáb (نِصَاب), (حولى) and that he has been in possession of the same for a full year. (4 .Ibn 'Ábidín ii شرط افتراض الزكاة عقل و بلوغ و اسلام و حرّية و ملك حولى) The Nisáb is the amount, or value of property, which is subject to this tax. A smaller amount than the fixed Nisáb is not subject to the payment of the tax.

The Zakát of various kinds of property is to be paid on the following conditions :

(1) Animals زكاة الحيوان : of these the Zakát is due on the following five conditions :

(a) they must come under the term cattle (نَعَم), such as camels, oxen, sheep, horses, which are not kept as articles of merchandize. Mules, donkeys, etc., are not subject to this tax.

(b) they must be cattle kept out at pasture (سَائِمَه). Animals fattened at home (معلوفه) are not subject to tax.

(c) they must have been in the possession of the owner for a whole year (الحَوْل لا زكاة فى المال حتى يحول عليه الحَوْل).

(d) they must have been the absolute and full property and under the full control of the owner (كمال المُلْك والتصرّف).

(e) the quantity or number of the property must amount to what is called the nisáb:

The Nisáb of camels (الابل) is five, that is, no Zakát is due on less than five camels, on 5 to 9 camels the tax due is one sheep of the second year, or a goat of the third year. (جذعة من الضان اوثنية من المعز) ; for 10 to 14 camels the tax is two sheep ; from 15 to 19, three sheep ; from 20 to 24, four sheep ; for any number from 25 to 35, the Zakát due is a yearling female camel (بنت مخاض) ; from 36 to 45, a two-year old female camel (ابنة لبون) ; from 46 to 60, a three-year old female camel (حقّة) ; from 61 to 75, a four-year old female camel (جذعة); from 75 to 90, two two-year old female camels (بنتالبون) ; from 91 to 120, two three-year old female

(حِقَّتان) ; from 120 to 133, three three-year old female camels; from 133 camels upwards a three-year old female camel (بنت لبون).

No Zakát is due on oxen, cows, buffaloes (زكاة البقر), till they reach the number of thirty. From 30 to 40 cattle a one-year calf (تبيع) is due; then up to 40 a two-year old female calf (مسنة) ; when the number exceeds 40 the Zakát is to be calculated according to this rule.

No Zakát is due on sheep, goats (زكاة الغنم) for less than 40 ; from 40 to 120, a two-year old sheep is due ; from 120 to 200, two goats or sheep ; above this one for every hundred. Thus the Zakát on sheep and goats is about 1 per cent. (Kashf i. 258).

(2) Zakát of the fruits of the field is the tenth (زكاة المعشرات); of wheat, barley (حبوب), dates, (تمر), raisins (زبيب) honey (عسل) the Zakát due is the tenth (العشر); but only when these amount to 800 من (مِنّ), weight of two katil); nothing is due on smaller quantities or on fruit before they are ripe and dry. The delivery takes place when they are quite ripe and dry (بعد التجفيف) Land watered by means of buckets or machinery pays only half of the tenth.

ان كان يُسقى ينضح أو دالية) Kashf i. 262.)

(3) Money, gold, and silver (زكاة النقدين): No Zakát is due on silver (فضة) till it amounts to 200 dirhem by the weight of Mecca, and of gold till it amounts to 20 Mithqál (مثقال), which is the Nisáb of silver and gold respectively. On 200 dirhems of silver the Zakát due is five dirhems or about the fourth of the tenth of the value. Of gold the Nisáb is 20 Mithqáls; when it has reached this amount, half a Mithqál is due, and for every additional four Mithqáls the tax due is two Qírát (قيراط). On objects made of silver or gold, such as cups, rings, bracelets, necklaces, etc., the same taxes are due, but only if they have been in the full possession of the owner for a whole year.

(4) Merchandize (زكاة التجارة): Articles of merchandize should be appraised; they are subject to the same tax as gold and silver (2½ per cent.) if they exceed 200 dirhems in value. The year (حول) commences with the possession of the capital with which the merchandize has been purchased; if the capital did not amount to the taxable sum, then the tax is to be paid from the time when the merchandize has been bought.

(5) Minerals and buried treasures, (زكاة الركاز والمعادن) : If a person find a deposit of buried treasure, one-fifth is due upon what consists of gold and silver, nothing is due on precious stones. There are differences on the subject between the Imáms of the various Schools, but they are of little importance.

(6) Alms of the feast of Fitr (زكاة الفطر ـ صدقة الفطر) : The distributing of alms at the feast of Fitr (and of the fast of Ramadán) on the first day of Shawwál (شوال) is obligatory on every Muslim. These alms consist of a measure, or half a measure or wheat or barley (صاع), or raisins or dates, taken from the best of what is used for food. The head of the family is bound to give these alms not only for his own person, but also for his wife, his children, his Muslim slaves or any other person dependent on him for their support. Muhammad commanded his people to distribute these alms to the poor early on the day of the feast, before going to assemble for prayer, saying : "Relieve the poor from going about (begging) on this day." Ibn 'Abbás says : "God commanded the giving of these alms as a purification of the person, who has fasted, from any forbidden act he may have committed, or any evil words he may have used ; if he distributes them before the prayer of the feast, they are accepted as Zakát ; if he does so after the prayer service, whatever he gives is only common alms (صَدَقة) not Zakát (Kashf i. 264-265). As to the manner of giving the Zakát كيفية اخراج الزكاة five points are to be considered :

(1) The intention ; the giver must intend the payment of the obligatory Zakát.

(2) The speedy delivery of the Zakát when due, that is after the year.

(البِدَار بعد الحَوْل)

(3) One kind must not be changed for another.

(لا يخرّج بدلاً بل يخرّج المنصوص عليه)

(4) The Zakát of one place must not be delivered in another place.

(لا يُنقل الصدقة الى بلد آخر)

(5) Zakát is to be distributed among the various classes of people who are entitled to the same, namely, the following eight classes (Súra ix. 60) (1) the poor (الفقير), who possesses nothing and are unable to acquire anything ; the (2) needy (المسكين), whose income does not cover their expenses ; (3) the collector of the Zakát (العاملون) including messengers, scribes ; (4) chiefs and influential men who have embraced Islám, to whom gifts (subsidies) are given in order to keep them steadfast and encourage others to embrace Islám (المؤلفة قلوبهم على الاسلام) ; (5) the slave who works to buy his liberty (المُكَاتَب) ; (6) those who have got into debt without being guilty of fraud ; (7) those who fight for Islám (الغُزَاة); (8) the wayfarer according to his want. The giver of the alms has to ascertain how many of these classes there exist in his place and to distribute them among the same. (Ghazáli i. 132 and 138-139.)

The qualifications for the recipients of the alms are (1) that they understand that the support they receive is to make their minds free from

FASTING.—The third foundation of Islám is Fasting
(صَوْم - صِيَام) which consists of total abstinence from
food, drink and cohabitation from sunrise to sunset.

(هو امساك عن المفطرات حقيقةً او حكماً)

Bathing, smoking, taking snuff, smelling a flower are
equally forbidden during fast time.

Muhammad used to say: "By God the odour of the
mouth of him who fasts is more acceptable to God than
the odour of musk."

With regard to the degree of obligation, a fast may
be divided into (1) obligatory Ramadán; (2) meritorious,
but not in the same degree, (3) supererogatory, such as
fasting certain days in the month.

There are various kinds of fasts :

(1) Obligatory, Ramadán fast (صوم الفَرْض - صوم رَمَضان).

(2) Atoning, redeeming fast (صوم القَضاء), a fast observed
at another time instead of one which has been omitted.

(3) Expiatory fast (صوم الكَفّارَة), by way of expiation
for some sin committed.

---

worldly cares and enable them wholly to give themselves to the worship
of God ; (2) that they thank the giver and invoke blessings upon him ; (3)
that they only accept such gifts as they know are lawfully acquired (حلال) ;
(4) that they take no more than they are lawfully entitled to : the debtor
what suffices to pay his debt, the poor and needy ought not to ask for more
than the support of one year ; (5) that they ascertain from the giver of the
Zakát the amount he has to dispose of, in order not to ask for an undue
proportion.

Muhammad allowed rich people to pay their Zakát for two years in advance, if they liked to do so. At first he ordered his people to give alms
only to Muslims, but later on he allowed them to give to people of all
religions. Muhammad used to give presents to those whose hearts he saw
favourably inclined to Islám.

(4) Vowed fast (صوم النذر), a fast vowed to be observed under certain circumstances.

(5) Supererogatory fast (صوم النفل), including all kinds of voluntary fasts.

The Fast of Ramadán is absolutely obligatory on every individual Muslim. It rests on a direct command of the Qur'án : " O believers ! A fast is prescribed to you, as it was prescribed to those before you that ye may fear God for certain days." (Súra ii. 179-184.)[1]

---

[1] Ramadán, is the ninth month of the Muslim year. In the month of Ramadán the Qur'án is believed to have been sent down by God, wherefore it is held to be sacred. This fast of thirty days (not the nights) is obligatory on every Muslim, male and female, who has reached the age of puberty. Very young children, idiots, the sick and infirm and aged, pregnant women or women who are nursing their children, are exempted from observing this fast.

The fast of Ramadán begins as soon as the appearance of the new moon of the month of Ramadán has been seen by two trustworthy witnesses. When the weather is overclouded and prevents the new moon of Ramadán from being distinctly seen, the testimony of one witness is sufficient ; but when the beginning of the fast rests on the testimony of one witness only, the fast must be continued and cannot be broken till the appearance of the new moon of the following month (Shawwal) is affirmed by two trustworthy witnesses. One is not sufficient in this case.

Things to be observed with regard to the fast of Ramadán are :

(1) Watching for the beginning of Ramadán (مراقبة اوّل مهر رمضان).

(2) The proposal. The believer must propose to himself to observe the fast ; and must reiterate this proposal every night for the fast of the next day....

(3) Total abstinence from food and drink (الامساك عن ايصال شىء الى الجوف). Bleeding, cupping does not invalidate the fast, nor what enters the mouth involuntarily or out of forgetfulness (ناسيًا).

(4) Abstinence from sexual intercourse during the day time (الامساك عن الجماع) except it be out of forgetfulness. At night cohabitation is permitted, and the fast is not thereby broken.

(5) Abstinence from pollution (الامساك عن الاستمناه بالكفّ).

(6) Abstinence from vomiting (الامساك عن إخراج القىء), unless it is involuntarily. Spittle may be swallowed.

The Sunna (السُنَن) to be observed during the fast of Ramadán in imitation of the Prophet are the following: (1) delaying as long as possible the Suhúr (تَاخِير السحور). The Suhúr is the meal taken at the time of the Sahar (سحر), that is, a little before day-break, (2) taking a date or drinking a little water before prayer, (3) giving up the use of the siwák from noon to sunset, (4) giving alms, (5) reading the Qur'án.

Voluntary fast (صوم التطوّع). Besides the thirty days fast of Ramadán, there are certain days of the month and the week, which it is considered most praiseworthy and meritorious to observe as days of voluntary fasting.[1]

If the fast is omitted or broken it must be made good by one of the our following acts (لوازم الافطار فاربعة) Ghazáli ii. 145-146) :—

(1) a redeeming fast (صوم القضاء), from قضى, to perform, to redeem, to make reparation for). A Muslim who has not observed the fast for some valid reason or otherwise (بعذرٍ او بغير عذر) is bound to make up for it by observing the fast omitted at some other time. He may do so either on consecutive or on separate days most convenient to him. A woman who omits her fast, on account of physical occasions, has to make good the omission some other time. The Companions, if on a journey they did not fast, were not required to make this redeeming fast.

(2) Expiatory fast (صوم الكفّارة), is incumbent on him who has transgressed the command of abstinence from sexual intercourse. It consists in setting free a slave or, if he be not able to do that, in fasting two consecutive months, or feeding sixty poor persons.

(3) Fasting the remainder of the day (امساك بقيّة النهار) is incumbent on him who has committed the sin of eating or drinking on a fast day.

(4) Ransom (فديّة). A woman with child, mothers giving suck, who do not observe the fast on account of their being afraid to do harm to their children, are to give a ransom of a measure of wheat to a poor person for every neglected fast day, besides observing the 'redeeming fast'...

1 (1) Annual: the fast of 'Arafa; the fast of 'Ashúra' on the 10th of Muharram, and the first ten days of the month of Zu'l-Hijja and Muharram, and all the holy months.

The vowed fast (صوم النَّذر). When the believer has vowed a fast to God, he must strictly observe it. The neglect of it requires a redeeming fast; and, if it was vowed with an oath, the neglect requires an expiatory fast of sixty days.

Fasts may not be observed on the so-called forbidden days, *viz.*, the first day of the festival of Fitr and the four days of the festival of Adhá.

Muhammad used to say: "Fasting is one-half of patience, and patience is one-half of faith." Muhammad used to fast two days in the month, and he commanded his people to do so also, until the fast of Ramadán was revealed. Most of them disliked it and considered it a burden. Everyone who disliked fasting, used to feed sixty poor people; but when the verse 'Whosoever is present in the month of Ramadán, let him fast was revealed, the Prophet commanded all who were able, to keep it." He said: "God has said: 'fasting belongs to me, and I will reward it.'"

At first, sexual intercourse was prohibited also at night; but when Muhammad found that people transgressed the command, he allowed it, and the verse: "It is allowed to you to go into your wives" was revealed. Muhammad recommended his people to eat immediately after sunset, before performing their prayers; he also advised them to eat the meal called Suhúr a little before day-break, as it would strengthen them for the fast of the day, and afterwards to say the morning prayer. He used to say,

---

(2) Monthly fasts: the privileged days for fasting are the first day and the middle days, *i.e.*, 13th, 14th, 15th, which are called the white, bright days (الايّام البيض) and the last days of a month.

(3) Weekly fasts: the best days of the week for fasting are Monday, Thursday and Friday.

"The handles of Islám and the pillars on which it is built up are these,—Confession that there is no God but God, the appointed prayer and the fast of Ramadán—he who forsakes one of them becomes an infidel, whom to deprive of his wealth and his life is lawful."

It is the duty of devout Muslims to seclude themselves in the mosque during the month of Ramadán and abstain from all worldly business, devoting this time to reading and meditating on the Qur'án, the Hadíth and other religious literature. Muhammad used thus to spend the last ten days of Ramadán and to exhort his people to follow his example. This seclusion is called I'tikáf [1] (اعتکاف). Women also may spend I'tikáf, not however in a mosque, but in a room in their houses (تعتکف في مسجد بیتها).

THE HAJJ. The pilgrimage (الحج) to the Ka'ba, the holy house at Mecca (البَیت الحرام), is the fifth foundation on which Islám is built up. [2] The performance of this

---

[1] There are three kinds of I'tikáf: (1) the I'tikáf of Ramadán, which is a Sunna duty; (2) the I'tikáf a believer vows to observe at a certain time which is Wájib, (3) the I'tikáf observed at any other time, which is considered mustahabb.

The seclusion a man vows may be consecutive and is preferable in Ramadán, or it may be separate. If he has vowed a consecutive I'tikáf, he must not leave the mosque during the days of the same, except for the most necessary natural wants, or for performing his ablutions. He eats and sleeps in the mosque.

کانوا یحرجون و یقضون حاجتهم فی الجماع ثم یغتسلون و یرجعون الی معتکفهم فنزل قوله تعالی ولا تباهرو هنّ و انتم عاکفون فی المساجد (Súra ii. 188 ; Ghazáli i. 146).

The great fast day of 'Áshúra عاشورا, observed by Muhammad and many of his followers, is no doubt borrowed from the Jews who kept a fast on the 10th of the month of Tisri (Leviticus xvii. 29.) See Sale on the subject ; also Dictionary of Islám, 534.

[2] The object of this pilgrimage is the Ka'ba, a square primitive stone building at Mecca, which Muslims believe to have been built by Abraham,

pilgrimage, once at least in his life, is incumbent on
every Muslim, male and female, who is possibly able to
do it. (من استطاع اليه سبيلا) This duty rests on a special
command of the Qur'án. Súras xxii. 28 ; ii. 153, 192 ; iii.
90 ; v. 2.

---

and to which the pagan Arabs had from ancient times performed pilgrimages as to their national sanctuary, on which occasion they performed
the very same rites and ceremonies now observed by the Muslim pilgrims. The so-called black stone (الحَجَر الأسود), built up in one of the
corners of this temple, forms an object of special veneration to the pilgrim.
The Ka'ba has been adopted as the central sanctuary of the whole
Muslim world.

The conditions (شرط لزوم الحَجّ) under which a Muslim is bound to perform the pilgrimage are these: (1) full age; (2) Islám ; (3) sound reason ;
(4) fredom, a slave is not to perform it ; (5) ability, that is, he must be in
good health, and possess the means to defray his expenses and, at the
same time, to provide for the family he leaves behind ; the roads must be
safe. A woman must be accompanied by her husband or some near
relation.

The time during which the pilgrimage may be undertaken are the
months of Shawwal, Zu'l-Qa'da and the first nine days of Zu'l-Hijja, for
a pilgrimage undertaken at any other time is not the Hajj (the great pilgrimage) but is called ' Umra (عُمرَة), or minor pilgrimage or visitation,
in which all the rites and ceremonies of the Hajj, except the offering of
the sacrifices, are observed.

The Muslim before setting out on his pilgrimage must (1) repent of his
sins, restore what he has unjustly taken (رّد المظالم), pay his debts, pay
the allowances up to his return (نفقة), return pledges (ودائع), provide the
means for his journey, give alms to the poor, sick, etc., (2) choose a suitable
companion, a pious and charitable man ; (3) before starting say a prayer
of two rak'as and read suitable verses of the Qur'án ; (4) on arrival at the
door of his house say: "In the name of God, in Him I trust;" (5) on
mounting the animal say : "In the name of God, etc. ; " (6) perform the
greater part of the journey at night, and not to dismount till the day has
become hot; (7) not linger behind the caravan, at night one pilgrim
watches while the other sleeps ; (8) on ascending to say : " God is great ! "
on descending : " Praise be to God." For a detailed account see Ghazáli
i. 153-154 who treats of these subjects under the heads.

فى الحراسة - فى النزول - فى الركوب - اذ حصل على باب الدار - فى
الخروج من الدار - فى الرفيق - فى المال - مهماعلا

The Miqát (ميقات) are the starting places. On each of the various
roads leading to Mecca, there are, at the distance of about five or six miles
from the city, stages called Miqát, or starting places, where the pilgrims
collect and from whence they start in a body on their further journey to
Mecca, after having assumed the Ihrám (احرام) the pilgrim's garb. Muhammad appointed five such places of meeting.

(1)   For pilgrims coming from Madína a place called Al Halfa (الحلفة),
about six miles from Mecca ; (2) for those coming from Syria, Jukhfa
(جحفة) ; (3) for those from Irak, Zat 'Irk (ذات عرق) ; (4) for those coming from Yemen, Yalamlam (يلملم) ; (5) for those from Nejd, a place called
Qarnu'l-Manázil (قرن المنازل) ; (Ibn 'Abidín ii. 165).

When the pilgrim has reached his respective Miqát, he has to observe
the following five customs (آداب) : (1) he bathes and cleans his whole
body, proposing to himself to do it for the sake of the pilgrimage, he pares
his nails, combs his beard ; and (2) he divests himself of his clothes and
assumes the pilgrim's sacred robe, consisting of two seamless wrappers, one
being wrapped round the waist and the other thrown loosely over the
shoulder, the head being uncovered. Sandals may be worn, but not shoes
or boots. After he has assumed the pilgrim's garb, he must not shave any
part of his body, nor pare his nails, nor wear any other garment than the
Ihrám. He now enters upon a state or time, in which what before was
allowable or lawful to him is forbidden.

The pilgrim having now entered upon the Hajj, faces Mecca and makes
the Níyya, that is, he proposes to himself to perform the pilgrimage,
either Hajj or 'Umra as the case may be. It is laudable if he recites
the talbia, تلبية, (from لبى to declare one's readiness) : " Here I am for
Thy service, O God, I am ready." (لبيك اللهم لبيك).

It is laudable now to say the petition : " O God, I purpose to perform
the Hajj ; make it easy to me....O God, I offer to Thee my flesh and my
hair and my blood....I have vowed to abstain from women and perfume
and clothes out of desire to please Thee ! "

Then he repeats the talbia, every time he ascends a hill, or descends
into a valley.

Things prohibited to the Muslim (محظورات الحج والعمرة), as long as he
wears the pilgrim's garb, are : (1) wearing a shirt, drawers, shoes, turban
(قميص و السراويل و الخف و العمامة) ; (2) perfume (طيب), the atonement
for having used perfume is a sheep (الفدية دم شاة) ; (3) shaving, paring
nails, the atonement for trangression is a sheep ; (4) sexual intercourse,
the atonement for transgression is a cow or seven sheep ; (5) things leading

to sexual intercourse such as kissing and self-pollution, the expiation is a
sheep ; (6) killing game. The expiation for transgressing is cattle of the
value of the animal killed (Ghazáli i. 153).

The customs to be observed from the entrance into Mecca to the Tawaf,
or the going round the Ka'ba, (آداب دخول مكة الى الطواف) are as
follows:

(1) At a place called Zu-Túwa (ذو طوى), the pilgrim washes (bathes)
himself. Before the entrance into Mecca the pilgrim has to bathe nine
times.

(2) On approaching Mecca (أوّل الحرام وهو خارج مكة) he says : " O
God this is Thy sanctuary and the place of security; preserve my flesh
and blood....from hell-fire."

(3) It is desirable that he should imitate the Prophet by entering
Mecca from the side of Al-Abtah (الابطح) and leaving it by Al-Kuda
(الكُدَى).

(4) When he enters Mecca and obtains sight of the Ka'ba, he says:
" There is no God but God! God is great! "

(5) On entering the holy mosque (المسجد الحرام), he does so by the
gate of the Beni Sheiba (باب بنى شيبة) saying : " In the name of God,
by God, from God " on approaching the Ka'ba he says : " Praise be to God,
peace on his servants."

(6) After this he approaches the Black Stone and touches it with his
right hand and kisses it saying : " My pledge I have delivered, my vow I
have fulfilled, bear thou witness that I have done it."

(اللّهمّ امانتى اديتها و ميثاقى و فيتهُ – اشهد لى بالموافاة). When it is not
possible for him, on account of the throng, to touch the black stone
with his hand, it suffices to touch it with a stick and to kiss the end
which has come in contact with the stone (Ghazáli i. 155). After this he
performs the circumambulation, during which the following is to be observed : " He must be careful to be in a state of outward and legal purity.
He then takes up part of the Ihrám under his right arm and throws
it over his left shoulder (يطبع قبل الطواف), " making " one end hang
down on his back and the other on the chest, thus he repeats the talbia and
appropriate petitions. This is called the Tawáf of the arrival. When he
has thus arranged his pilgrim's garb (اذا فرغ من الاطباع), he stands so
as to have the Ka'ba on his left, at a distance of about three steps, and the
black stone in front and then passes before it with his whole body
(يمر بجميع الحجر بجميع بدله)."

Before the black stone he says : " In the name of God, God is great "
.... and then goes round the sanctuary, beginning on the right and

leaving it on the left .... after this he reaches the door of the sanctuary, when he says certain petitions, and praises God till he reaches the Ruknu'l 'Aráqí (الركن العراقى), and after it the Mizáb (ميزاب), then the Ruknu'l Shámi (الركن الشامى), then the Ruknu'l Yamáni (ركن اليمانى), reciting at each of these places the appointed ejaculations and petitions. He has now performed one turn or procession (طَوُف) round the Ka'ba. In the same manner, and repeating the same petitions, etc., he encompasses the Ka'ba seven times (سبعة أشواط).

The first three processions he performs at a quick step; the last four times at the usual walking pace. It is desirable that every time he passes before the black stone, he should touch it either with his hand or with a stick and kiss it. It is also desirable that he kiss the Ruknu'l Yamáni.

After having thus encompassed the Ka'ba seven times, the pilgrim approaches the Ka'ba between the black stone and the door called the Multazim (الملتزم) and presses his body against the wall, placing his right cheek upon it and stretching out his arms and hands upon it and saying: "O God, O Lord of the ancient house! Save my neck from hell-fire." This is considered a place where prayers are answered.

The pilgrim now performs a prayer of two rak'as behind the Makám Ibrhimá in the first of which he recites Súra ii. 119, and in the second the Suratu'l-Ikhlas, 112. These are the two rak'as of the Tawáf (ركعتا الطواف); he then closes his processions by once more touching and kissing the stone.

(السَّعى بين الصَّفَا و المَروَة)

After having performed the seven processions round the Ka'ba, the pilgrim issues from the temple gate, called the gate of Safá, and ascends the hill of Safá a little so that he can see the Ka'ba; here turning his face towards it he repeats praises and petitions; then he walks alternately at a slow and quick pace till he reaches the top of the hill Marwa. Between these two hills he walks backward and forward, sometimes slowly, sometimes quickly, seven times repeating each time the same petitions. . . (Súra ii. 153). Women are dispensed from observing this custom. This is called the بين الصَّفَا و المَرُوَّة the walking between Safá and Marwa. This custom is said to be observed in remembrance of Abraham when he searched for water for his son Ishmael and ran backwards and forwards in great trouble of mind.

When the pilgrim has performed these rites he is at liberty to leave the sanctuary and return to his house in the town. He must, however, continue to wear the Ihrám and keep his mind in the same state of devotion and reverence. He may not as a duty but as an act of merit, repeat the processions round the Ka'ba up to the 7th of Zu'l-Hijja.

(الوقوف فى عرفات و ما قبله).

On the 7th of Zu'l-Hijja, three days before the feast of the sacrifice (عيد الاضحى), immediately after the noon prayer, the Imám, standing near the Ka'ba, informs the pilgrims of the approach of the feast and preaches a sermon in which he exhorts them to prepare themselves for the solemn rites to be observed and instructs them how to observe them. On the following day, the 8th, which is called يوم التَّروية, the day of watering, (so called because the pilgrims give drink to their camels, as a preparation for standing on 'Arafát, where there is no water), immediately after morning prayer, the pilgrims proceed to Mina where they spend the night. It is laudable to walk on foot, reciting the appropriate petitions. The next morning, the 9th, after having spent the night at Miná and performed morning prayer, the pilgrims proceed on their way to mount 'Arafát. On arriving there they pitch their tents in the plain of 'Arafát near the mosque. After the requisite ablutions they repair to the mosque where the Imám, after the decline of the sun, ascends the pulpit and after the Mu'azzin has called to prayer preaches a sermon, consisting of two parts; after this he performs, with the congregation, the noon and afternoon prayers together. The pilgrims then take their stand on 'Arafát, in any place of the hill, but not in the valley. While standing there one behind the other, they must not cease to pronounce words of praise and prayer and repentance (انواع التمجيد و التسـبيح و التهليل ; و الثنا - و الدعاء والتوبة), they must not leave 'Arafát till after sunset, so as to have spent there part of the day and the night (Ibn 'Ábidín ii. 187).

Leaving 'Arafát after sunset the pilgrims proceed to a place called Muzdalífa repeating petitions and praises. Arrived there it is desirable that they perform their ablutions in honour of the same. There the Imám and the assembled pilgrims perform sunset and night prayers together with one Azán and two Iqáma at the time of the ' Ishá and spend the night at Muzdalífa.

After midnight they prepare themselves to start and provide themselves with little stones or pebbles (seventy may suffice).

Very early after morning prayer on the 10th of the month, the procession begins to move towards Miná. On reaching the further end of Muzdalífa, they stop awhile and recite the appropriate petitions for this holy place (المشعر الحرام) ; then, leaving it before the sun rises, they press on till they reach the Wádi Muhassir (وادى مُحَسَّر) which they traverse in speed. When the sun of the great day of the sacrifice has risen, the pilgrims raise their voices in praise and prayer till they have reached Miná and the three heaps or pillars of pebbles not far from each other. The last one is called the Jumratu'l-'Aqaba (جمرة العقبة), known as 'the great devil,' (الشــيطان الكبير); the middle one is Jamratu'l-Wasita (الوسطى); and the first one Jumratu'l-Aula (الاولى). The first two heaps or pillars are on this occasion passed without taking any notice of them; but on reaching the Jamratu'l-'Aqaba, each pilgrim throws the seven stones of the 'Aqaba. This is done thus: "When the sun has risen about the length of a spear above the horizon, the pilgrim seizes one after the other of the seven pebbles between the thumb and the forefinger of the right hand and throws them at the pillar, saying, every time he throws a pebble: In the name of God....I do this in obedience to the Most Merciful and in spite of the devil." The object is to confound the devils who are supposed to be there. This ceremony is called the throwing of stones (رمى الجمر).

The pilgrim having thus performed the rite of throwing stones returns to Miná and there offers the sacrifice (يذبح الضحية) of the Feast of the Sacrifice. The victim may be a sheep, or a goat, or a cow, or a camel, according to the means of the pilgrim. It is a meritorious act for the pilgrim to slaughter the sacrifice with his own hand. This he does in the following manner: placing the head of the victim towards the Ka'ba, its forelegs being tied together, he stands on his right side and plunges the knife into its throat with great force crying with a loud voice: "In the name of God, God is great"....Part of the flesh of the sacrifice ought to be roasted and eaten by him who offers it, and the remainder distributed among the poor. The sacrifice offered on this occasion is called ضحية (pl. ضحايا) a word not used in the Qur'án, but in Traditions. It is derived from ضحى the advanced morning, (about 10 A.M.), because this is the time when this sacrifice is to be offered.

Besides this obligatory sacrifice of the pilgrim, there are other voluntary sacrifices and gifts, presents, offerings called هَدىّ (singular هَدْيَة), consisting of animals (camels, oxen, sheep) which a Muslim, who cannot perform the pilgrimage, sends as offerings to the sacred temple. These offerings are branded and sent off with strings, necklaces (قلائد) round their necks, (Súra v. 2, 96, 98) in sign of their being set aside as offerings to the sanctuary, so that they may not be interfered with (see Ibn 'Abidín ii. 269. باب الهدى). The sacrifice (camel) of thanksgiving is to be thus designated, but not the sacrifice of obligation (بدن الجمر دم الاحصار والجناية). Such offerings are often presented as voluntary gifts by pilgrims besides the obligatory sacrifice and are dealt with like the obligatory sacrifices, except that their being presented at 'Arafát is not strictly required. Muhammad on his first pilgrimage slaughtered sixty-three camels.

The pilgrim now gets his head shaved, during which operation he repeats the appropriate petitions: for the bald it suffices to pass the

This lesser pilgrimage called the 'Umra can be performed at any time except the 8th, 9th, or 10th of Zu'l-Hijja, these being the days fixed for the Hajj, the great pilgrimage. It can be performed before or after the great pilgrimage, jointly with or separately from the same. It is not of the same importance or meritoriousness, nor a

---

razor over his head, for women to cut off a bit of hair. He has now fulfilled the greater part of his duties as a pilgrim and is restored to the first degree of his former freedom (التحلّل الاوّل). All things which had hitherto been illicit to him in his capacity of a pilgrim are now again licit to him, except sexual intercourse with women and hunting. He now returns to Mecca and encompasses the Ka'ba seven times in the same manner as the first time. This is called the Procession of visiting (طواف الزيارة) in distinction from the first, which is the procession of the arrival. This procession properly concludes the pilgrimage and the pilgrim may now put off the Ihram.

He has, however, two more duties to perform during the three days of the 11th, 12th and 13th which are called the days of tashriq (ايّام التشريق), days of exposing to the sun, drying the flesh, because now the pilgrim prepares provisions for the return journey by cutting slices from the flesh of the victims offered on sacrifice and drying them in the sun. The duties involved are spending the night at Minâ and repeating the act of throwing stones. The night thus spent at Minâ is called the Night of Rest (ليلة القر). On the second day of the feast he performs his ablutions for the act of throwing the stones (اغتسل للرمى) and then repairs to the first pillar which is near 'Arafât, and throws at it seven stones, then to the second pillar and then to the third pillar, where he again throws stones with the same petitions as before.

These duties fulfilled, he returns to Mecca and performs the procession of farewell (طواف الوداع) in going round seven times with the same petitions as formerly, then he performs a prayer of two rak'as behind the Makâm Ibrahim; he also drinks of the holy well of Zamzam (زمزم) and goes again to the place of the Ka'ba called Multazim pressing his body against it and reciting the appropriate petitions. Retiring backwards and steadily keeping his eyes fixed on the Holy House till it is out of sight, he makes his exit, and the Hajj with its obligatory and praiseworthy rites and ceremonies is completed. (For more details, and the proper petitions see Ghazáli i. 100.)

duty of the same obligation as the Hajj ; but still it is a
Sunna duty in imitation of the Prophet's example and in
obedience to his exhortation : "Join the 'Umra with the
Hajj, for truly the joining of both brings a blessing on
your days and your possessions, and wipes out your sins
and purifies you." [1]

---

[1] اِعْتَمَر - أَحْرَم بالعمرة, he performed the 'Umra. He who desires to
perform the 'Umra washes himself and puts on the pilgrim's garb and
begins the pilgrimage from one of the appointed stations; he proposes to perform the 'Umra and recites the talbia, then goes to the mosque of 'Áyesha,
and then says a prayer of two rak'as and the appointed petitions. He
then returns to Mecca and encompasses the Ka'ba seven times and runs
between Safá and Marwa. He then has his head shaved and the 'Umra
is completed.

It consists of the same rites and ceremonies as the Hajj, with this
exception that there is no sacrifice required. Residents at Mecca should
perform the 'Umra frequently. These are the four kinds of pilgrimages :

(1) The joined pilgrimage (حَجّ قِرَان), which requires the putting on
of the Ihrám once for both.

(2) The pilgrimage of enjoyment (حَجّ التَّمتُّع), which consists of first
performing the 'Umra, then, after having taken off the pilgrim's garb,
putting it on again at the proper time and performing the great Hajj.

(3) The great Hajj alone (اِفراد بالحَجّ).

(4) The 'Umra alone (اِفراد بالعمرة).

There are punishments of various degrees, according to the gravity
of the sin or negligence committed by the pilgrim. He has to offer a
sacrifice, or fast, or give alms (يجب دمان أودم أوصوم أوصَدَقة) for having
been in an unclean state, while encompassing the Ka'ba, for having had
sexual intercourse with his wife or slave after standing on 'Arafát. A
smaller expiation is inflicted for the use of perfume, covering the head
and so on.

If a pilgrim is prevented by an enemy, or illness (or, if a woman,
by the death of a near relation who was her protector during the pilgrimage,) he is at liberty to give up his pilgrimage and to defer it to the
following year.

A Muslim who is not able to perform the pilgrimage personally may do
so by proxy. This kind of pilgrimage is legal, and the merits of it are
placed to the account of him in whose favour it is undertaken, even if

JIHÁD.—The fighting against unbelievers - مَغَازِي - سِيَر الجِهَاد with the object of either winning them over to Islám, or subduing and exterminating them in case they refuse to become Muslims, and the causing Islám to spread and triumph over all religions is considered a sacred duty of the Muslim nation. It is not a duty incumbent on every individual Muslim, but on the nation as a whole. This is meant by calling it a general duty and not an individual duty. It rests on a direct command of the Qur'án. (Súras ix. 5, 6, 29 ; iv. 76-79 ; ii. 214, 215, 186 ; viii. 39-42.)[1]

---

it be a dead person. It is an acknowledged doctrine of Islám that the merit and reward of every kind of worship and good actions may be acquired for another person. He who performs the pilgrimage by proxy does not derive any merit for himself.

After the completion of the Hajj, it is considered most desirable and meritorious to visit Madína. Muhammad said : " He who visits me after my death is as if he had visited me during my life-time." The visitor performs a prayer of two rak'as near the pulpit, after which he visits the tomb of the Prophet (القبر الشريف) with the appropriate salutations.

On returning home it is a laudable custom for the pilgrim, whenever he ascends a hill, to say three takbírs, and when he comes in sight of his place of residence to say : " O God let me live in it in peace and grant me my portion," then to apprise his family of his arrival and to go first to the mosque and there perform a prayer of two rak'as.

Muhammad said : " Man does nothing, on the Day of the Sacrifice more pleasing to God than the shedding of blood, the blood which flows on the earth is accepted of God."

[1] A learned Muslim doctor gives the following definition of Jihád : " It is the calling on unbelievers to receive the true religion and fighting those who do not receive it." (الدَعا الى الدين الحق و قتال مَن لم يقبلهُ Ibn 'Abidín iii. 285-308 ; Bukhári ii. 110-168.) Muhammad used to say : ' Paradise is under the shade of the swords." الجنّة تحت ظلال السيوف " War is permanently established until the day of judgment." " One day of fighting is of greater value with God than fasting a whole month." رباط يوم فى سبيل اللّٰه خير من صيام شهر " He who dies without having ever

proposed to himself to engage in holy war dies the death of a heathen."

فرض كفاية Fighting is a. من مات ولم يحدّث نفسَه بالجهاد مات ميتة جاهلية
but should the infidels invade a Muslim territory, and the Imám under
such circumstance issue a general proclamation, then it becomes the duty
of every Muslim, man and woman, to fight the invaders, *i.e.*, it then
becomes a فرض عين.

At the beginning of his career Muhammad propagated the religion of
Islám by means of teaching, preaching and argumentation, and never had
recourse to force or compulsion. In several of the early Meccan Súras he
declared that he was sent only to preach and admonish. At Madína, when
at first he wished to win the Jews over to his side, he said that he had no
authority to compel any person to embrace Islám. There was to be "no
compulsion in religion" (لا اكراة فى الدين) Súra ii. 237; *see* Sell's Historical Development of the Qur'án, S. P. C. K., on this verse, p. 89, 206).
He exhorted his followers also to bear patiently those injuries which were
offered to them on account of their faith (Súras xxxiv. 2; xxxv. 22; ii. 113;
xvii. 106; xxv. 58; xxxiii. 44; xv. 94; iii. 19; lxxxviii. 22); but no sooner
was he, after the space of about twelve years' peaceful work, on his
flight to Madína, enabled, by the assistance of his adherents (انصار) in that
city to make head against his enemies, than he gave out that God had
allowed him and his followers to defend themselves against the infidels,
and, at length, pretended that he had Divine leave even to attack them
and destroy idolatry and set up the true Faith by the sword. The passages of the Qur'án sanctioning the use of the sword are considered by
Muslim divines as abrogating (ناسخ) those passages which recommend
peaceful means and which are then called abrogated (مَنْسوخ).

This progress from peaceful means to compulsion is thus stated by Ibn
'Abídin in iii. 237-238.

اعلم ان الامر بالقتال نزل مرتّباً. كان صلعم ماموراً بالتبليغ والاعراض - فامدع
بما توٴمر و اعرض عن المشركين . ثم بالمجادلة بالاحسن أُدع الى سبيل ربّك
الآية - ثم أُذن لهم بالقتال - ثم أُمروا بالقتال - ثم أُمروا بشرط السلاخ الاهـهر
الحرم ثم أُمروا به مُطلقاً

"Know thou that the command of fighting was revealed by degrees, for
the Prophet was at first commanded to deliver his message, then to
discuss and dispute and endeavour to convince the unbelievers by arguments, then the believers were permitted to fight, then they were commanded to fight at first at any time, except the sacred months, then
absolutely, without any exception." So it remains to this day. The
condition of fighting the unbelievers when they begin war and the prohibition of fighting during the sacred months are annulled (منسوخ) by

War is to be carried on with three classes of people.[1]

When a Muslim ruler conquers a country inhabited by non-Muslims, the inhabitants are to be offered three alternatives.[2]

---

the general and unconditional command: "Fight the unbelievers wherever you find them," (Súra ix. 5). This is called the verse of the sword. Muhammad himself gave the example to his followers. Ibnu'l Athír says: "The number of the battles (غَزَوَات singular غَزْوَة) fought under the orders of the Prophet is twenty-seven; that of the smaller warlike expeditions (سَرَايَا singular سَرِيَّة) is forty-six." He himself fought in nine battles, the others were commanded by some of his Companions.

[1] With all idolaters and infidels, who refuse to submit to the Muslim rule by either embracing Islám or paying tribute.

With those who are under Muslim dominion, but rebel and refuse to continue paying the tribute.

With such as rebel against the Imám, even though they are Muslims, and with all who begin war.

It is the duty of the Imám to send an expedition, at least once or twice a year, to the land of warfare (دَارُ الحَرب) to fight the unbelievers. If he neglects to do so, he commits a sin, except when he knows that they are not strong enough to subdue the enemy.

[2] The reception of Islám, in which case they become secure as to their persons, families and possessions and enjoy all the privileges of Muslims, whose brethren they have become.

If they do not embrace Islám, they have to pay the tribute, or poll-tax (الجِزْيَة), by which they obtain protection and become Zimmis (ذِمِّي), that is, subjects, allowed to profess their own religion, provided it be not gross idolatry. It is the duty of the Imám to explain to those who have to pay the poll-tax the amount to be paid and the time at which payment is required. This capitation-tax is of two kinds: (1) that which is established voluntarily and by composition, when people make peace with Muslims before war takes place; and (2) that which the Imám imposes after conquest on every person, according to his means.

If they will neither embrace Islám nor pay the poll-tax; then the women and children will be made captives and so become slaves, while the men will be slain, or otherwise disposed of at the pleasure of the Imám.

Muslims ought to call upon non-Muslims to embrace
Islám before they attack them.   If they do embrace

The capitation-tax is called Jizza (جِزْيَة from جَزَى, to satisfy, to com-
pensate), because it is a compensation for the life of the unbeliever.   It is
a kind of tax (خَرَاج) and may be called capitation-tax (خَرَاج الرَّاس).   It is
also called by some captivity-tax (الجَالِيَة from جلا to lead into capitivity),
as it was first applied to the Zimmis who were by order of the Khalif
'Umar carried away from Arabia into captivity.   Muhammad had spared
the lives of the Christians of Nijrán, on condition of their delivering annually two thousand cloaks, and 'Umar spared other Christians on condition
of their paying double the taxes required of Muslims.   The taxation takes
place at the beginning and the payment at the end of the year, or at the
end of every month or two months.   This poll-tax is taken from "people
of the book " (كتابى), that is, Jews, Samaritans and Christians of all
denominations and from the Magi and idolaters on condition that they
are not from Arabia.   Idolaters from Arabia and apostates must choose
between Islám and the sword.   Women, children, the blind, crippled and
monks are exempt from paying the tax.

The capitation-tax must be delivered by the person who owes it himself ; it cannot be sent by another person ; but the person who owes it
must himself hand it over, stand while the Muslim, who receives it, sits
and strikes him on the neck, saying : "Give it, O, thou enemy of God "
(Ibn 'Abidín iii. 294).   The Zimmis who are under the protection of
Muslims are not allowed to build either churches or synagogues, or con-
vents, or burying places, or any other place of worship ; their churches in
Arabia must be pulled down, and they themselves must not be allowed
to reside in any of the towns or villages of Arabia, for the Prophet declared that the existence of two different religions cannot be allowed in
Arabia (لا يجتمع دينان فى جزية العرب) (Ibn 'Abidín iii. 295-297).   A
church when destroyed, or in ruins, cannot be built up again.

The Zimmi must distinguish himself from the Muslim by wearing
different clothes " lest he receive the marks of honour and respect due to
the Muslim only."   He is to be kept in a state of subjection and abject
humiliation.   He must not ride on saddles like Muslims.   When the
Muslim stands, he may not sit.   No Muslim ought to show him respect
and honour.   If he meets him in the street he must make him go aside.
They must not live in large numbers in the midst of Muslims, and, if they
possess houses of their own, they must be forced to sell them to Muslims.
Their houses must be lower than those of Muslims.   A Zimmi loses his

Islám, it is not necessary to go to war with them, because
that which was the design of the war is then obtained
without war.[1]

DÁRU'L HARB, DÁRU'L ISLÁM.—The world, according
to the doctrine of Islám is divided into great divisions : [2]

---

right of protection (أَمَان), if his country becomes a land of warfare or if
he does not pay the poll-tax. If he should insult the Prophet he is to
be killed.

[1] If a Muslim attacks unbelievers without first inviting them to embrace
Islám he is an offender, but still if he do attack them before so inviting
them, and slays them and take their property, neither fine, expiation nor
atonement are due by him, because that which protects them, *viz.*, Islám,
does not exist in them, nor are they under protection by place (living in
a country of Islám). It is laudable to invite people to Islám, when a call
has already reached them, but it is not obligatory, as it is recorded of
the Prophet that he plundered and despoiled the tribe of Al-Mustalik by
surprise, and he also agreed with Usama to make a predatory attack on
Kubna at an early hour and to set it on fire, and these attacks " were not
preceded by a call."

Some doctors, however, say that such a call and invitation to unbelievers were required in the beginning of Islám when it was not generally
known, but that at the present time, when Islám has spread far and wide,
and is well known, the Imám has full liberty either to call unbelievers to
accept Islám, or to attack them without any previous call. (Ibn 'Ábidín
iii. 241-242).

When unbelievers resist, then it is the duty of the Muslims, with God's
assistance, to attack them with all manner of warlike engines, and they
must also set fire to their habitations, even at the risk of burning them,
their wives and their children, and inundate them with water, and tear
up their plantations and break down their grain, because by these means
they will be weakened. . . These means are, therefore, all sanctioned by
the law ضرب و هدم و قطع اشجار و نحو ذلك. (Ibn 'Ábidín iii. 242).

[2] The Land of Warfare (دار الحرب) is any country belonging to infidels,
which has not yet been subdued by Islám, or " a country in which peace
has not yet been proclaimed between Muslims and unbelievers."

The Land of Islám (دار الاسلام) is one governed according to the laws
of Islám. It again becomes a Land of Warfare under the following circumstances : (1) when the country is governed according to the laws of
unbelievers instead of the laws of Islám (باجراه احكام اهل الشرك) ;
(2) when the country in question becomes joined to a Land of Warfare

PLUNDER (غَنِيمَة).—This, taken from the enemy by
force during the war, is distributed among the combatants.   The tribute received from unbelievers is paid over
to the general treasury for the benefit of the Muslim
nation at large.[1]

---

and no other Muslim country lies between them; (3) when no more
protection (أَمَان) remains for either Muslim or Zimmi, though they had,
at first, enjoyed protection when the country was conquered by Muslims.
The Land of Warfare becomes a Land of Islám when the laws of Islám
are promulgated in it and it is governed in accordance with the same, so
that the Friday prayers and Muslim festivals are observed.

It is not allowed to disfigure people by cutting off their ears and noses.
Though it is related that the Prophet disfigured the 'Uníín (العَرَنِيِين),
such actions are abrogated by subsequent prohibitions. Muslims should
not slay women or children, or aged bed-ridden and blind persons, or
monks in their cells devoting themselves exclusively to the service of the
church.   It is allowed in war to cut off the head of the unbeliever and
carry it about, and to dig up the graves of infidels in search of objects
of value.

If the Muslim, in fighting, meet his father in the host of the infidels he
must not begin fighting him. Anyhow he must not slay him; but hold
him in view till some other come and slay him "for thus the end is
answered without the son's slaying his father, which would be a sin." If
a free Muslim, man or woman, has granted pardon to an unbeliever or
a company of them, the promise must be respected by Muslims. The
infidel who asks for pardon is to be spared.

If the Imám consider it desirable in the interest of Islám to make peace
with any particular tribe or people, he is allowed to do so. He may either
accept a ransom from them or pay them a sum of money to obtain peace,
if he feels that he is not strong enough to overcome them. If after such
an agreement he should, however, perceive that it is more advantageous to
break it, he may lawfully renew the war; due notice must, however, be
given.   In case a country submits to Muslim rule peacefully, the land remains the property of its original inhabitants, on condition of their paying
the land-tax (خَرَاج) for the same.

1 If the Imám conquers a country by force of arms, he is at liberty to
leave the land in the possession of the original proprietors, on condition
that they pay the land-tax besides the capitation tax, or he may divide it
among the Muslims. Muslims who become proprietors of the same, have
to pay the tenth and nothing else. With regard to movable property, it

CAPTIVES.—Unbelievers taken in war, except idolaters of Arabia and apostates who must be killed, who do not embrace Islám may either be killed, or made captives, (أُسِيرٌ plural أَسَارَى,) or be granted their liberty on condition of their becoming Zimmis, according to the decision of the Imám.[1]

---

is not lawful for the Imám to leave it in the possession of the infidels, but he must bring it away with the army and divide it among the soldiers.

Four-fifths of the spoil belong to the troops, and one-fifth must be divided into three equal portions (1) for the relief of orphans, (2) feeding the poor, (3) the entertainment of travellers; this latter class includes the poorer members of the Prophet's family of the Bani Háshim. Captives form part of the plunder. All cattle and baggage which cannot be carried away upon a retreat must be destroyed. For the proper distribution of the booty, the Imám ought to appoint competent men, who, on the army's entering the territory of the enemy, make a list of the combatants, distinguishing foot-soldiers from horsemen. He who goes to war on foot receives one portion, the horseman receives two. Women, children, slaves, non-Muslims may receive gifts (not portions) from the booty. The Imám may also promise the Muslim warriors additional rewards, in order to encourage them to fight bravely.

On the first considerable success of Muhammad in war, the dispute which happened among his followers in relation to the dividing of the spoil rendered it necessary for him to make some regulation concerning it. A divine commission was produced authorising him to distribute the spoil among the soldiers, at his own discretion, reserving the fifth part for the uses above mentioned. "They will question thee about the spoils, (الانفال) say: 'the spoils are God's and the Apostle's'...... and know ye that when ye have taken any booty, a fifth part belongeth to God and the Apostle and the near of kin and to the orphans and to the poor and to the wayfarer." (Súra viii. 1.)

Muhammad was entitled to a portion of the spoil like other members of the expedition; but he enjoyed the privilege of choosing and appropriating to himself, before the general distribution, as part of his portion, any object he desired to possess. This is called صَفِيَّة. Thus he took possession of a valuable sword called Zu'l-fiqár and Safía, the beautiful girl, from the spoil taken from the Jewish tribe of Khaíbar.

(هو الصفىّ كان يصطفّه لنفسه).

[1] It is not lawful to release infidel captives in exchange for the release of Muslim captives from the infidels (فداؤهم) nor to release them

PROTECTION, SECURITY (امان).—This is granted to infidels in the lands of the Muslims as well as to Muslims
in unconquered lands and must be scrupulously observed.
Protection given to a non-Muslim to enter and reside in a
Muslim place is not to be extended over a year, lest he
become a spy (جَاسوس - عَيْن). If he desires to remain
longer, he must become a Zimmi, and pay the capitation
tax.

BEITU'L-MÁL.—This is the name given to the public
treasury and is the place where the fifth of the spoils and
booty, the capitation tax levied on Zimmis, presents
received in return for protection, land taxes, the produce
of mines and treasure-trove, property for which there is
no owner and the Zakát are deposited.[1]

APOSTASY[2].—This is the forsaking of Islám by express-
ing such disbelief with the tongue, after one has been a
believer.

(الارتداد هو اجراء كلمة الكفر علي اللسان بعد الايمان).

---

gratuitously. Some, however, consider it lawful. Cattle and implements
of war must be destroyed. Women and children of infidels who cannot be
carried away must be left in a desert place, where they find neither water
nor food so that they may die of hunger and thirst, because it is not
lawful to kill them. The bodies of Muslim women, who die in the land
of warfare and cannot be buried in a safe place, must be buried so that
they may not be exposed to ill usage by the enemy.

1 From this property various expenses such as salaries, allowances, subsidies, expenses for the public good are defrayed. The salaries of Imáms
and Mu'azzins and other persons appointed in connection with Mosques,
of learned professors teaching the Qur'án and Traditions, of Qádis, soldiers,
and those who defend the boundaries also come from it. It defrays the
expenses of building bridges and mosques and of making ponds.

Lying is allowed in war. He who slays an enemy, takes his weapons
and no fifth is due on the same.

2 Some say that the mere forsaking of the faith, without giving expression to unbelief (كفر), constitutes apostasy, but the majority of the men
of the Hanafi School are of opinion that it is the forsaking of Islám

inwardly, together with the confession of one's unbelief that constitutes apostasy.

A Muslim who apostasizes is to be brought before the Imám and called upon to give up his unbelief and return to Islám. He is imprisoned for three days and invited every day to recant; if he asks for a further delay, he is to be granted the same; but if after that delay, he does not recant, he is to be killed. A female apostate is not subject to capital punishment, but must be kept in confinement till she recants. Some doctors say she is to be imprisoned and beaten every day till she recants or dies. The person who thus kills her, is not guilty. If either the husband or the wife apostasize, a divorce takes place *ipso facto*, no sentence of divorce is necessary. A boy under age who apostasiszs is not to be put to death, but to be imprisoned until he comes to full age (seven or eight years); if he continues in his unbelief he must be put to death. An insane person, a drunkard, or one forced is not held responsible for apostasy. If a person is so compelled by force to apostasize, his wife is not divorced, nor are his lands forfeited.

It is a controverted question whether, in the case of an apostate, (مُرْتَدّ) who repents and returns to Islám, his repentance and confession of faith are sufficient, or whether besides this he must abjure the religion he had adopted. Some affirm, others deny the sufficiency of the confession and return to Islám (لايكون مُسْـلماً حتى تبرأ من دينه و يقرّ انّه دخل فى الاسلام) Ibn 'Ábidín iii. 313). If the declaration of apostasy can possibly be explained in a different way, this must be done so as to clear the person from infidelity.

An unbeliever who insults (سَبّ) one of the prophets is to be killed; if he insults or curses God (انْ سبّ اللّه تعالى) and repents, the punishment must be remitted, for, in the case of transgression of man, the punishment is necessary, but in a transgression against God, the punishment can be remitted, for "God is forgiving and merciful." According to the Sunni doctrine, he who insults or curses the two first Khálifs, Abú Bakr and 'Umar, becomes an infidel; if he considers 'Ali superior to these he is an innovator, a heretic (مُبْتدع).

The sorcerer (الساحِر), that is, one who practises sorcery or considers it lawful, is an infidel and deserves death. The repentance of the Zindíq (زنديق hypocrite), as well as the sorcerer, if he repents before he is seized, is accepted and the punishment is remitted; but if he repents, after he is seized, his repentance is of no avail, and the sentence of death must be carried out. Whether the apostate who returns to Islám will lose or keep his former good works is a controverted question, some affirming others denying it.

REBELLION (البغاة ـ الفتنة).—A Rebel[1] is a person who withdraws from obedience to the rightful Imám, or rises against him without sufficient cause. If rebels have sufficient cause to refuse allegiance to the Imám and disobey his orders, they are not rebels. In this case, Muslims not implicated in the matter must abstain from assisting either party.

THINGS LAWFUL AND UNLAWFUL.—It is the duty of Muslims to exhort and assist people in doing good, and to dissuade and, whenever possible, to prevent them from doing evil. This is not the duty of every individual, but it is sufficient if some of the nation perform it. The two parts of this duty: exhorting to good works and dissuading from evil are included in the technical term Hisba (حِسْبَة). He who performs the duty is called the Muhtasib (مُحْتَسِب). On all the questions concerning the duties of a Muhtasib, the curious will find a detailed description in Ghazáli's *Ihyá*. Before the exhortation one must be sure that the person to be reproved has committed or intends to commit an unlawful action, and that he is likely to accept and act according to the advice. If it appears that the person will not listen, then the exhortation

---

'Alí says: "A Jewess insulted the Prophet, whereupon a man strangled her till she died. Muhammad declared that nothing was due for her blood " (ابطل دمها).

[1] There are three classes of rebels thus described (1) highway robbers (لصوص ـ قُطّاع الطريق), (2) rebels who disobey or rise against the rightful Imám without sufficient cause, (3) the Khawárij who reject the rightful Imám, whom they consider an infidel, and who hold it to be lawful to shed the blood of the orthodox Muslims, to plunder their property and to make their women and children captives. These are not to be considered infidels, as they build their false opinions on verses of the Qur'án which they misinterpret. These rebels must first be made aware of their error; if they refuse to be persuaded, they must be brought to allegiance by the force of arms.

is not a duty. If the duty can be exercised, it must be done gradually, first gentle reproof, then admonition, and then strong measures.

TRANSACTIONS (المعاملات).—Thus far in the consideration of Fiqh, we have dealt with the laws and regulations concerning worship and religious duties (عِبَادَات), such as Prayer, Almsgiving, Fasting and matters more distinctly religious. We now proceed to the second part, technically called المعاملات or transactions, which treats of the laws and regulations by which the private relations of Muslims among themselves and with unbelievers are ordered.

This part comprises

(1) Contracts (عَقَادَات) and agreements to which the mutual consent of the contracting parties is required such as marriage, buying and selling, etc.

(2) Orders (إيقاعات), treating of all matters depending on the will of a single person such as divorce, slavery, vow, etc.

(3) General laws and regulations (أَحْكَام), treating of various general laws and regulations which relate to the civil concerns of Muslims, chiefly such as concern inheritance, testimony and the power of the Qádi.

MARRIAGE (زِكَاح).—Marriage[1] is enjoined upon every Muslim and celibacy (عزوبة) is discouraged. Muhammad is reported to have said on the subject: " When the servant of God marries, he perfects half his religion," and also: " Marriage is my custom; he who dislikes it does not belong to me." " Marry and multiply, so that I may be glorified by my nation over other nations." Consequently

---

[1] Ibn 'Ábidín says: " There is no other devotional service instituted and practised on earth from the time of Adam, and which will continue in Paradise except marriage and faith. Marriage is considered a kind of

in Islám even the members of the ascetic Orders are
generally married.

Marriage is defined by Muslim jurists to be " a contract
by which the husband obtains possession of the wife, and
is allowed to enjoy her, if there be no legal impediment
preventing the same."[1]   The husband has power over the
wife, but not the wife over her husband.

The validity of the contract depends on the consent
of the parties, that is, the assertion and declaration of the
husband, and the acceptance by the wife, or her representatives.   The Qur'án says : " Marry what seems good
to you of women, by twos or threes, or fours, or what your
right hand possesses " (*i.e.*, slaves).   (Súra iv. 3.)

There are three kinds of marriage :

(1)   Legal permanent marriage (نكاح دائم).

(2)   Temporary marriage (نكاح المتعة), now illicit
according to the Sunni law, but not so with the Shí'ahs.

(3)   Marriage with a slave (نكاح الأمة).

---

devotional service, as it is the means of increasing the number of Muslims, and of keeping the believer in a state of chastity. If a man feels,
inclined to marry, it is his duty to do so, and if he fears that he will
be tempted to fornication, it is obligatory on him to marry.

[1] Liberty is allowed a woman who has reached the age of puberty to
marry, or to refuse to marry a particular man, independent of the wishes
of her guardian, who has no power to dispose of her in marriage, without
her consent or against her will. If she has been promised in marriage
during her infancy by her guardian, she has the right, on reaching her
majority, to ratify or dissolve such a promise. When a woman, adult and
sane, chooses to be married through an agent, she empowers him, in
the presence of competent witnesses, to convey her consent to the bridegroom. The expression of consent on the part of the woman may also
be given in an indirect way, without words. If a virgin is silent, or
smiles or laughs, it is taken as her consent.

In the selection of a wife, the Muslim is advised to look for the following qualifications in her (1) piety (ان تكون ذات دين), (2) good

As regards the validity of the marriage,[1] the Muslim is permitted to marry four free women (اربع من الحرائر), and to have as many slaves as concubines [2] (سرية) pl. (سَرَاري) as he may like (له التسرّي بماشاء من الإماء) Súra iv. 3).

The legal disabilities to marriage (اسباب التحريم) are (1) consanguinity (قرابة - نسب) ; (2) affinity (مُصَاهَرة) i.e., mother-in-law, step-grand-mother, daughter-in-law; (3) fosterage (رضاع), a man cannot marry his foster mother, his foster sister; (4) a man may not marry his wife's sister (الجمع بين المحارم - الجمع) ; (5) a man married to a free

---

character (حُسْن الخُلق), (3) beauty (حسن الوجه), (4) a small dowry (حفيفة المهر), (5) power to bear children (ان تكون ولودا), (6) that she be a virgin (ان تكون بكرا), (7) a good family, (ان تكون نسيبًا), (8) that she be not a near relation (ان لا تكون من القرابة القريبة). A free woman is preferable to a bond woman. (For further details see Ghazáli and Dictionary of Islám 674).

1 The conditions of the validity of the marriage are sound reason, puberty, freedom, that there be no degree of affinity which prevents marriage, and the declaration, on the part of the husband, and the acceptance on the part of the woman.

Ghazáli (ii. 22) says on the subject : '' There are four conditions which must be considered in the contract of marriage : (1) the consent of the guardian (اذن الولي و ان لم يكن فالسلطان). (2) the consent of the woman (رضاء المراة ان كانت ثيبًا بالغًا او بكرًا), (3) the presence of two trustworthy witnesses (حضور بالغًا شاهدين ظاهرى العدالة) (4) declaration and acceptance (ايجاب وقبول), pronounced in due form by two men (not females) authorized thereto. According to the Hanafi school there is no necessity for the intervention of the guardian.

2 Only slaves can become concubines. These may be either captives, taken in war or purchased by money, or descendants of slaves. Even married women, if taken in war, are, according to the injunctions of the Qur'an (Súra iv. 28), at the disposal of the Muslim conqueror.

woman may not add to her by marriage a female slave زِ إدخال أَمَة علي حرَّة (6) a man may not marry the wife or Muladda of another man, before the expiration of the woman's 'idda (عِدَّة), i.e., her period of probation ; (7) a Muslim may not marry an idolater or Majusiyya مشركة; (مجوسِـيّة - و ثنيّة) he may marry a Jewess, a Christian or a Sabean woman ; (8) a man may not marry his own slave, or a woman her bondsman (ان تكون مملوكاً للناكح مُلك يمين). (9) If a man pronounces three divorces upon his wife who is free, or two upon a slave, she is not lawful to him till she has been regularly married to another man called the Muhallil محلِّل, i.e., one who makes marriage lawful. He, having duly consummated the marriage, afterwards divorces her or dies, and when her 'idda from him is accomplished, she can remarry her former husband. (Sura iv. 26, 27 ; See Ghazáli ii. 22). A woman who has been divorced by the form called li'án (لعَان) can never be married to her former husband again.[1]

---

[1] After a man has made the choice of a female for marriage, the law allows him to see her first. He, accompanied by some friends, goes to the house of the agent and there settles the amount of the dowry which is paid at an early day. This is called the "writing of the contract." The Muslim law appoints no specific religious ceremony or rites to be observed on the occasion of marriage. Mutual consent in the presence of witnesses is sufficient to make the marriage valid. On the day appointed for the marriage, the bridegroom, accompanied by some friends, goes to the place agreed upon. They are received by the guardian, or agent and some friends. Two trustworthy witnesses must be present. All persons present then recite the Fátiha, and the bridegroom delivers, the dowry. The bridegroom and the agent of the bride sit upon the ground face to face and grasp each other's right hand, raising the thumbs and pressing them against each other. Having placed a handkerchief over

A temporary marriage is called mut'a (نِكَاح مُتْعَة). This is a marriage in which the time for which it is contracted is mentioned. This kind of marriage was allowed by Muhammad for some time, but afterwards he prohibited and abolished it. The Shi'ahs, however, still consider such a temporary marriage perfectly legal, and establish the legality of it not only from Traditions but also from declarations of the Qur'án (Súra iv. 29 ; see Dictionary of Islám, 424).

The Guardian is called al-Wali (الوَلِيّ from وَلِيَ, to be near, to be intimate, patron, helper). The guardianship may be established by relationship (father, mother), or possession (of male or female slave by the master), or friendship. According to the Hanifa School a free woman, of age, and of a sound mind, whether virgin or married before (بِكْرٌ اوْ ثَيِّب), is entitled to give her consent and to contract a marriage without the intervention of the guardian.[1]

---

their hands, a Faqíh generally pronounces a kind of Khutba or sermon, consisting of a few words of exhortation and prayer with quotations from the Qur'án and Traditions, on the excellence and advantages of marriage. He then requests the guardian or agent of the bride to say: "I marry to thee my daughter for a dowry of such and such an amount." The bridegroom thereon says : "I accept from thee her marriage with myself and take her unto my care and engage myself to afford her protection, and ye who are present bear witness of this." Before the persons assembled on this occasion disperse, they settle when the "night of the entering" (لَيْلَة الدَّخْلَة) is to take place, that is, when the bride is to be brought to the house of the bridegroom. (For a description of the rejoicings and the customs observed between the time of the contract of the marriage and the bride's being conducted in procession to the house of the husband, see Dictionary of Islám 323-327.)

[1] This mediation is, however, considered more becoming to female modesty. In case of young persons and slaves, the guardian is absolutely required (الوَلِيّ شَرْط نِكَاح صَغِير و مَجْنُون و رَقِيق). According to Sháfi'í the

There must be a certain degree of equality (كَفَاءَة) between husband and wife as regards family, social and financial condition, freedom and religion. This sufficiency is required, however, more on the husband's than on the wife's side. It is the duty of the guardian to see to this (العَجَمَ مَنْ لا يَكُونُ كَفوًّا للعربيَّة). A person from a town may marry one from a village (القَرَوِي كفوء للمَدَني).

The dowry is also called صَدَاق ـ صَدَقَة ـ نَحْلَة ـ عَطِيَّة ـ عَقر. This is the money due by the husband to the wife for the right of cohabitation with her.[1] It is a sum settled by mutual agreement. It may be specially mentioned, or it may not be mentioned and left to a subsequent agreement.

Marriage by exchange (نِكَاح الشَّغَار) is that when a man marries the sister or daughter of another, and in return gives his sister or daughter, and does this in order

---

guardian is required in all cases. According to the Shi'ah law a woman who is "adult and discreet" requires no guardian to make marriage valid.

Ibn 'Ábidín (ii. 318) mentions that marrying a woman "for the day-time only" (النهاريَّات) is legal, on condition that the man mention to the woman that he will stay with her only in the day-time, while he will spend the night with another wife.

(أن يكون عندها فى النهار و فى الليل عند ضُرَّتها)

1 Dower is generally divided into two parts, termed مُعَجَّل, or prompt, which is paid on entering into the contract, and مُوَجَّل, or deferred, which is paid upon dissolution of the contract, or on the demand of the wife. In case of divorce, if the husband has consummated the marriage with the wife, or has only met her alone and seen her, without consummating the marriage (which meeting is called الخَلْوَة, retired, solitary place), she is entitled to her full dowry. If the husband divorce her before the consummation of the marriage, and without his having seen her in a solitary place, she is only entitled to half of the dowry.

to avoid paying the dower. It is considered by some authorities blamable, though not absolutely unlawful; they considered the right of cohabitation (بضع) to be the dowry given by both contracting parties. The majority consider such a marriage illegal, since the Prophet has clearly prohibited it. An adulteress may only marry an adulterer or polytheist; this is according to the Qur'án :

الزانية لا اينكحها الا زان او مشرك

Marriage of a slave (نكاح الرقيق) is governed by certain rules. An unbeliever who is taken in the enemy's land (دار الحرب) is called a رقيق, not مملوك. After he is removed to a Muslim country he becomes مملوك; consequently every مملوك is a رقيق, but not every رقيق, is a مملوك. A رقيق is a slave, who belongs to his master in part or as a whole (كلا او بعضا). A slave, the whole of whom belongs to his master, is called اقن عبد ـ قن. The marriage of a slave, male or female, whether he or she is مدبر ولد قن or أمة مكاتب, can only take place with the permission of the master; and no dowry is given before the slave consummates the marriage.

The duties of the husband to his wife and the duties of the wife to her husband are described by the term آداب المعاشر (Súra ii. 320). The husband ought to be careful to maintain a middle course in dealing with his wife in twelve points.[1]

---

1 (1) The marriage feast (الوليمة); (2) kindness, (حسن التخلق); (3) playfulness (مزح ـ ملاعبة ـ مداعبة); (4) policy, maintaining his dignity (سياسة); (5) jealousy, not to be carried away by it (الاعتدال فى الغيرة); (6) pecuniary allowance (نفقة) he must give her a sufficiency; (7) teaching (تعليم); (8) equally dividing (القسمة), i.e., granting every wife her due; جماع

The customs to be observed on the birth of a child are as follows :—(1) excessive joy should not be shown on the birth of a boy, nor great sadness at that of a girl ; (2) to recite the call to prayer into the child's ear ; (3) to give the child a good name ; (4) to offer two sheep for a male and one sheep for a female child on the seventh day, when the hair is shaved off the child's head for the first time. Muhammad used to say : " Shed blood on his account, and remove evil from it." (اهرِقوا دماً و أَميطوا عنهُ الأَذَى) (5) to rub its palate with a date or some sweet thing.

Abortion (حُكم اسقاط الحمل) is unlawful under certain conditions. When the child is formed in the womb, and the spirit has been breathed into it, and has given it life, which takes place about one hundred and twenty days after the conception, it is generally considered that it is unlawful to bring about an abortion. Whether it can be done lawfully before this takes place, is a controverted question. Some hold it to be blamable (مكروه) ; but the majority are in favour of its being licit, if there be good reasons for it, and the husband gives his consent.

Súra ii. 224) ; and not to prefer one to the other ; (9) chastisement (تأديب النشور) inflicted by the husband by abstaining from spending the night with a wife in case of her disobedience ; (10) observing the proper rules in cohabitation (آداب الجماع) ; and (11) in childbirth (ولادة) ; and (12) in divorce (طلاق). (For detailed explanations see Ghazáli and Dictionary of Islám 674). Ghazáli says : " Marriage is a kind of slavery, for the wife becomes the slave (رقيق) of her husband, and it is her duty absolutely to obey him in every thing he requires of her, except in what is contrary to the laws of Islám."

" If the wife be disobedient and obstinate, the husband has the right to punish her and to force her to obey him, but he must proceed gradually : exhort, admonish, threaten, abstain from intercourse with her for three days (انفرد عنها بالفراش و هجرها من ليلة الى ثلاث ليال), beat her so as to let her feel the pain, but be careful not to wound her in the face or make her blood flow abundantly, or break a bone." (Súra iv. 38).

DIVORCE.—Divorce,[1] in Law, means a release from the marriage tie in the manner commanded in Law, *i.e.*, by the use of certain expressions, conveying either an immediate and irrevocable, or a conditional and revocable divorce, which can be made definitive later on.

(الطلاق رفع قيد النكاح في الحال او المآل بلفظ مخصوص)

---

[1] The Muslim law of divorce is founded upon express injunctions contained in the Qur'án as well as in the Traditions. The teaching of the Qur'án upon the subject is contained in Súras ii. 226-233 ; lxv. 1-7. Divorce, though allowed, is considered blamable (مُبَاح), and, if possible, to be avoided (الطلاق ابغض المباحات الى اللّه تعالى).

Divorce may be pronounced to take effect immediately and irrevocably (الطلاق البآئن) or at some future time (فى المآل) which is the revocable divorce (الطلاق الرجعى). It may be given verbally or in writing.

The words by which a divorce is given to a wife are of two kinds, either (1) express, clear, as when the husband says : "Thou art divorced" (انت طالقه طلّقتك) or (2) metaphorical, as when he says : "Thou art free ; put on thy veil, arise and seek for a mate, etc., etc."

The express divorce may be revocable or it may be irrevocable. It is of the first kind, if the husband use no expression pointing to his intending a definitively separating divorce or does not pronounce the divorce three times. The figurative divorce is given by such expressions also as : "go out, go away, stand up, etc " (قومى - اذهبى - اخرجى). Whether such a divorce is revocable or irrevocable depends on the intention of the husband, "for by no metaphorical language is divorce effected, except it be intended."

Divorce is either divorce according to the Sunna (طلاق سُنّى - طلاق السنّة), or heterodox, heretical divorce (الطلاق البِدْعى) which, though lawful, is not considered religious.

The best mode (الطلاق الأَحسن) is when the husband once expressly and clearly pronounces to his enjoyed (المدخول بها), but unpregnant wife, the sentence : "Thou art divorced" when she is in a state of purity (طُهر), during which he has had no carnal connection with her, and then leaves her to complete the prescribed period of probation of three months (العدّة). Until the expiration of this time of probation, the divorce is revocable ;

but after the period is elapsed it is irrevocable, and, if the husband wishes to take back his wife, they must go through the ceremony of marriage again. To divorce a wife when she has her courses, or in the time of 'purity', in which the husband has had intercourse with her is heterodox and unlawful (بدعی حَرام) (Ghazali ii. 32).

The good divorce (الطلاق الحَسَن) is when the husband repudiates his enjoyed wife by three sentences, either express or metaphorical, not pronounced at one and the same time, but giving one sentence in each period of purity (تفریق الثلاث فی ثلاثة اطهر لا وطئه فیها).

The heterodox, irregular form of divorce (الطلاق البِدعی), is when the husband repudiates his wife by three sentences of divorce, pronouncing them either at one and the same time, or separately during one and the same period of her purity. In this case the husband cannot under any circumstances take back his wife again, until she has been regularly married to another husband, enjoyed by him and then divorced. This intermediate husband, who makes the marriage of the former husband to his irrevocably divorced wife legal again, is called the Muhallil (المُحَلِّل, who makes a thing otherwise unlawful, legal). This arrangement rests on a direct command of the Qur'án (Súra ii. 230). The Muslim doctors are very particular in explaining that it is not sufficient for the Muhallil to contract the marriage with the divorced wife, but that he must necessarily consummate it, and that, in certain cases, the birth of a child of this marriage is required, in proof of the marriage having actually taken place. Should the woman desire to return to her first husband, she may make it a condition that the Muhallil should divorce her, after the consummation of her marriage, and if he refuses to do so, the Qádi may compel him (Ghazáli ii. 32). A husband may divorce his wife without any misbehaviour on her part and without assigning any cause, and his divorce is effective, if he be of sound understanding, of mature age and free to choose. The divorce by a boy or a lunatic, would not be effective. If the husband pronounce divorce in a state of drunkenness from drinking fermented liquor, or from taking opium or hashish, or if he pronounces it in jest or by a mere slip of the tongue, still the divorce takes place.

There are also other reasons which sanction divorce, if required, *viz.*:

(1) جَبّ, Jubb, *i.e.*, if the husband has by any cause been deprived of his organ of generation, (from جبّ to cut off). A man suffering from such a defect is called (مَجْبوب).

(2) عُنّه, Impotence, in either husband or wife. A year of probation may be granted in these cases by the Qádi.

(3) Inequality of race or tribe. A woman cannot be compelled to remain the wife of a husband who belongs to an inferior tribe.

(4) Insufficient dower. If the stipulated dowry is refused when demanded, divorce can take place—(*See* Dictionary of Islám, 88).

In addition to the above modes of divorce, there are several other modes of effecting a separation between husband and wife. These are:

(1) Khula (خُلْع - خُلْعة) from خَلَع, to remove, to put away, send away) is a divorce obtained by the wife at her request, on the offer of a compensation to her husband. The validity of this divorce rests on the demand (by her) and acceptance (by him) of the fixed compensation (ايجاب قبول العوض). The words used are: (خالعني,) "Release me for such and such a sum." Answer: (خلعتُك), *i.e.*, "I have released thee for such and such a sum." This mode of divorce is also sanctioned by the Qur'án (Súra ii. 229). The woman so divorced is not entitled to the payment of her dower. (Bukhári . 226. Dictionary of Islám, 274). The compensation must be fixed.

(2) Mutual discharge, or Mubárá' (المُبَارأَة), is a divorce effected by a mutual release (الابراء من الجانبَيْن), each releasing the other of the rights and duties of marriage, by the wife saying (بارئني على الف دينار) "Release me for a thousand dinars". The husband replies: "I release thee for a thousand dinars" (بارأتك على الف دينار), or the husband asks to be released from the marriage tie, and the wife agrees to it.

(3) Zihár (ظِهَار) is a divorce effected by the husband likening his wife to the back (ظَهْر) or any other part or member of the body of any of his kinswomen within the prohibited degree, *e.g.*, he may say to his wife: "Thou art to me like the back of my mother" (انت على كظهر أمي). The intention of the husband decides whether divorce takes place or not; if he intended divorce, his wife is not lawful to him until he have made expiation (كفّارة) by freeing a slave, or fasting two months, or feeding sixty poor men. This rests on the command of the Qur'án: "To those who put away their wives by saying: 'Be thou to me as my mother's back.'" (Súra lviii. 2-4.)

(4) Swearing, vowing Abstinence (ايلاء), is a form of separation in which the husband declares with an oath that he will not have carnal intercourse with his wife for a period not less than four months, in the case of a free woman, and two months in the case of a slave. This also rests on the injunction of the Qur'án (Súra ii. 226). At the end of the specified time he offers the usual expiation due for an oath, and either returns to his wife or divorces her.

(5) Mutual cursing, Imprecation (لعان), is a form of divorce which takes place under the following circumstances: "If a man accuses his wife of adultery, and does not prove it by four witnesses, he must swear before

God four times that he is the teller of the truth " and then adds : " If I am
a liar God curse me." The wife then also says four times : " I swear
before God that my husband lies " and then adds : " May God's anger be
upon me if this man be a teller of the truth. "

اههد بالله انهٔ لمن الكاذبين ـ اههدُ بالله انی لمَن الصادقين فيما رميتها ـ

لعنة الله علٰی ان كنتَ من الكاذبين ـ غضب الله علٰی ان كان من
الصادقين) ٠

After this, a divorce takes place *ipso facto*. This form of divorce also
rests on the Qur'án (Súra xxiv. 6-10). Such a woman may, according to the
Hanafi doctrine, marry again ; according to the opinion of the Shi'ahs she
is prevented from contracting a marriage again.

Besides these, there are other modes of divorce to be mentioned : such
as :

(1) When the husband authorizes his wife either by clear words, or in
some other way to divorce herself or charges some other person to do it.
This may be done either by authorization, or by appointing an agent or by
writing a letter. The words are : " Divorce thyself ", or " the matter is in
thy hands," (أمرك بيدك ـ اختاری ـ طلّقی نفسك) to which the wife
replie " I have divorced myself, I have chosen "

(اخترت نفسی ـ طلّقتُ نفسی)٠

(2) Conditional Divorce (التعليق) is when the husband says to his wife
" If thou goest out of the house, thou art divorced."

(3) Divorce of the sick (طلاق المريض). A sick man may divorce his
wife, even though he be on his death-bed.

The 'Idda period of probation (العدة) designates the number of days a
divorced woman has to wait before she is allowed to marry again. It is a
time of probation during which it may be ascertained whether she is
pregnant or not, and lasts for three months. After this time, if it is ascertained that she is not with child, she is at liberty to contract another
marriage ; but if not, she has to wait till she have given birth to her child.
After divorce, the ' Idda is, as before mentioned, three months ; after the
death of her husband, four months and ten days. The observation of
these periods of probation is enjoined in the Qur'án. (Súras lxv. 2-4 ; ii.
232). During this time of probation, the wife lives in the lodging assigned
to her by her husband and has to obey him. She may not leave the
house, nor undertake anything without his permission.

Restitution (الرَّجعة) designates the receiving back of a wife who has
been divorced by a revocable divorce. A man may do this if the period of
her 'Idda has not expired. Should he, however, allow the time of her
probation fully to elapse, he may not take her back unless by means of the
Muhallil. In case of the legal restitution, the husband says to his wife :

" I take thee back." A woman divorced by a reversible divorce must adorn herself for her husband during her time of probation. It is not so with a woman who has been definitely divorced or whose husband is dead. A woman definitively divorced must on no account allow her husband to have carnal intercourse with her, and if he insists, she must offer him a compensation or flee from him; but if this is of no avail, she may kill him, if possible not openly, but by giving him poison (so that she may not be found out). No punishment must in this case be inflicted on her. If she kills him with a weapon, she has to pay blood-money. Some theologians hold that killing the husband under such circumstances is not allowed. The woman must not, under any circumstances, commit suicide.

Maintenance (النَّفَقَة) implies all those things which are necessary to the support of life such as food, clothes, and lodging. There are three causes of providing maintenance established by Law: (1) Marriage, (2) Relationship, (3) Possession, property (of a slave. اسباب النفقة ثلاثة) (زوجيَّة و قرابة و مَلك) In this place we have to deal with the maintenance of the wife. The husband is held to give the necessary support to his divorced wife during her 'Idda or until her delivery, if she is pregnant. The support given must be in accordance with the means of the husband and the condition of the wife. It may be paid day by day, week by week, or month by month, and the woman has the right to ask for the appointment of a surety who will guarantee the payment. No such support is due to a wife who has brought on her divorce by her misconduct, or to a woman who has lost her husband by death, whether she be pregnant or not. Her lodging, however, is to be provided.

As regards the suckling of a child the mother, when divorced, is not obliged to do so except she desire it, and be appointed to do so for the same wages which the husband would have to pay to a nurse. If the father should be too poor to pay the nurse's wages she is obliged to give suck to the child. The father has to pay three maintenances (1) for suckling, (2) for the guardianship of the mother, (3) sundry expenses for the child. The longest time of fosterage fixed by the Qur'án (Súra ii. 233) is two years (حَوْلَين كَاملين). This may by agreement be shortened. (Súra lxv. 6.)

The acknowledgment of the father is a sufficient proof of the legitimacy of the child. Should there be any doubt, the birth of the child rest on the testimony of the mid-wife and other trustworthy witnesses. The following are considered legitimate children : (1) children of legitimate wives; (2) children born by a slave to her own master, without her being a lawful wife. Such children inherit like the children of legitimate wives, (3) the children of a woman with whom a man has had carnal intercourse by mistake, thinking her to be his wife or slave. The child born of the wife,

SLAVERY.—Slavery (رِق ـ عَبُودِيَّة) existed in Arabia before the rise of Islám. Muhammad did not abolish it, but
adopted it as part of his system, kept slaves himself, and
laid down certain laws and regulations, and made slavery
a permanent institution of Islám.[1]

---

before the legitimate marriage has been contracted, is considered illegiti-
mate, and cannot inherit.

The guardianship of the child (حِضَانَة) is the right of the mother,
even if divorced, unless she be an apostate, or wicked or unworthy to be
trusted. According to the Hanafi School she has the custody of her
daughter, until she has reached the age of puberty. The custody of male
children is limited to the seventh year. The mother loses her right of
guardianship when she marries a stranger.

A widow has to observe mourning (حِدَاد) for her dead husband for the
period of four months and ten days. During this time she must abstain
from wearing any kind of jewelry or ornaments and from using perfumery
and paint. Except for her husband a married woman may not observe
mourning longer than three days, and the husband may force her to abstain
from it, for he has a right to claim that she adorns herself. A definitely
divorced woman may not wear her ornaments (some say the revocably
divorced wife also), " lest by so doing she tempt her husband to have illicit
intercourse with her."

Polygamy is undoubtedly an institution sanctioned by Islám and cannot, as some liberal-minded Muslims pretend, be abolished and declared
illegal. It is declared legal by Muhammad's example, who took to himself eleven wives, besides concubines.

[1] A slave is مَمْلُوك ـ عَبْد ـ رَقِيق : a female slave is أَمَة. The condition of slavery is عَبُودِيَّة ـ رِق, the term generally used in the Qur'án.
Any student, thoroughly conversant with what the Qur'án and Traditions
teach on the subject of slavery, will agree that it is incorrect to say that
Muhammad disapproved of the institution and considered it as temporary
in its nature and that it would ultimately disappear. The orthodox
Muslim may be forced to liberate his slaves ; but he can never be forced to
acknowledge the system of slavery as wrong and unlawful, as it is an institution sanctioned by the Prophet and legislated for by him, and which,
therefore, stands and falls with the Qur'án and the religion of Islám.
War with unbelievers is enjoined as a permanent duty of Muslims till

there be no other religion on earth but Islám. The captives made in these wars, therefore, yield a constant supply of slaves, male and female. They are the absolute property of the owner, with whom he can deal as he likes.

Muslims are permitted to cohabit with any of their female slaves made captives in war (Súras iv. 3, 29 ; xxxiii. 49), even if they are married women whose husbands are still alive. They are enjoined to show kindness to slaves (Súra iv. 40).

With regard to enslaving captives in war, the Imám may either kill the males or enslave them, or release them by making them Zimmis. The idolators of Arabia and apostates are, however, to be killed without choice. If captives embrace Islám they become slaves, but must not be killed. If infidels become Muslims on the field of battle, before their capture, they are free men ; but after they are caught they become slaves. Slave traffic is allowed, and the slave, being the property of his master, may, like other property, be sold and bought.

It is, however, unlawful for a Muslim to enslave, (1) his mother (2) the ascendants on the mother's side, (3) the father, (4) the ascendants on the father's side, (5) the sons, (6) the ascendants of the sons, (7) the sisters (8) the aunts on the mother's side, (9) the uncles on the mother's side, (10) the daughters of brothers, (11) the daughters of sisters, (12) the descendants of the father, (13) all persons related by the nurse (بالرضاعة). Infidels possessing Muslim slaves may not keep them, but must sell them to Muslims at the current price. The children of a female slave are also the property of her master, except those children which she has of him, and whom he acknowledges as his who are free. If a female slave is the property of several masters, her children are also joint property of these masters, except special agreements have been made. If of a married couple one is free, the other a slave, the children born to them are free and are given over to the free one, except the master has, on marrying them, made it a condition that the children of this marriage should be his own property.

The liberation of a slave can be effected in five ways :—

(1) Manumission (تَحْرِير - اعتاق - عَتْق) designates the act by which the owner of a slave gives up his right to the same and gives him, of his own free-will, immediate and unconditional freedom (اسْقاط المولى حَقّة) (عن مملوكـه بوجة يصير المملوك من الاحرار) This act is binding, when it proceeds from a person who is free, sane, of age, and the actual owner of the slave in question. If such a person say to his slave : "Thou art free, I set thee free," and such like expressions, the slave becomes free, whether the owner mean emancipation or not. If the liberated female slave be with child, her child is also free on her account.

The infidels, who are at war with Muslims become slaves as soon as they are made captives and come into possession of the Muslims; but not till they have been removed to a land of Islám do they become Mamlúk (مملوك).   Part of a slave may also be liberated (اعتق بعض عبده); on his paying the remainder of his price he becomes quite free.   A slave who is the joint property of several masters, if one of them liberate his part, the others may do the same with their part, or demand the payment of their portion from the slave.   The liberation of a slave who is a believer, is considered a most meritorious act.   In certain cases, the liberation of a slave is obligatory, in expiation of certain sins, e.g., for breaking the fast of Ramadán, swearing and not keeping an oath.

(2)   Liberation of a slave by means of a writing (كتابة) designates the liberation of a slave by means of a bond of freedom, granted to a slave (male or female) in return for a sum of money agreed upon to be paid within a specified time.   The owner declares that he has given M. N. such a writ, on condition of his paying such and such a sum.   The slave having obtained such a writ is called a مكاتب, until the ransom is fully paid.   During the interval between the promise of freedom and the payment of the money the Mukátab enjoys a certain freedom; but is placed under certain restrictions, e.g., he is free to move from place to place; but he cannot marry or make a pilgrimage without the permission of his master.   As soon as he pays the total sum agreed upon, he receives his full liberty.   Only a Muslim can be liberated in this way.   A Mukátab cannot be sold or given away as a present or pawned, and, if he is unable to pay the sum due, it is to be paid from the public treasury. Liberation on condition of the slave's agreeing to the proposal of his master of giving an equivalent (عتق على جعالة - عتق على جعل) is some-what similar to this mode, but differs from it in several points.   Here the master proposes to his slave to liberate him on his giving an equi-valent, money or work, for a certain time.   If the slave agrees to the master's proposal, he obtains his liberty at once, before he has fulfilled the conditions, for in this case, his liberation does not depend on his ful-filling (اداء), but on his accepting the condition.   The Mukátab obtains his liberty only on his having fulfilled the condition.

(3)   The liberation of a slave after his master's death is by an arrange-ment called tadbír (تدبير)   This tadbír is a declaration made by a master to a slave (male or female) that he or she shall be free at his death.   This the master does by saying: ' Thou art a mudabbar (مدبّر), or " thou art free at my death " (انت حرّ بعد وفاتى).   The slave may then claim his liberty at the death of his master.   In case of a female slave, the children she has born in the interval are also free.   This declaration may be made either in writing or before two witnesses.   The owner of the slave is at

OATHS.—Acknowledgment (الإقرار) is a legal term for the avowal of the right of another person upon one's self

---

liberty to take back his promise and thus annul the arrangement at any time. A mudabbar may neither be sold, nor given away as a present nor pawned, but he may be hired out, and the female slave may be enjoyed by her master, or married by force, against her will. If a man, whose sole property consists in slaves, liberates all his slaves by tadbír and his heirs object to this arrangement, the third only of every slave is liberated and the remaining two-thirds are to be paid by them.

(4) Liberation by Istíláid (استيلاد). When a man has a child born to him of a female slave, and claims and acknowledges the child as his own, this acknowledgment becomes *ipso facto* the cause of the freedom of the female. This freedom is not gained till after his death, because she is then included in the portion which the child inherits. The woman becomes "a mother of offspring" (أم ولد); the child is free from its birth, and the right of the master of the "Umm Walad" becomes restricted, as he may neither sell her nor give her in marriage to another man. It is the duty of the father to acknowledge (ينبغى أن يشهد) the child, when born, or even before its birth before witnesses, lest at his death it may be considered a slave. He declares: حملها وما فى بطنها منى.

(5) Liberation of a slave as an act of expiation (كفّارة). Liberation of a slave may also take place as an act of expiation for certain sins and transgressions.

A female slave, captive, bought, or otherwise acquired by a Muslim, must not be touched by him till he has ascertained whether she is pregnant or not. For this purpose the master of the female slave takes her to his abode and abstains from intercourse with her for the space of a month, in the case of an old woman or a girl under age. (صغيرة وآئسة) He who does not observe this time of probation (استبراء) from برى to be clear, free) commits a sin (إثم). This probation is called استبراء الجارية الاستبراء. A female slave having a child cannot be sold separately from her child, till the child has reached the age of seven years; but some doctors are of opinion that the child can be sold away as soon as it has been weaned at the proper time.

Muhammad ordered his followers to treat slaves kindly (Kashf ii. 168, 169, 284.) Slavery is in the eyes of every Muslim a divinely sanctioned institution, and, as such, cannot be declared illegal or abolished; it stands and falls with Islám.

in sales, contracts, etc., such as that he owes M. N. a sum of money, a number of camels, or that he has received an object in deposit (وديعة), or as a loan. He who acknowledges is the مُقِرّ ; the person to whom one acknowledges is the مُقَرّ له ; the object of avowal is the مُقَرّ بِهِ. Such an avowal ought to be clear (صريح), not ambiguous (مُبْهم), otherwise it is of no value before the Qádi. Making a sign with the head (الإيماء بالرأس) is not considered a sufficient avowal.[1]

---

[1] The teaching of the Qur'án on the subject of oaths (يَمِين pl. أيمَان) is to be found in Súra ii. 225 : " God will not punish you for a mistake in your óaths," and Súras v. 91 ; xvi. 93, 96. Muhammad used to say " Whosoever swears to a thing and says : ' if it please God,' and then acts contrary to his oath, it is no sin."...Ibn 'Ábidín gives the following definition of an oath : " It is a solemn assertion made by him who swears that he will do or leave a thing." The oath necessarily requires the mention of one of the names or attributes of God, mentioned in the Qur'án. To swear by the Prophet, the Qur'án, the Ka'ba or an attribute or name of God, not mentioned in the Qur'án, is not an oath. The letters to be prefixed to the name of God, in order to express an oath are وَ ت بِ, e.g., تالله - بالله - والله, Walláhi, Billáhi, Talláhi ; for brevity's sake this letter may be omitted. An affirmative oath necessarily requires the title of confirmation : (حَرف التأكيد) which is or نَ, e.g., والله لأ نَفعلَنّ كذا " by God I shall do so."

The false oath is of three kinds :

(1) The grievous oath (اليمين الغَمُوس from غَمَس, to plunge, because it plunges the swearer deeply into sin) is a false oath sworn with intention (على كاذب عمدًا). A person swears he has not done a certain thing, while he knows he has done it. A Muslim thus intentionally swearing a false oath commits a great sin and must repent. No expiation is required in this case, as the sin is considered so grievous that only true repentance can wipe it out.

The Vow (النَّذْر pl. النذور) is a solemn declaration by which a person promises to perform a certain act such as fasting, or giving of alms, or offering a certain sacrifice, it may be of a camel, lamb, or sheep. It must be lawful, and something in addition to what is incumbent on him. No foolish or unlawful vows are to be redeemed, and expiation is to be made for not redeeming them. A legal vow not redeemed by a person before his death is to be fulfilled in his stead by some one else. Muhammad said:

لزم النَّاذِر الوفاء بما سمي .

A conditional vow (نذر معلق) is to be redeemed when the condition is found, e.g., a man vows to do a thing if he is healed from a disease. Ignorant people often make vows that they will offer money, oil, etc., to Saints (Auliyya), but such vows are foolish and unlawful (باطل و حرام).

THE QÁDI.—Authority and power in Muslim lands belong to the Sultán (Imám). He appoints the Qádi or judge, whose office and duty it is to examine law-suits,

---

(2) The inconsiderate oath (يمين اللَّغو) is an oath by which a man affirms what is false, but still believes that he is saying the truth (ان حلف كاذباً يظنّهُ صادقاً). It is hoped that God will forgive this sin.

(3) The oath concerning the future (اليمين المُنْعَقِد على آت) concerns an incident or transaction which is to come. A man swears that he will do or not do such a thing; if he fails in this, expiation is incumbent on him by which his transgression is wiped out, even if it be not combined with repentance. يمين منعقد على آت و فيه كَفَّارة ان حنث فقط وهى ترفع الاثم و ان لم توجد التوبة معها و لو مُكْرهاً Ibn 'Abidín iii. 50-53). The expiation for a false oath is the freeing of a slave, or fasting or feeding ten poor persons, as at one time. It would lead too far to mention all the expressions, conditions, mental reservations (تَوْرِية), dissimulations which according to the teaching of the Muslim doctors, make a solemn assertion not a legal oath. Muhammad says: "He who in swearing adds to his oath: ' If it please God,' can never swear a false oath."

brought before his court and to give a decision according to the law (الشرع). He is competent to give a decision on all matters treated of in Fiqh. The word قَضَى means to decree, to command. The term قَضاء, in law, designates the decision, or decree of the judge in law-suits, and his making thereby an end to quarrels and strife.[1]

(القضاء هو شرعاً فصل الخُصومات و قطع المنازعات)

---

1 The six chief points (أَرْكَان) to be considered are (1) (حُكم) or sentence of the judge, which is given either in words (قولى) such as: " I decide, give sentence " (فعلى), or in acts (الزمتَ – قَضيت – حَكَمتَ), *i.e.*, the carrying out the sentence at once (تَنفيذ الحُكم). (2) The object of judicial decision (محكوم به), which may be a thing concerning God exclusively (حق الله تعالى المحض) *e.g.*, adultery, drunkenness, or such as concerns man exclusively (حق الله المحض), or such as concern God and man ; but God in a special manner (ما فيه الحقان و غلب فيه حق الله تعالى) *e.g.*, calumny, theft, or such as concerns both God and man also, but chiefly man, *e.g.*, retaliation, chastisement (قصاص – تعزير). (3) The person in whose favour the sentence is pronounced is المحكوم لَهُ ; the com-plainant plaintiff is المُدَّعى ; the law-suit is الدَّعْوى ; the defendant is المُدَّعى عليه. (4) The person against whom the sentence is given is المحكوم عليه. (5) The judge (الحاكم) is either the Imám, or the Qádi, or the Arbitrator (المُحَكَّم). (6) The way in which the judge forms his judgment and gives sentence differs according to the object of litigation. It is either by proof, or confession, or the oath, or clear and undoubtful evidence.

The persons qualified to exercise the office of Judge are Muslims, whose testimony is accepted in the court of law (اهلها اهل الشهادة). An un-believer may not be made judge in Muslim affairs (تقليد الكافر لا يصح) ; but he may give a decision in matters concerning non-Muslims.

A Muslim appointed Qádi by the proper authority may exercise the duties of his office, though he be a wicked man (و ان كان جاهلاً او فاسقاً). As to the Mufti, (المُفتى), the majority are of opinion that a wicked person cannot exercise this office, and that his decision cannot be relied upon (لا يستحل استفتاءُهُ – لا يعتمد على فتواهُ). The Mufti is a learned

INHERITANCE فَرَائِض (عِلْم الميراث ـ فَرَائِض)—The term فَرَائِض
is an abbreviation of عِلْم الفَرَائِض or the science of the portions, ordered, appointed for the heirs by divine command
in the Qur'án. The heir is الوارث (pl. وَرَثَه), the heritage
is الميراث ; property left, or heritage is تَرِكَة the portion
which each of the heirs receives is سَهْم (pl. سِهام أَسْهُم).
The verses of the Qur'án upon which the law of inheritance is founded are called the أيات المواريث. They are
Súra iv. 8-18.[1]

Jurist who gives decisions or legal opinions in difficult questions of law.
If the Qádi has obtained his office by means of bribery his decisions are
void, as he is not to be considered a lawful Qádi. If the Qádi accepts
bribes (يَرْتَشِى) in giving sentence, the opinions concerning the validity
of the same are divided. If the Qádi at the time of his appointment
is a pious man and then becomes wicked, the Sultán may depose him.

The right and duty of the imprisonment (حَبْس) of offenders is believed
to be laid down in the Qur'án (Súra v. 37) and the Sunna. The prisoner
is not allowed to have a comfortable bed, nor may friends keep him company. His wife may not share the prison with him. It is not lawful to
imprison a person on mere suspicion (تُهَمَّة) (Dictionary of Islám 205).

[1] The property of the deceased Muslim is applicable, in the first place,
to the payment of the funeral expenses; secondly, to the discharge of his
debts; thirdly, to the payment of legacies as far as the third of the
residue. The remaining two-thirds, with so much of the third as is not
absorbed by legacies, are the patrimony of the heirs. A Muslim is, therefore, disabled from disposing of more than a-third of his property by will.

The residue of the estate, after the payment of funeral expenses, debts
and legacies, descends to the heirs (وَرَثَة) and among these, the first are
persons for whom the law has provided specific shares or portions and
who are, therefore, called sharers (ذَوُو الفُرُوض). After the sharers have
been satisfied, any residue remaining is divided among the distant relations (عَصَبَة).

During his life-time a Muslim has absolute power over his property, and
may dispose of it as he likes. He must, however, deliver the property to
the donee in his life-time. As regards testamentary dispositions in the

EVIDENCE, WITNESS, TESTIMONY (شَهَادَة).—Evidence is the statement of the truth for the confirmation of the truth in the office of the Qádi with the special formula: أَشْهَدَ "I testify." It is the duty of every Muslim to bear testimony when the same is demanded of him (يجِبُ اذاها بالطلب), as it is enjoined in the Qur'án (Súra ii. 282).

----

making of donations, endowments, and legacies, the amount so left is limited to one-third of the property. The law of inheritance, is acknowledged to be an exceedingly difficult branch of study (Ibn Khaldún. i. 376).

One-half (نصف) is due to the husband when there are no descendants, the sister when there are no other heirs, the daughter when she is the only child.

One-fourth (الرُّبع) is due to the husband surviving with children, the husband and wife when there are no descendants.

One-eighth (الثُمن) is due to the wife surviving with children.

One-third (الثلث) is due to the wife during the life-time of her father-in-law, when the husband has left neither children nor other relatives entitled to inherit.

Two-thirds (ثُلثان) are due to two or more daughters when there are no sons.

One-sixth (السُدس) is due to the father and the mother of their child, when the latter has left descendants. (For details see Dictionary of Islám, 200-213).

The hindrances (موافع الارث) which prevent a person from sharing in the inheritance which are many, are :—

(1) Infidelity. An infidel cannot inherit from a Muslim, but a Muslim can inherit from an infidel.

(2) Murder (قتل). A man who has wilfully killed another cannot inherit from him. Man-slaughter does not, however, exclude from inheriting.

(3) Slavery (رق). A slave cannot inherit from a free man, nor a free man from a slave.

(4) Li'án (لِعَان), imprecation, separation between husband and wife, prevents mutual inheritance.

(5) Flight, disappearance (غَيبَة).

Persons, in order to be able to give evidence, which can be legally accepted, must have the qualifications of full age, sound reason, faith, good reputation, absence of suspicion, and partial knowledge of the subject concerning which evidence is required. They may be eye-witnesses (شاهد أصل), or witnesses from hearsay (شاهد فرع).[1]

USURPATION OR TAKING BY FORCE (غَصَب). — This is the taking of the property of another, which is valuable, without the consent of the proprietor. Usurpation is also exacting service from the slave of another, or putting

---

[1] In cases inducing bodily punishment, witnesses are at liberty either to give or withhold their testimony. The concealment of vice is preferable, because the Prophet said to a person who had borne testimony : " Verily it would have been better for you if thou hadst concealed it." In the case of theft it is a duty to testify that a certain person took such property, in order to preserve the right of the proprietor ; but the word taken (اخذ) ought to be used instead of stolen (سَرَق), in order to conceal the crime (رعاية للسَّتر).

The evidence required in case of whoredom (زنا) is that of four men (Súra xxiv. 4). The testimony of a woman is not admitted in such a case.

The evidence required in other criminal cases is that of two men : that of women is not admitted.

In all other cases the evidence required is that of two men or of one man and two women.

The Imám Sháfi'í rejects the evidence of woman, except in certain cases such as childbirth and female defects, on account of the deficiency of woman's understanding. If two Christians testify that a certain Christian woman has embraced Islám, their testimony is valid, and she is forced to become a Muslim (تُجبَر على الاسلام). The testimony of Muslim heretics is valid.

As regards retraction of evidence, if witnesses retract their testimony, prior to the Qádi's having passed sentence, by saying : " I retract what I have testified" (رجعت عمّا شهدت به), or similar expressions, it becomes void ; if sentence has been already given, it does not become void by such a retraction (لا يُفسَخ المُحكم). The retraction of the evidence, in order to be valid, must be made in the presence of the Qádi.

a burden upon the quadruped of another person. The person willingly doing so (الغاصب), transgresses, and is responsible to the person injured (المغصوب منه) for compensation for the thing usurped or injured (المغصوب). But if he has done so unwillingly, thinking the object usurped his own, he is not an offender in law, but is still liable for a compensation. As soon as a Muslim sees an object, slave, animals, house, etc., which has been wrongfully appropriated, he is to restore it to its rightful proprietor, for it is unlawful.

PRE-EMPTION (شُفعة).—This is the right of preference which a partner or co-sharer (شريك) in the possession of a certain object such as a house, or landed property, enjoys when that object is being sold, or his taking possession of it for the same price, if it has already been sold to a third party. The person who desires to make use of this right is the advocate (شفيع) ; he must make his claim as soon as he hears of the sale, or if he be present, before it is concluded ; otherwise he loses his right (الشفعة تملّك البقعة جبراً علي المشتري بما قام عليه و شرطها ان يكون المحلّل عقاراً) The right does not apply to movable but only immovable property (عقار). Only Muslims enjoy this right.

LOST PROPERTY, TROVES (لقطة ـ لقيط).—This comprises : (1) a found child, a foundling, which the person who finds it must take up, and restore it to the parent. If these cannot be found, he must bring it up, but the expenses are paid from the public treasury ; (2) property found and taken up for the purpose of preserving it in the manner of a trust.

A trove under ten dirhams must be advertised for some days; if it exceed ten dirhams in value, it must be kept at the disposition of its rightful owner for the space of a year.

The capture of a runaway slave is considered a praise-worthy act, and the captor is entitled to a reward of forty dirhams. The Qádi imprisons the fugitive slave till his owner claims him and proves him to be his property; if no owner claims him for a long time, the Qádi sells him and keeps the money realized by the sale at the disposal of the owner.

If a person who is lost or has disappeared had been married, the Qádi appoints an agent. His wife cannot marry again for four years, and he cannot be legally declared dead till the period expires, when he would have reached the age of ninety; then only can his property be divided among the heirs.

SLAYING OF ANIMALS (نَبِيح).—It is said that slaying of animals in Law means the act of slaying an animal agree-ably to the prescribed forms, without which the flesh is not lawful for the food of man (Bukhári iii. 253 et seqq.) It is of two kinds: (1) by choice (اختياري), or (2) by necessity (اضطراري). The former is slaughtering animals " in the name of God " with the knife, the latter is slaugh-tering[1] effected by a wound, as in shooting birds or animals, in which case the words: " Bismilláhi, Alláh Akbar ! " must be said at the time of the discharge of the arrow from the bow or the shot from the gun. The Muslim may eat with Jews and Christians, as long as the food is of lawful kind (Súra v. 7).

---

1 The proper mode of slaughtering is to draw the knife across the throat and the windpipe. The carotid arteries and the gullet must be cut through, while the words " In the name of God, God is great" are repeated. The proper slaughtering is considered to be effected by the shedding of blood.

FOOD AND DRINK (اَطْعِمَة , اَشْرِبَة).—Muhammad used to say on this subject : " What God has declared lawful in His book is lawful, and what He has declared unlawful in His book is unlawful, or what He has been silent about is unlawful " (Súra ii. 167). All kind of fish is allowed for food, except those which have no scales, and resemble snakes. Oysters and tortoises are also unlawful. The Sháfi'ites consider them lawful. Quadrupeds such as camels, cattle, and sheep are lawful. The horse and the donkey are considered as مكروه disliked. Dogs, swine, cats, mice, and dead animals may not be eaten. Birds of prey are unlawful ; but pigeons and sparrows are lawful. Intoxicating drinks are forbidden. For the customs to be observed on eating (آداب الاكل) *see* Ghazáli ii. 2, 225. Fermented liquor (خَمرة) is unlawful; unfermented liquor (نبيذ) is lawful. If a man is in danger of dying of hunger, any unlawful food becomes licit for him.

WASTE LAND.—It is the law that all land is either culti-vated land (عَامِر), or waste land (خَراب - حَوات). All

---

(الذبح الاختياري هو ذبح بين الحلق واللبة و عروقة الحلقوم والمرىء والودجان و حل بقطع اى ثلاثة منها), It is absolutely necessary that the person who slays should be a Muslim or a Kitábi, *i.e.*, a Jew or Christian not a heathen or Majian, or an apostate (أَضْحِيَّة). The term applied to the sacrifice slaugh-tered on the day of the great festival (ايام لأضحى - يوم النَّحر) is أضحِية. It is so called because it is slaughtered at the time called ضحى or the time of the day when the sun has risen high on the horizon (Bukhári viii. 285). A Muslim is allowed to hunt (الصَّيد مُباح), with arrows or weapons of iron, as spears, or better still with trained animals, with dogs or panthers or hawks or falcons. The sign of a dog's training is his catching game three times without eating it. A hawk is considered trained, when she attends to the call of her master. If the dog eats any part of the game, it is unlawful. Hunting is not allowed on the pilgrim-age, nor within the limits of the sacred cities of Mecca or Madína.

waste land which is not cultivated, either from want of
water or some other cause, and is at a distance from a
town or village, may be taken possession of for the object
of reclaiming and cultivating it, if the Imám gives permission to do so.

Regulations concerning the right to water are that a
man may in his turn, use the water of a river, a rivulet,
or a canal for the purposes of irrigation, giving water
to animals, etc., (see Dictionary of Islám, 546, 665).

الشرب شرعاً نوبة الانتفاع بالماءِ سقياً للزراعة والدوابّ.

SALE.—A sale in law signifies an exchange of property
for property, with the mutual consent of the parties
(مُبادلة شيء بشيء علي وجٍﮧ مخصوص). The points to be
observed are (1) (المال) the property, which can be taken
possession of, and preserved, treasured up to the time
when it is wanted, (المال ما يميل اليه الطبع و يمكن اذخارُﮧ
لوقت الحاجة) i.e., objects, money, but not rights and
debts which cannot form the objects of sale; (2) the seller
(البائع); (3) the buyer (المُشتري); (4) the object of sale
(المَبيع); (5) the equivalent price (الثَمَن). The objects of
sale may be divided into (1) things which, if they perish,
can be replaced by an equal quantity of something of the
same kind. They are called مثلي; and (2) into things
equal in value and quantity, called كَمَي. When something is sold the object and the price must be mutually
delivered at once. Offer and acceptance (ايجاب and قبول)
are necessary. The contracting parties must have the
qualifications of full age, sound reason and full liberty.
For the full possession of the object of sale there must
be delivery and reception (قبض and تَسليم). The object
of sale must be lawful (مُبَاح), the description and speci-
fication of the object of sale must be clear (وصف), the

statement of price, definite (ثمن), and the possibility of
realizing a gain, by such a sale or purchase, must be
evident. Treasuring up wheat, barley, in order to raise
the price, is unlawful.[1]

-----

[1] At the sale of domestic animals and slaves, the purchaser has the right
to annul the agreement for three days. This privilege is called the
Option (الخيار). A female slave cannot be delivered to the purchaser before she has had her menstruation. Should this not appear, a time of
probation of forty days must be observed, in order to ascertain whether
she is pregnant or not. If the purchaser is doubtful, he may himself
subject her to this probation, but may not have any carnal intercourse
with her during the forty days, otherwise he is subject to the punishment
of atonement. If a Muslim purchases a female slave, who is pregnant,
it is best for him not to cohabit with her till she has been delivered of her
child; otherwise the child she bears will be considered as his own and
entitled to inherit, and its mother will become (ام ولد) the "mother of offspring." Male or female slaves may be bought by partners who equally
share the right of their services. If one of the partners cohabit with such
a female slave and she brings forth a child, he has to take her over as his
property and to pay his co-partners their share of the value of the slave.
It is unlawful to sell young infidel slaves to non-Muslims, as their conversion to Islám may be hoped for. The Qur'án prescribes the presence
and testimony of witnesses on the occasion of sales (Súra ii. 282).

Such an agreement of sale can only be dissolved with the mutual consent of the contracting parties. It can, however, be dissolved under the
following circumstances, when there is :

(1) Option of place (خيّار المجلس), when the contracting parties have
not yet left the place of agreement.

(2) Option of previous condition (خيار الشرط), when the option of dis-
solving the contracts within a specified time has previously been agreed to.

(3) Option of fraud (خيار الغبن); when the purchaser discovers that
the seller has deceived him.

(4) Option of delay (خيار التاخير), when the object of sale has not been
delivered by the seller, or the price paid by the purchaser at the proper
time.

(5) Option of appearance (خيار الرؤية), if the object of sale, on being
delivered, has a different appearance, or different qualities from what it
had at the time of the sale.

٠(الربا شرعاً فضل خالٍ عن عِوض) USURY (رباً) is unlawful

The profit (فضل) or excess, which is considered usury, is

(6) Option of defect (خيار العَيْب), when defects are discovered which were not evident at the time of the sale. When of two slaves purchased one dies before their delivery, the purchaser has the choice of either annulling the agreement, or of letting it stand, in which case, however, he has to pay the price of both slaves.

Cancelling (اقالة) is the term for the dissolution of the sale. If one of the contracting parties wishes to annul a sale, he says: "Release me" and the other says: "I have released thee." (أَقِلنى - أَقَلْتُك).

There are many different kinds of sale. Of these the following may be mentioned :

(1) Selling for a profit (المرابحة), when the seller distinctly states that he purchased it for so much, and sells it for so much.

(بيع ماملكة بما قام عليه و بفضل)

(2) Selling at the original price (بيعة بثمنه الأوّل - التولية).

(3) Sale of things for things, or barter (مقايضة).

(4) Sarf (صَرْف), a special kind of sale or exchange, a change of money, or of silver for gold (و يشترط عدم التاجيل والخيار).

(5) Sale by advance (سَلَم), when the price is immediately advanced for goods to be delivered at a future fixed time.

(6) Loan (قَرْض), a transaction in which a man borrows certain things, money or other things, and engages himself to return an equal quantity of things of the same kind without any definite understanding as to the time of the repayment.

(القرض عقد مخصوص يرد على دفع مالٍ مثلى لآخر ليرد مثلهُ)

(7) بَيْعُ الّوَفاه, is an operation by which a person delivers, as a kind of pledge or mortgage, to another person certain movable or immovable objects, valued at a certain specified price, on condition that, if he returns the sum lent at the assigned term, the pledge is returned to him; if not, it remains the property of the lender, on condition, however, of his paying the borrower the difference between the value of the pledge and the sum lent to him. This operation is also called the pledge to be returned (رَهُن المَعَاد) ; or sale of trust, deposit (بيع الامانة).

that demanded by one of the parties in a sale of homogeneous articles, estimated by weight or measurement, as
an obligatory condition, without his giving any equivalent
for it in return. For example, the sale of two loads of
barley in exchange for one load of wheat does not constitute usury, since the articles are not homogeneous, and
the sale of ten yards of cloth for five yards of cloth is not
usury, since they are not estimable by weight or measurement of capacity (كَيْل او وزن). The Qur'án strongly forbids usury (Súra ii. 276 ; *see* Dictionary of Islám, 656).

Sale may be either fully valid, (بَيْع لازم) or, it may be
suspended, (بيع موقوف) or invalid (بَيْع فَاسد)

DEBT, ADVANCE (سَلَف ـ سَلَم ـ دَيْن).—Debts are of two
kinds : (1) money or other articles of value delivered to
a person, on condition that he pay back after a specified
time articles of the same value or quantity, without any
compensation or interest ; (2) سَلَف ـ سلم, *i.e.*, an advance
of money or articles of a certain value delivered to a
person, on condition that after a specified time he give
in return for the same certain specified articles, implying
a certain profit in addition to what had been advanced
to him. The lender is called المقرض : the borrower is
known as المستقرض.

LOAN (عاريّة).—This is an agreement by which the owner
of a certain object delivers the same over to a person to
make use of and profit by it, without any payment or
compensation, on condition of his returning it in good condition when it is claimed back (العاريّة تمليك المنافع مجانآ).
The person who makes the loan is the مُعِيار ; he who
receives the loan is the المستعير ; the object loaned is
المستعار.

Deposit (وديعة ـ إيداع).—This is an agreement by which a thing is entrusted to the care of another with the injunction to carefully preserve it in good condition (الإيداع تسليط الغير على حفظ ماله صريحاً او دلالةً).

The object deposited is called وديعة; the proprietor of the deposit is مُودِع; the person entrusted with the deposit is the مُستودَع ـ مُودَع ـ أمين.

When the deposit is seriously damaged or destroyed, the trustee is only held responsible for it, in case of excessive negligence (تفريط), or transgression of the authority given him by the depositor (تعدّي).

Hire, Lease, Rental, Wages (إجارة). — This is an agreement by which the owner of a certain object gives it over to a person for a specified time, to use and profit by it, or by which a person promises to render certain services to another, for which the person who makes use of the hired object, or to whom services are rendered, makes a certain payment (الإجارة تمليك نفع بعوض). The hirer is مُؤجِر; the renter, tenant, lessee is مستأجر; the servant or hireling is أجير; the rent or wages is أُجرة.

Partnership (شركة).—This is an agreement by which two or more persons unite in one concern, or business. (الشركة هي عبارة عن عقد بين المتشاركين في الاصل و الربح)
The partners put together capital with the object of sharing in the profit, in proportion to the capital contributed. The jurists also mention various kinds of partnership[1]

---

[1] (1) شركة العنان social contract; (2) شركة ابدان و اعمال partnership of people of the same profession, sharing the profit of their joint work; (3) شركة وجوه a person of reputation and credit associating with a person

COMMISSION, CO-PARTNERSHIP (مُضَارَبَة)—is an agreement by which a person delivers a capital or stock to another, who is to traffic with the same, and the profit is to be divided according to agreement. The partner who gives the capital is the ربّ المال or صاحب المال; the one who traffics with it is the عَامِل ـ مُضَارِب or manager. (المضاربة هي عقد شركة في الربع بمالٍ من جانب و عملٍ من جانب)

FARMING OUT LAND (مُزَارَعَة ـ مُخَابَرَة ـ مُحَاقَلَة).—Land may be given into the charge of another, on condition that a fixed proportion of its produce is transferred to the owner. He who farms out is the صاحب ارض; the farmer is the زارع; the land farmed out is مُزرعَة. The owner of the land has, however, to pay the land-tax (الخَراج).

WATERING A GARDEN (مُسَاقَاة).—The owner of a garden, vineyard, or plantation, containing fruit trees, may deliver over the same to a person for a specified time to care for it, on condition that the produce be divided between them, in the proportion of one-half, one-third or the like, as may be stipulated.

RACING AND SHOOTING (سَبَق و رِمَايَة).—The free consent of those who take part in the competition and fix the rewards is necessary. Horses, camels, elephants, donkeys, and mules may be used in these competitions.

AGENCY, ATTORNEYSHIP (وَكَالَة).—This is an agreement by which a person appoints another person to be his agent

---

of no credit, with the object of equally sharing the profit of an under-taking; (4) شركة معاوضة when each partner promises to divide the profit of his particular undertaking with his partners.

in the conducting of business, sale, collecting debts, or in executing certain orders in his stead, and as his substitute. The agent is a وَكِيل ; the person appointing him is the المُوَكِّل ; an agent with limited authority is a وَكِيل خَاصّ with general authority a وَكِيل مُطْلَق ـ وَكِيل عَامّ.

PLEDGING, PAWNING (رَهْن).—This designates the detention of a thing as a sign and surety of a claim or a debt. The Qur'án says : "Let pledges be taken" (Súra ii. 183). The person who gives the pledge is الرَّاهِن ; the receiver of the pledge, or pawn is المُرْتَهِن ; the object pawned is الرهن ومَرْهُون.

(الرهن حَبْس شيء مالي بِحق يمكن استيعاءه منه كالدَّيْن)

SURETYSHIP, SECURITY, BAIL.—(ضَمَان) These are in Muslim law of three different kinds.

(1) ضَمَان by which a person becoming a surety (ضَامِن) and promises to pay the creditor the debt of a third person, in case the latter should not pay it himself at the specified time. The surety is الضَّامِن ; the debtor is المَضْمُون عنه ; the creditor is المَضْمُون عليه.

(2) حَوَالَة is an agreement by which a debt is removed from the original debtor to another person, who thereby becomes alone responsible to the creditor for the payment of the debt. The drawing of bills of exchange (بُولِيصَة، سَفْتَجَة) is said to be blamable.

(3) كَفَالَة is an agreement by which a person becomes surety for the payment of debts or for the property or for the debtor. There are two kinds of such kafála, that is, (1) security for the person, engagement to find and produce the debtor, should he abscond or flee كَفَالَة حُضُور

and كَفَالَةُ النَّفْسِ ; (2) security for property or the payment of the debt is كَفَالَةُ الْمَال ـ كَفَالَةُ بِالْمَالِ.

(الكَفَالَةُ هِيَ ضَمُّ ذِمَّهِ الكَفِيل ذِمَّةَ الاصِيل فِي المُطَالَبَة مُطلَقاً بِنَفسٍ او بِدَيْنٍ او عَينٍ) ; the person who is surety is الكَفِيل، the person for whom one is surety is المَكفُول عَنهُ ; the object of security is المَكفُول بِه.

DONATION, GIFT (هِبَّة)—This is an agreement by which a person gives property of his own to another person to become his sole and entire property, without compensation (بِلا عِوَض). The donor is الوَاهِب ; the receiver of the gift is المَوهُوب لَهُ ; the gift is هِبَة. The donation must be made in the presence of witnesses. The retractation of a gift (الرُّجوع فِي الهِبَة) is not unlawful, but a blamable action which is to be avoided.

WILL, BEQUESTS (وَصَايا ـ وَصِيَّة)—These are means by which the testator (المُوصِي) leaves to a legatee (المُوصَي لَهُ) money or property, to be delivered up after his death. The person appointed to carry out the will is called the وَصِيّ or executor. Guardianship (وِلايَة ـ الوَلِيّ) naturally belongs to the father or grandfather of the deceased. When there is neither a guardian, nor executor appointed by will, a Qayyam (قَيِّم) is appointed by law to act as guardian. The will should be executed in writing and is to be certified by two male witnesses, or by one male and two females. Bequests are lawful and valid to the extent of one-third of the testator's property. A will may be altered by the testator.

PROXIMITY, KIN, FRIENDSHIP (وَلاء).—This designates in Law a peculiar relationship, voluntarily established, and which confers the right of inheritance on one or both parties connected. It is of two kinds :

(1) ولاء العتاقة, or relationship between a master and a manumitted slave, in which the former inherits any property the latter may acquire after his emancipation.

(2) ولاء الموالاة, or relation arising out of mutual friendship, especially between a Muslim and a convert to Islám.

COMPULSION (اِكراه).—This designates an unlawful action which a Muslim commits under unjust compulsion. There is the absolute compulsion (تام), when he is forced to commit such an unlawful act by him who has power over his life, and the relative compulsion (ناقص), when the danger of resisting is less imminent.

ENDOWMENT, RELIGIOUS FOUNDATION (وَقف).—Endowment, or Wakf, designates appropriation or dedication of property to charitable and pious uses and to the service of God. The object of such an endowment must be of a perpetual nature, and such property or land cannot be sold or transferred or pawned (لا يَملَك ولا يَمَلَّك ولا يَعار ولا يرهن). The person who dedicates such a thing must expressly declare it by such words as : "I dedicate it as alms for ever for the benefit of the poor, or for the cause of God." The person who dedicates is المَوقِف ; the object dedicated is وَقف , مَوقوف ; the person or object for whose benefit the endowment is made is مَوقوف عليه.

Such an endowment may be made for the benefit of particular persons, e.g., children, or for the public in general. It must be separated from private property, and it must be expressly declared to be perpetual in character.

A female slave who is made "Wakf" can only be married to a slave, so that she and her offspring may remain slaves and be a profit to their owner.

COMPROMISE OR RECONCILIATION (صُلح).—This is an understanding come to with the object of terminating a litigation (الصُّلح هو عقد برفع النزاع و بقطع الخصومة). The mediator is المُصلِح; the claimant is المُصالِح; the respondent is المُصالَح له; the object of litigation is المُصالَح عنه.

Muhammad said: "Reconciliation is more meritorious than prayer and fasting." In order to bring about a reconciliation between husband and wife it is said to be lawful to tell an untruth (Súra iv. 127-128).

EXCLUSION (تخارج).—This designates an arrangement by which the heirs-at-law exclude a person who has a share in the inheritance, by giving him an object, or money which he accepts as his share.

BANKRUPTCY (افلاس).—In Law this designates the state of a person who is not only unable to pay his debts, but lacks the necessary means for supplying his own pressing wants. The bankrupt person is المُفلِس. When the Qádi has duly ascertained that the property of the bankrupt is not sufficient to pay his debts, he declares him insolvent, and places his property under sequestration. The Qádi then distributes it to the debtors, and after that the bankrupt person has no more obligations to his debtors and has full liberty of action.

INHIBITION, INTERDICTION, SEQUESTRATION (حجر).—These are terms which designate an order to prevent a person from disposing of his property.[1]

---

1 The causes of inhibition are three: infancy, insanity and servitude (صِغَر ، رِق ، جُنون) The acts of a child, who has not reached the stage of puberty, are not legal, unless they are sanctioned by his guardian. A boy or girl are of age if the signs of puberty appear on them, otherwise fifteen years is admitted as the age of puberty of both; some allow

We now come to the third part of Fiqh which deals with punishments.

PUNISHMENT (عقوبات).—Punishments inflicted according to the Muslim law for various crimes and offences, are: (1) حَدّ (pl. حُدُود) that is punishments for certain crimes, fixed by the law of the Qur'án or Traditions; (2) تعزير or chastisement for offences, not fixed by the law, but left to the option and discretion of the Imám; (3) قِصاص or Retaliation.

عَقُوبَة is from تَعَقَّب to follow, because the punishment follows the transgression. حَدّ (حدود اللّه) in its primitive sense means prevention, hindrance, impediment, limit, boundary.[1] In Law it means the punishment appointed by the Law of the Qur'án or the Traditions for certain crimes and transgressions. The Hadúd are the limits, which man is not to transgress, and for the transgression of which he will be punished. No intercession ought to be made, and is of no avail when once the case has come before the Qádi. Before this time intercession may be made and the punishment be cancelled. The guilt, however, remains, and it is only repentance which can remove it.

(ليس الحدّ مُطَهِّرًا بل المُطَهِّر التوبة و اذا حُدَّ ولم يَتُب يَبقي عليه اثم المعصية)

Some are of opinion that the punishment removes the guilt. If a man commits a sin such as drunkenness, or

---

twelve for the boy and nine for the girl. مَأذون is a legal term to designate a licensed or privileged slave who has received remission of the inhibition which prevented his buying and selling.

[1] The transgressions which are punished by Hadd punishments are: (1) adultery, (2) fornication, (3) false accusation of a married person of adultery, (4) apostasy, (5) drinking wine, (6) theft, (7) highway robbery.

adultery which deserves the punishment of Hadd, and repents of it sincerely before it is reported to the Qádi, it is praiseworthy not to inform the Qádi of it for the "concealing of such acts is a laudable thing."

As regards the crimes which are to be punished by the infliction of the Hadd, it is laid down as follows:

(1) Adultery.—Only that kind of adultery is punishable which an adult Muslim of sound reason commits of his own free will with a woman, who is not his own, in the land of Islám, (Daru'l Islám). In the land of the enemy (Daru'l Harb) it is not punishable by Hadd. Adultery is to be proved either by the confession of the transgressor or by witnesses. If by witnesses, it is necessary that four witnesses testify at one and the same time before the Qádi that they have seen N. N. commit adultery, with N. N. and explain how and when and where and with whom. To prove adultery by confession it is necessary that, on being asked four times, the person persists in his confession and no one contradicts his statement. Should he, before the punishment is inflicted, retract his confession by saying: "By God I have not pleaded guilty," he is to be considered innocent, and must be released immediately; the same applies to other crimes also, such as theft and drunkenness. It is considered desirable to suggest to a man accused of adultery that he should say that he has done it by mistake, or that he has only kissed or touched the woman in which case he escapes punishment. If he should pretend that the woman with whom he had illicit intercourse is his wife, even if this be not true (and no proof is required of him), or if he buys or marries her afterwards, he is not to be punished. A married man (مُحْصَن from حصن, to be fortified, protected, viz., by marriage from unlawful intercourse), who commits adultery is to be stoned in a public place till he dies; the married woman (الْمُحْصَنَة) is to be stoned, standing in a hole dug in the earth, up to the waist. The witnesses on whose evidence the adulterer is stoned must begin to throw stones at him, then the Qádi and the people standing there in rows, also cast stones. After death, the burial takes place as in the case of other Muslims. An unmarried man (غير الْمُحْصَن) who commits adultery is not stoned, but punished by the infliction of one hundred stripes (مائة جَلْدَة), if he be free; fifty, if he is a slave.

(2) Fornication.—Four witnesses are required to prove fornication (Súra xxiv. 2-5). In the beginning of Islám women found guilty of fornication or adultery were to be imprisoned till they died (Súra iv. 19). The man must suffer the punishment standing upright, the woman sitting.

DRUNKENNESS (الشُّرب).—The drinking of wine under which all sorts of strong and inebriating liquors are comprehended, is strictly forbidden in the Qur'án (Súras ii. 216 ; v. 92, 93). The drinking of wine (شرب الخَمر), if it be but a single drop, and drunkenness (سُكَر) are both unlawful. In the beginning of Islám, wine was not prohibited; the Companions used to take it. If a Muslim drinks wine and two witnesses testify to his having done so, stating

---

If there are any doubts, they must be mentioned and the transgressor allowed the benefit of them. Muhammad himself said : "Endeavour to prevent the execution of punishments by suggesting doubts whenever you can do so." For unnatural crimes with beasts (وطاء بهيمة) the punishment, whether of a man or a woman, is not 'hadd,' but تعزير and is left to the judgment of the Qádi. The beast is to be killed and burned.

For pederasty (وطاء دُبُر) the punishment is also تعزير, which is left to the judgment of the Qádi.

Onanism (الاِستمناء).—This is considered unlawful. Some doctors say it may be excused under certain circumstances and may even become a duty, if practised in order to escape from the sin of fornication.

Sodomy (لِوَاط).—This is to be punished. The question whether it will be allowed and practised in Paradise is one which has been seriously discussed by learned dogmatists, some affirming, others denying it. Certain dogmatists maintain that he who practises it, being of opinion that it is not unlawful, does not thereby become an infidel. Unnatural intercourse of women with each other (السِّحق) is to be punished by one hundred stripes.

(3) False accusation of a married person of adultery or fornication (القَذْف).—When this is made against a virtuous married man or woman, and cannot be proved by four trustworthy witnesses, he who thus brings a false charge receives eighty lashes (Súra xxiv. 4). To accuse married people of adultery is considered one of the great sins; to accuse unmarried persons of this sin is considered as only one of the little sins. This sin, not being considered as grievous as adultery, fornication, drunkenness, the stripes are not to be applied to the naked body. The culprit is allowed to keep on his underclothing.

how and when and where, or if his breath smell of wine, or if he confesses, or is found in a state of intoxication, his punishment is eighty stripes, if a free man ; forty, if a slave. The proof of a man's being drunk is his being unable to distinguish between heaven and earth, a man and a woman, or if he be confused in his speech. The use of opium and hashish is unlawful (حرمة اكل البنج وحشيشة و أفيون).

THEFT (سرقة).—Theft, according to Muslim law, is the taking away of the property of another in a secret way (خفية) at a time when such property was in safe custody (في حرز). Secresy is necessary to constitute theft, for public robbery or open plunder is not theft. Custody (حرز) is of two kinds : (1) place, i.e., house or shop ; and (2) by personal guard, i.e., by means of a personal watch over the property. If a Muslim adult of sound understanding steals out of undoubted custody ten dirhems or property to the value of ten dirhems, his punishment is the cutting off of his hand (قطع اليد Súra v. 42). The punishment is the same for a free man and a slave.[1]

---

[1] The theft must be proved by the testimony of two reliable witnesses, who are to explain the manner, time and place of the theft. The thief must be held in confinement on suspicion till the witnesses are fully examined. If the owner of the stolen property should declare, even after the thief's confession and the pronouncing of the sentence by the Qádi, that he had given the stolen property to him, the thief is set at liberty. It is desirable to exhort him not to make any confession. If a party commit a theft, and each receive ten dirhems, the hand of each is to be cut off. For less than ten dirhems, or objects which were not in custody, the punishment is not inflicted. If thieves make a hole in the wall, and one of them inside put objects through this hole into the hands of others who are outside, this cannot be considered theft, nor can a man be punished for theft if, after having made a hole in the wall, he enters the room and places the object he intends to take into the hole, then comes out and carries them away from outside.

HIGHWAY ROBBERY[1] (قطع الطريق).—This is considered a very heinous offence, the punishment of which has been thus fixed by the Qur'án (Súra v. 37) : "The recompense of those who war against God and His apostle, and go about to enact violence in the earth, is that they be slain or crucified or have their alternate hands and feet cut off, or be banished from the land." [2]

CHASTISEMENT, TAZÍR (تعزير).—This designates in Muslim law the infliction of a punishment for an offence, for which no special punishment has been fixed in the Qur'án

---

[1] Highway robbers are of four kinds : (1) those who are seized before they have robbed or murdered any person or put any person in fear : their punishment is to be imprisoned till they repent or die ; (2) those who have robbed, but have not murdered: these have their right hand and left foot struck off ; (3) those who have committed murder but have not robbed : these are punished with death ; (4) those who have committed both robbery and murder ; their punishment may be of six different kinds at the option of the Imám. He may cut off hand and foot, or have them then put to death by the sword, or crucified, or kill them at once. The same punishment is inflicted on freemen and slaves, men and women (Dictionary of Islám, 174).

[2] The right hand is to be cut off at the joint of the wrist, and the stump afterwards cauterized (تقطع يمين السارق من زنده وتحسم). For the second theft, the left foot is cut off, and for any theft beyond that he must suffer imprisonment, till he show signs of sincere repentance. Besides suffering the punishment, the thief has to restore the stolen object. (Dictionary of Islám, 284).

If the man accused of theft maintains—no proof is required of him—that the stolen object is his property, or that he has received and accepted it as a present (هبة), or mentions a circumstance, which makes it doubtful whether the punishment ought to be inflicted, the sentence (حَد) cannot be carried out.

The punishment cannot be carried out if a man steals from the public treasury, because everything there is the common property of all Muslims in which the thief as a member of the community has a share.

or the Traditions and which may, at the option of the Imám, be punished in some other way.[1]

CRIMES, OFFENCES, AND TRANSGRESSIONS حِنَايَات.— These designate in Law certain acts committed to the detriment of either property or life or members of the body. In acts detrimental to property are included highway robbery, theft, etc., and in acts detrimental to life and members of the body murder, manslaughter, injuring or destroying members of the body such as hand or eyes.[2]

---

1 أَدَب - عَزَّر means to censure, to reprimand, to chastise. If the punishment decreed by the Imám is to consist in stripes, it may be three to thirty-nine stripes تسعه; which may be severe, as they are limited.

The Qur'án allows husbands to chastise their wives for the purpose of correction and amendment (Súra iv. 38).

Chastisement is inflicted on a person who abuses a Muslim by calling him a fornicator, an infidel, a thief, a Jew, a Christian, etc.

If the Imám inflict either the Hadd punishment or merely Tazír on a person and the same should die in consequence of such punishment, his blood is lost (هَدَر), i.e., it is not to be avenged; and nothing in the shape of a fine is due upon it (مِن حَدّ او عُزِّر فهلك فه مه هدر); it is homicide by misadventure. It is different from the case of a husband who inflicts chastisement on his wife, and in so doing kills her. A husband who beats his wife cruelly is chastised for it.

If a woman apostatises from Islám in order to be separated from her husband, she is forced to return to Islám, and receives seventy-five stripes and may not marry another husband.

Various kinds and degrees of punishments and fines are inflicted for these offences, viz., (1) Retaliation, Revenge, (قَوَد ,قصاص); (2) Price of blood (دِيَّة); (3) Expiation (كَفَّارة); (4) Loss of inheritance (حِرمان الإرث);

2 Acts detrimental to life are:

(1). Wilful murder (قتل العَمد - قتل عمداً - قتل النفس).—Every act of wilful murder of a person whose blood is under continual protection. Muslim or Zimmi, subjects the person who commits the crime to the fine of Qisás (قصاص), which consists in doing to the person who has committed the crime the very same thing he has done to another (ان يُفعَل بالفاعل مثل ما فعل), i.e., shedding of blood for shedding of blood, hand for hand, tooth for tooth. The murderer deserves hell, (Súra iv. 94-95) and his punishment is the jus talionis according to Súra ii. 173, "A free man to be slain for a free man, a slave for a slave, a woman for a woman." A father however is not to be slain for the murder of his child, but the child is to be slain for the murder of his parent. A master is not to be slain for his slave. Retaliation is to be executed by the next of kin with some metal weapon or sharp instrument, capable of inflicting a mortal wound. The heir, or the next of kin to the murdered person, is at liberty to forgive or to compound the offence.

(2) Manslaughter (قتل شبة آلعمد), which is similar to wilful murder (خطأ العمد and شبه الخطأ). Killing with a rod or stick is only manslaughter, as a rod and stick are not mortal weapons. The fine for manslaughter is expiation and blood money, and the manslayer is excluded from inheriting the property of the slain (موجبة الاثم و الكفّارة و ديّة معلّظة).

(3) Homicide by misadventure (قتل الخطأ)

(4) Homicide similar to the above (ماجرى قتل الخطا), for example, if a man in his sleep falls upon another and kills him.

(5) Homicide by intermediate cause (قتل بسَبَب) e.g., when a man digs a ditch and sets up a stone and another falls into the ditch and the stone kills him.

The punishment of retaliation is inflicted for the murder of every person whose blood is perpetually (not temporarily only) protected, that is, the Muslim and the fully protected Zimmi; not the temporarily protected, or the enemy, on condition of the slayer being a fully responsible person and there being no doubt; but if a thief enters a house, and the owner of the house runs after him and kills him, he is not subject to retaliation, nor is he who kills an outlaw a robber, a drunkard, subject to it either. If a person deserving death takes refuge in a sanctuary, he is not to be killed there; but no food is to be supplied to him, and when he comes out of the sanctuary he is to be killed.

Retaliation for acts of less vital importance القود فيما دون النفس is to be observed as much as circumstances allow that is, hand for hand foot for foot. If a member which is to be cut off in retaliation be defective, a compensation (أرش) may be accepted.

Retaliation may be commuted for a sum of money (ديّة pl. ديات). The term أرش used commonly for the fine inflicted for injury or destruction of part of the body, is sometimes also used as synonymous to ديّة. Where compensation is offered, it is desirable to accept it. The sum paid for the murdered person is a matter to be settled between the parties. The fine due for manslaughter consists of one hundred female camels, to be delivered in the course of three years, or ten thousand dirhems (silver) or one thousand dinars (gold). If camels are required it is called ' the heavy fine ' الدية المغلّظة.

The Expiation (الكفّارة) due for manslaughter and homicide is the liberation of a believing slave by which it differs from expiation due in other cases : if the slayer be unable to do this, he may fast two consecutive months. The price of blood for a woman is half of that due for a man.

Swearing an oath with regard to a murdered person is done when the body of a dead man, on whom wounds are seen which indicate his having been killed, is found, and his near relatives suspect the people of the place of having killed him and they deny it. Then fifty of them have to swear an oath by God that they have neither killed him, nor have any knowledge concerning the person who killed him. If the prosecutor has strong proofs that the people of the place have killed him, or know the murderer, he has to swear an oath to that effect. If the corpse be found between two villages, the nearest is responsible.

The legal term used to designate the price of blood is مُعَقَّلة. It is so called because it is intended to prevent the shedding of blood. The term عاقلة designates the assembly of the relatives or, in certain cases, the corporation or guild who are responsible for the payment of the price of blood or any other fines,

(العاقلة هى اهل الديوان - فيجب عليهم كل دية وجبت بنفس القتل)

Compensation may be given for inflicting wounds on the head and face. These wounds may be of different kinds : mere scratches or such as cause the blood to come in drops but not to flow ; or, a scratch which causes the blood to flow freely ; or a cut through the skin merely ; or a wound which lays bare the bone ; or a fracture of the skull ; or a fracture which causes the removal of part of the skull ; or a wound extending to the brain. No retaliation is due for such wounds, but various fines are inflicted. A Muslim is not to be killed for an unbeliever.

CHAPTER V.

THE SECTS OF ISLÁM.

Muhammad predicted that his followers would be divided into numerous religious sects. According to a tradition recorded by 'Abdu'lláh Ibn 'Umar, he said: "Verily it will happen to my people even as it did to the children of Israel. The children of Israel were divided into seventy-two sects, and my people will be divided into seventy-three."

ستفترق أمّتي علي ثلث و سبعين فرقة الناجية منها واحدة و الباقون هلكي · قيل و من الناجية · قال اهل السنّة و الجماعة قيل وما السنّة و الجماعة · قال ما انا عليه اليوم و اصحابي · و قال لا تزال طائفة من أمّتي ظاهرين علي الحقّ الي يوم القيامة ·

The Muslims, at the time of Muhammad's death, are said to have been all one in matters of belief and practice. There existed no differences between them, excluding those who were hypocrites professing Islám outwardly and opposing it secretly. Afterwards differences arose between the true followers of the Prophet; but only on subjects of minor importance which did not affect the faith or salvation. On these unimportant matters every one was at liberty to adopt what opinion seemed preferable to him.

(الخلاف في امور اجتهادية لا توجب ايماناً ولا كفراً)

Towards the end of the period of the Companions of the Prophet, serious differences on more weighty subjects began to arise, especially when Ma'badu'l Jahani, Ghulánu'd Dimishqe and Yúnasu'l Aswári rose and opposed the doctrine of Predestination, and from that time a variety of additional conflicting opinion was set

up and discussed, and differences multiplied, till at last
the Muslim nation became divided into seventy-three
sects. (Sharastání i. 4). The chief subjects on which
these sects differed from the orthodox school and among
themselves are the following :

(1)   The Attributes of God and His unity القاعدة الاولي

الصفات والتوحيد فيها و ما يجب لله تعالي و ما يجوز عليه و ما

يستحيل و تشـتمل علي مسـائل الصفات الازليّة ـ و بيان صفات

الذات و صفات الفعل .

On these points, differences of opinion existed between
the Ash'ariyya, the Mujassima and the Mu'tazila.

(2)   Predestination and God's Justice (القدر والعَدَل)

القاعدة الثانية : القدر والعدل وهي تشـتمل علي مسـائل القضاء

والقدر ـ والجبر والكسب ـ و ارادة الخير والشر ـ والمقدور والمعلوم ـ
Differences of opinion on these points existed between
the Qadariyya, the Nejjaríyya, the Zabariyya, the Ash-
'ariyya and the Karramiyya.

(3)   God's Promises and Threats القاعدة الثالثة الوعد

والوعيد والاسماء والاحكام ـ وهي تشتمل علي مسائل الايمان

والتوبة والوعيد والارجاء والتكفير والتضليل .

(4)   Revelation, Reason, the Apostleship and the Imámate القاعدة الرابعة السمع والعقل والرسالة والامامة وهي تشـتمل

علي مسائل التحسين والتقبيح والصلاح والاصلح واللطف والعصمة

في النبوّة و شرائط الامامة .   Shahrastáni i. 4.

Ibn Ahmadu'l Iji (الايجي), the author of Sharhu'l
Mawáqif, divides the Muslim sects into eight classes :

(1)   The Mu'tazila, (2) the Shí'ah, (3) the Khawárij,
(4) the Murjía, (5) the Nijjariyya, (6) the Zabariyya, (7)
the Mushabbiha, (8) the Nájia (the saved).

1. THE MU'TAZILA (المُعْتَزِلَة) were the followers of Wásil bin 'Atá' (واصل بن عطاء), who was born at Madína A.H. 80. The circumstances of his becoming the founder of this sect are thus related : " Hasanu'l-Basri, a famous divine, was one day seated in a mosque at Basra when a discussion arose on the question whether a believer who committed a mortal sin became thereby an unbeliever. The Khawárij affirmed that it was so, while the orthodox denied it. On being asked to give a decision on this question, Hasanu'l-Basri began to revolve the matter in his mind, but before he had time to give an answer, Wásil, one of his followers, rose up and said : ' I maintain that a Muslim who has committed a mortal sin should be regarded neither as a believer nor an unbeliever, but as occupying a middle station between the two.' (ان مرتكب الكبيرة ليس بمؤمن ولا كافر و يثبت له المنزلة بين المنزلتين) He then retired to another part of the Mosque where he was joined by a number of his friends to whom he explained his opinion on the subject. Thereupon Hasanu'l-Basri said : ' Wásil has now separated from us ' (اعتزل عنا واصل) and they were then called Mu'tazila, or Separatists and Seceders. They were emphatically the liberal party, and the freethinkers or rationalists of Islám (Shahrastáni i. 29). They are also known as the Qadariyya' (القَدَرِيَّة), because they ascribed the actions of men to their own power (لاسنادهم افعال العباد الي قدرتهم) and denied their being decreed by God (يُنكرون القدر فيه) and also as the Men of justice and of the Unity of God (اصحاب العَدَل والتوحيد). As they denied the existence of eternal attributes in God they were also called the ' deprivers,' the Mu'attila (المُعَطِّلَة) Shahrastáni i. 29-31;

Sale, 113). The Mu'atazila are sub-divided into twenty sub-divisions, holding the general opinions of the sect but separating on various points. The curious will find a list of these various sects together with a description of their peculiar tenets in Shahrastáni, Mawáqif 620 *et seqq*, and a summary of the same in Sale's Preliminary Discourse.

1. THE SHI'AH SECT الشـيعة—This name comes from شاع from يشيع to follow, to conform with, to obey, and means party, partisans, followers, because they are the followers of 'Ali, the cousin of Muhammad, and husband of his only daughter Fátima. He is considered to be the lawful Khalíf and Imám after Muhammad. It is also held that the Imámate belonged by divine declaration and the command of the prophet (نصاً و وصيّة) to him and his descendants. (Ibn Khaldún i. 164 *et seqq*). The Shí'ahs are divided into twenty-two divisions, each declaring the others to be infidels. The chief sub-divisions are: (1) the Ghálía (الغالية) that is الغلاة or zealots, fanatics (from غلا to exceed the bounds, to over do, exaggerate); (2) the Zaidiyya and (3) the Imámiyya. The Ghálía exceeded all bounds in their veneration for their Imáms and raised them above created beings and attributed divine properties to some of them. Sometimes they made them like God, and sometimes made God like man

حكمت باحكام الا لهية في حق بعض الائمة ـ اما انهم بشــروا
تصفوا بصفات الاوهيّة او ان الا له حل في ذاته البشرية و هو القول
بالحـلول ـ (Ibn Khaldún i. 165).

"These ideas, says Shahrastáni, they borrowed partly from those who believe in metempsychosis (التماسخ), and partly from Jews and from Christians. The Persians and many of the Muslims of India are Shí'ahs.

For a list of the Shí'ah sects and their special tenets *see* Shahrastáni i. 132 *et seqq.* Mawaqif 624 *et seqq.*

3. THE KHAWÁRIJ (الخوارج).—They are termed the rebels, revolters. Every one who rebels against the Imám, lawfully appointed by the Muslim nation, is called a Khawárij, whether it be in the days of the 'Companions' against the first Khálifs, the 'rightly directed Imáms', (الأئمّة الراشدين) or at a later period.

The first who were called Khawárij were 12,000 men who revolted from 'Ali, after they had fought under him at the battle of Siffin, and took offence at his submitting the decision of his right to the Khalifate to the arbitration of men, when in their opinion it ought to have been submitted to the judgment of God. There are twenty, more or less important, sub-divisions of this sect. (Shahrastáni i. 85 ; Mawáqif 629-631 ; Dictionary of Islám 270.)

4. THE MURJÍA, المرجئة or مُرجيه—The word إرجاء has two meanings : (1) التأخير to delay, put off, postpone ; (2) to cause to hope, to give occasion to hope. Some, therefore, say that this sect is called مُرجئة from أرجاء to postpone, defer, delay, because the subordinate works to intention, *i.e.*, esteem works to be inferior to intention (نيّة) and profession of the faith (يرجئون العمل عن النيّة و عن الاعتقاد) others again say that they are so called because they hold that the judgment of the believer who has committed mortal sin will be deferred till the resurrection ; others again think that they are so called from رجاء (to hope), because they allow hope by asserting that "disobedience joined with faith hurteth not" (لا يضرّ مع الايمان معصية) Shahrastáni i. 103; Mawáqif 631; Sale 122; Dictionary of Islám 421). This sect is divided into five sub-divisions.

5. THE NIJJÁRIYYA النجّاريّة.—These are the followers of Muhammad-binu'l-Husainu'n-Nejjár. The greater part the Mu'tazila adhered to his doctrine. They were sub-divided into three divisions (Shahrastání i. 61).

6. THE JABARIYYA (الجبريّة).—This word comes from جبر to compel, to force, and is so called because they hold that God compels man to act as he does, and are consequently the firm opponents of the Qadariyya who hold the doctrine of free-will (الجبر اسناد فعل العبد الي الله). There are various divisions of this sect: such as the pure Jabariyya (الجبريّة الخالصة) the middle, moderate Jabariyya (الجبريّة المتوسّطه) (Shahrastání i. 59; Sale 121, 122).

7. THE MUSHABBIHA (المشبّهة, or Assimilators).—They allowed a resemblance between God and his creatures, supposing Him to be a body (جسم), composed of members, and capable of motion. There are various sub-divisions of this sect.

The abovementioned are what the orthodox call the erring sects (الفرق الضالّة) and of which Muhammad is re-ported to have said : " they are all in hell " (كلّهم في النار). These all have ceased to exist as distinct sects, except the Shí'ah.

8. THE ASH'ARIYYA ASHÁ'IRA (اشاعرة ـ الاشعريّة).—They are the followers of Abu'-l-Hasan 'Ali Ibn Ism'aíl al Ash'ari (ابوالحسن علي ابن اسمعيل الأشعري). The men of the orthodox school, the people of the Tradition and Sunna are included in them. They are called the " Sects which will be saved," (الفرق الناجية), and it is reported that they are the men of whom Muhammad said : " They

are the men who are of my and of my Companions' religion " (هم الّذين علي ما انا عليهِ و اصحابي). They hold none of the ' heresies ' (بِدَع) of the other sects.[1]

SÚFÍISM التصوّف—From the earliest days of Islám there has existed among the Muslims a kind of mysticism called التصوّف, Súfiism. Those who adopted the principles of this system were called Súfis صوفي (pl. صوفيّة) or مُتَصوّف (pl. متصوّفة). There are various opinions as to the derivation of this word. Some say it is derived from صُوف, wool, because the people adhering to this system are said to have worn the humble dress of wool (Ibn Khaldún i. 390). This opinion is rejected by others, because they say that they were not the only people who used to wear wool (لانهم لم يختصّوا بلبسهِ) ; others derive it from صفاء purity or, from σοφία wisdom. Súfiism in the days of the early Muslims consisted in spending one's time in pious exercises, entirely devoting oneself to the service of God, renouncing the pomp and vanities of the world, fleeing pleasures and amusements, despising riches and honours and retiring from the society of men in order to spend one's life in seclusion and acts of devotion. Many of the Companions of the Prophet and early Muslims used to lead such a life of abstinence. Sufiism as it has developed in the course of time is, according to learned Orientalists, mainly borrowed from Indian philosophers of the Vedanta School. Its chief doctrines are that the souls of men differ in degree, but not in kind from the Divine Spirit, of which they are emanations,

---

[1] Mawáqif 633-634 ; Shahrastáni i. 65-67; Sale 117; Dictionary of Islám, 24. Shahrastáni in his Book of the Religious and Philosophical Sects (ملل و نحل) gives a somewhat different list of these various sects.

and to which they will ultimately return ; that the
Spirit of God is in all He has made, and it in Him ;
that He alone is perfect love, and beauty, and that
hence love to Him is the only real thing and all besides is mere illusion ; that this present life is one of
separation from the Beloved ; that the beauties of nature, music and art revive in man the divine idea and
recall his affections from wandering from God to other
objects. They, therefore, taught that man must cherish
these sublime affections, and by abstraction concen-
trate his thoughts on God and so approximate to His
essence, and thus reach the highest state of bliss — ab-
sorption into the Eternal. They hold that the true
end and object of human life is to lose all conscious-
ness of individual existence—to sink in the Ocean ; of
Divine Life "as a breaking bubble is merged into the
stream, on the surface of which it has for a moment
risen."

Bayázidu'l-Bastámi said he was a sea without bottom,
without beginning and without end, that he was the
throne of God, that he was Abraham, Moses, Jesus.
He also said : "I am the true God, praise me." Towards the close of the second century of the Hijra,
al Halláj (الحلاج). one of the chiefs of Súfiism taught
at Baghdad thus : "I am the truth, there is nought in
Paradise but God. I am He whom I love, and He
whom is love is I ; we are two souls dwelling in one
body." This roused the opposition of the orthodox by
whom al Halláj was condemned as worthy of death.
By order of the Khalif he was flogged, tortured and
finally beheaded ; but Súfiism grew in spite of bitter
persecution.[1]

---

[1] *See* Tholuck's Súfismus, Brown's Darwishes, Palmers', Oriental Mysticism, 'Abdu-r-Razzáq's Dictionary of the technical terms of the Súfis,

The Súfís are divided into innumerable sects which find expression in the numerous Orders of Darwishes. Though they differ in name, customs, dress, meditations and recitations (ذكر); yet they all agree in the principal tenets, especially those which inculcate the absolute necessity of blind submission to the Murshid (المرشد), the leader, or instructor or guide.

Some of the chief Orders of Darwishes are:

The Bastámiyya founded by Bayázid Bastámi A.H. 261; the Qádiriyya founded by 'Abdu'-l-Qádír Jiláni at Baghdad A.H. 561; the Rufá'iyya founded by Sayyid Ahmad Rufá'i at Baghdad A.H. 576; the Sházaliyya founded by Ab'u-l-Hasan (Mecca) A.H. 665; the Maulá-wiyya founded by Jalálu'd-dín Rúmi A.H. 672; the Bedáwiyya founded by Abu'-l-Jitán Ahmad A.H. 675.[1]

THE WAHHÁBIS, الوهابيّه —The founder of this sect was Muhammad Ibn 'Abdu'l-Wahháb (عبد الوهاب) who was born at Ayenah in Nejd (A.D. 1691). After having received careful instruction in the doctrines of Islám according to the Hanbali rite and after visiting Mecca, Basra and Baghdad, he resided with his father at Horomelah, but after his father's death he returned to his native village Ayínah, where he assumed the position of a religious teacher. He was convinced by what he had observed on his journeys of the laxities and superstitions of the Muslims that they had widely departed from the strict principles of Islám, and that a return to the primitive teaching of their religion was required. The use of omens and augurals, the veneration of sacred shrines and the tombs of saints, the

---

published by Dr. Sprenger in Calcutta, 1845. Dictionary of Islám, 608. Sell's Faith of Islám, 2nd Edition, 106 *et seqq*.

[1] *See* a very full account in Sell's Essays on Islám, chapter on Religious Orders of Islám.

use of intoxicating drugs, the wearing of silk and satin and all sorts of luxury which had found favour in the Muslim world were all opposed to the principles of true religion, and Islám must be purged of these idolatrous practices; 'Abdu'l-Wahháb then determined to become the reformer of this corrupt Islám and to restore it to its early purity in conformity with the teachings of the Qur'án, the example of the Prophet and the practice of the Companions and early Muslims. His teaching met with the acceptance of many, but it also raised the enmity of others, especially the ruler of the district, and compelled him to flee to Deraiah, where he obtained the protection of Muhammad ibn Sa'úd, a chief of considerable influence, who himself embraced Wahhábism, and who, by marrying the daughter of Muhammad ibn Wahháb, still further united the interests of his own family with that of the reformer and became the founder of the Wahhábi dynasty, which to this day rules at Ryádh. 'Abdu'-l-'Azíz, the son of this marriage, after his father's death A.D. 1765, led the Wahhábi army to victory and pushed his conquests to the remotest corners of Arabia, destroying on his way the shrines of saints and everything he considered unlawful. In 1803 he was murdered by a Persian fanatic, but his eldest son, Sa'úd, became the great champion of the reformed doctrines. He conquered Karbala, the famous place of pilgrimage of the Shí'ahs, as well as Mecca, and at both places destroyed every vestige of idolatry. For nine years the Wahhábi rule existed at Mecca and Madína, but after this period they were driven out by the Turkish forces. Upon the death of Sa'úd (A.D. 1814) 'Abdu'lláh became the leader of the Faithful, but met with a series of reverses, and at last was taken prisoner by Ibráhím Pasha. He was sent to Constantinople and there executed in

the public square of St. Sophia, A.D. 1818. Turkí, the
son of 'Abdu'lláh, fled to Ryadh, where he was assas-
sinated. Faizul succeeded his father in A.D. 1830, and
established the Wahhábi rule in Eastern Arabia, making Riadh the capital of his kingdom. Faizul died in
A.D. 1866 and was succeeded by his son 'Abdu'lláh.

The Wahhábis speak of themselves as the Unita-
rians (مُوَحِّدِين) and call all other Muslims polytheists
(مُشْرِكِين.) They also reject the decisions of the four
orthodox Schools and the Ijmá', after the death of the
Companions of the Prophet.[1]

THE DRUZES الدروز — The Druzes are a sect which
arose about the beginning of the eleventh century in
the mountains of Syria. The founder of the religious
system of this sect was the fanatical and cruel Khalif
al Hákím bi-amr-illáh of the Fátimite dynasty in Egypt.
He affirmed that he was the representative of God
and the latest of His manifestations and incarnations.
In 407 A.H. (A.D. 1029) this was publicly announced
at Cairo, and his chief helpers were two Persians:
Hamza and Darázi, from the latter of whom the sect
derives its name. The new revelation was, however,
unfavourably received by the people and Darázi nar-
rowly escaped being killed by the mob. Retiring to
the fastnesses of Mount Lebanon, he there began to
spread the new faith. The chief tenets of this sect
are: Belief in one God; that God has shown Himself
at different epochs under a human form; that the last
manifestation and incarnation of the Divinity was in

---

[1] For details on these sects and their peculiar tenets *see* Burkhard's
Bedouins and Wahhábis; Bridge's Brief History of the Wahhábis; Pal-
grave's Central and Eastern Arabia, Dictionary of Islám, 659 *et seqq;*
Sell's Faith of Islám, 152-164.

Hákím bi-amr-illáh; that the latter disappeared in 411 A.H. to try the faith of his disciples, but that in a short time he will appear again in full glory to set up his kingdom and triumph over all his enemies.[1]

THE BÁBÍS.—Alhough the Bábís are not a Muslim sect, yet they have arisen on Muslim ground, and their opinions are closely connected with the Shí'ahs concerning the Imámate and they share the mystical mode of thought of the Súfís. Thousands of Shí'ahs in Persia have joined the movement and suffered cruel persecutions in consequence. It may, therefore, be useful to offer a few observations on their origin, development and their peculiar opinions.

'Abdu'-l-Kásim (Al Mahdi) the twelfth Imám disappeared in the year 329 A.H., but for a period of sixty-nine years he is said to have held intercourse with his followers through a successive number of men, who were called ' Doors ' (باب) or mediums of communication.

Abú'l Hasan, the last of these Doors, refused to appoint a successor, saying that " God hath a purpose which He will accomplish." Many centuries passed by, and it was not until the beginning of the present one that this curious theory of intermediaries between the concealed Imám and the faithful again took a definite shape.

Shaikh Ahmed (A.D. 1753—1826) the founder of the Shaikhi sect was a devout ascetic. He had a profound belief in 'Ali and was devoted to the memory of the true Imáms, whom he looked upon as creative forces, arguing from the words : " God the best of creators " (Súra xxiii. 14) that, if He be the best, He cannot be the only

---

[1] For full details refer to DeSacy's Exposé de la Religion des Druzes, Wartabet's Researches into the Religions of Syria and Sell's Essays on Islám, chapter, " The Khalíf Hákím and the Druzes."

one. The special point of his teaching was that God is immanent in the universe which proceeds from Him and that all the elect of God, the Imáms and just persons, are personifications of the divine attributes.

Shaikh Ahmad was succeeded by Háji Seyyed Kázim (A.D. 1843) who left no successor. After fastings, vigils and prayers for guidance, the Shaikhis began to consider what was to be done in the matter of a spiritual director. Mullá Husain proceeded to Shiráz and there met with Mírzá 'Ali Muhammad who produced before him the sign of his call to the divine mission. After a long and severe struggle Mullá Husain became convinced that he had found in the young and ardent enthusiast before him the 'True One,' the 'Illuminated One' and that he was worthy to be their Murshid. Mírzá 'Ali Muhammad was born at Shiráz (1820 A.D.) After having studied, meditated, and led an austere life till he was about twenty-four years of age, he announced himself as a duly authorized teacher and guide and assumed the title of the Báb, declaring that whosoever wished to approach God must do it through him. From being the Bab and mediator, he, after a time, proceeded to pretend that he was the Point or originator of the Truth, a divine appearance, a powerful manifestation. Notwithstanding the opposition of a number of Mullás, crowds of people, among whom there were learned men also, followed him and became his disciples. Later on an examination took place, after which he was kept in confinement. The most zealous at the time was Quratu'l 'Ayn, a most beautiful, intelligent and eloquent woman, who travelled about everywhere and made converts to Bábísm. In 1848 Nasru'd-dín, the Shah of Persia, severely persecuted the Bábís and put the Báb himself to death. A Persian author says of the Báb: "He spoke with much earnestness on the necessity of religious and social reform in Persia......we neither consider him an adventurer nor a fanatic, but an eminently moral man, a dreamer, brought up in the school of the Shaikhis and possessing some touch of Christianity. We regard him also as a man troubled by the direct influence of some of his devoted and ambitious disciples." In 1852 an attempt was made by some Bábís to assassinate the Shah, and the consequence was bitter persecution of the sect. The most awful persecutions, however, gave only fresh vigour and vitality to the movement. It is said that half a million of Persians are Bábís, others consider their number nearer to one million. " They are to be found in every walk of life, from the ministers and nobles of the Court to the scavenger or groom."

After the death of the Báb, Mírzá Yahyá and his half-brother Behá-ulláh became the leaders of the two sects, into which the Bábís are now divided : the Ezelis and the Beháis. There seems to be no doubt that the Báb nominated (1849) the former, whom he named Subh-i-Ezel (Morning of Eternity), as his successor and for a short time he really held the undisputed position as head of the Bábi community.

The Persian government, at last, prevailed on the Turkish authorities (1863-1864) to deport the two heads of the Bábí sect to Constantinople. The influence of Behá gradually increased, till he at last claimed to be the person to whom the Báb had referred as "Him whom God shall manifest." The two leaders were ultimately separated : Behá and his followers were exiled to Akka; Mírzá was sent to Famgusta in Cyprus.

The Bábí doctrines are to be found in the writings of the Báb called the Beyán. Many of the dogmas are very mystical, but the following is a brief summary : God is eternal and unapproachable. All things come

from Him and exist by Him. Man cannot approach
him, except through some appointed medium. So, distinct from God, there is a 'Primal Will' who became
incarnate in the prophets. The Báb came to perfect
the Law of Christ. Some say that he is Christ returned again on earth. The Primal Will, which spoke
in Adam, Noah, Moses, David, Jesus, and Muhammad,
now speaks through the Báb, and 'Him whom God shall
manifest,' and after him through others, for there is no
cessation of the divine manifestation. The Jews were
told to expect the Messiah, but they rejected him ;
the Christians were to expect Muhammad, but they
did not accept him ; the Muhammadans are taught to
look out for the Imám Mahdi ; now he has come
in the Báb, they persecute him. Bábism is now a
dispensation which has superseded Islám. The great
Teacher is one; but he manifests himself in different
dispensations, according to the needs and the capacity
of those to whom the dispensation comes.

A good many changes were introduced in the Muslim ceremonies. Prayers are said three times a day,
instead of five, the worshipper does not turn towards
Mecca as his Qibla, the fast of Ramadán is not kept ;
the traffic in slaves is forbidden, the holy war is abolished and friendly intercourse with all sects is enjoined.
Bábism is thus a revolt against orthodox Islám.[1]

---

[1] Sell's Essays on Islám, pp. 46-98. *See* also New History of the Báb
by E. G. Browne, p. 299 *et seqq.*